The Columbia Guide to West African Literature in English Since 1945

COLUMBIA GUIDES TO LITERATURE SINCE 1945

The Columbia Guides to Literature Since 1945

The Columbia Guide to West African Literature in English Since 1945

Oyekan Owomoyela

Columbia University Press

New York

Columbia University Press
Publishers Since 1893
New York   Chichester, West Sussex
Copyright © 2008 Columbia University Press

Library of Congress Cataloging-in-Publication Data
Owomoyela, Oyekan.
The Columbia guide to west African literature in English since 1945 / Oyekan Owomoyela.
    p.   cm.
Includes index.
ISBN 978-0-231-12686-1 (cloth : alk. paper)
1. West African literature (English)—20th century—History and criticism. 2. West African
    literature (English)—21st century—History and criticism. 3. Africa, West—Intellectual
    life. 4. Africa, West—In literature. I. Title.
PR9340.5.O96   2008
820.9'96609045—dc22   2007049090

Columbia University Press books are printed on permanent and durable acid-free paper.
This book was printed on paper with recycled content.
Printed in the United States of America
c 10 9 8 7 6 5 4 3 2 1

References to Internet Web sites (URLs) were accurate at the time of writing. Neither the
author nor Columbia University Press is responsible for URLs that may have expired or
changed since the manuscript was prepared.

For Isaac Mowoe, Jan Mumm, and Senna Oakley:
Ìwà lewà
(Character is beauty)

CONTENTS

The Columbia Guide to West African Literature in English Since 1945

PART ONE

The Literary and Cultural Context of West African Literature in English

THIS BOOK AIMS TO PROVIDE readers with a general background and a reliable reference source for West African literature written in the English language since 1945. The approach of the *Columbia Guide to West African Literature in English Since 1945*, combining language, geography, and history, is unique. It offers an overview of the development of post-1945 Anglophone West African writing, its formative influences as well as those that have impinged on it, and bibliographical and biographical information on the writers. The countries covered are The Gambia, Ghana, Liberia, Nigeria, and Sierra Leone. As should be expected, they do not receive equal space or attention. The main reason for the discrepancy is the unequal contribution of the countries to the literary output of the region, a fact that is itself explained by the disparity in the relative sizes of the countries and the resources (academic as well as economic) available to each of them. For example, close to a fifth (maybe even a fourth) of the entire continent's population claim Nigeria as their home, whereas The Gambia has fewer than two million people. Consequently, while Nigeria by itself produces more literature than all the other countries combined, Ghana being a respectable second—between them Nigeria and Ghana have produced the bulk of the writing from the region—The Gambia's output is quite modest.

Another imbalance worth mentioning pertains to gender: male writers predominate in the *Guide*, again because in real life they do in fact predominate in literary production. A number of factors explain this, including the initial advantages male members of the societies had over the female during the colonial period, especially in the area of education and employment; this caused the ranks of literary authors to remain almost exclusively male for several decades, even well into the postcolonial period. One consequence was that although a few female authors were published even in those early years, criticism tended to focus exclusively on the male authors. Marxist and feminist critics were first to decry the critical marginalization of female writers, and nowadays, with the ever-increasing number of highly educated women among the writers and critics, the imbalance has yielded to a state of near gender parity, with women's participation in the region's literary culture consequently receiving considerable attention.

Inasmuch as the literature under discussion is that written in the English language, the presupposition is that a linguistic unity exists over the geographical area of coverage, regardless of the fragmentation an indigenous language map of the same area will reveal. In the following pages, therefore, I will discuss the literature collectively rather than treat each country's writing as a discrete tradition, which it is not. That is not to ignore or minimize ethnic and cultural diversity—an issue that treating each country individually would not avoid anyway, given the heterogeneity within each of the countries in those regards. Moreover, the colonial practice of arbitrarily amalgamating discrete peoples into single countries, and in some cases splitting one ethnic community between (or among) countries dominated by different colonizers, has worked (or at least sought) to subordinate traditional identities to those resulting from shared colonial experience. To the extent that a country's literature displays peculiar tendencies for any reason and during any period—for example, the impact of the civil war in Nigeria on literature emanating from that country in the late 1960s into the 1970s and beyond—I will account for them in the introduction, specifically in the historical segment on each of the countries, or under pertinent subject headings in part 2.

This guide begins with an introductory overview of the entire subject, that is, a discussion of the salient points about post-1945 Anglophone West African literature—the historical background, the significant and noteworthy authors and texts, the shifts in thematic preoccupations and the reasons for them, the significance of foreign sponsorship, the debates about language and social commitment, gender matters, and so forth. A general bibliography concludes this section. The second part is an A–Z reference section that will, in encyclopedia fashion, present information on authors, texts, concepts, events, movements, and institutions that have played a role in the history of the literature. The length of each entry will reflect the relative importance of its subject, and a list of suggested readings will be provided where it is deemed appropriate.

Although the guide pays attention to the major genres—fiction, poetry, and drama—the reader will find that fiction enjoys the overwhelming attention in both the introduction and the A–Z entries. The reason for the bias is that fiction has been mostly responsible for attracting international attention to African literary production, poetry, drama, and creative nonfiction following at some distance. As an acknowledgment of this imbalance, while there do exist some volumes devoted to African poetry or African drama, many times their number deal with fiction, and even when a title suggests that the subject is African literature as a whole, fiction tends to crowd out the other genres. An attempt to offer equal space to all genres would be misguided, inasmuch as it would inevitably result in excluding some important fictional works and writers in favor of marginal ones in other genres.

Another caution about the coverage is that the guide has deliberately excluded the very substantial body of works known as "popular literature," which studies such as Emmanuel Obiechina's of Onitsha market literature (1972) and Stephanie Newell's edited volume on African popular fiction (2002) have amply discussed. This particular literature circulates almost exclusively in a tight geographical circle around its place of origin, is essentially ephemeral, and is often devoid of what most would recognize as literary merit. In general, in fact, it would be fair to conclude that the works and writers included in this guide are those that have a good chance of being accessible to the American reader—works and writers, that is, that are or could be part of the literary canon of the area.

The reference and critical works on African literatures currently available follow a variety of approaches. Some take the entire continent as a unit and cover it accordingly, while others divide the field according to the languages the writers employed; a few concentrate on specific countries or historical periods, and some define themselves thematically; finally, a number devote themselves to individual writers or groups of authors. Examples, to name but a few, are Janheinz Jahn's *Bibliography of Neo-African Literature* (1965); Hans Zell and Helene Silver's *A Reader's Guide to African Literature* (1971) and its successor, Zell's *A New Reader's Guide to African Literature* (1982); Albert Gérard's *African Language Literatures: An Introduction to the Literary History of Sub-Saharan Africa* (1981); Bernth Lindfors's series on the subject, the latest of which is *Black African Literature in English, 1982–1986* (1989); Oyekan Owomoyela's edited volume *A History of Twentieth-Century African Literatures* (1993); and, last, Pushpa Naidu Parekh and Siga Fatima Jagne's *Postcolonial African Writers: A Bio-bibliographical Critical Sourcebook* (1998). Other relevant reference works include the Twayne series on single authors and the *Dictionary of Literary Biographies*, which groups African and Caribbean authors together.

The European Origins of African Literatures

African literatures emerged out of the interactions between Africans and Europeans after the latter began to take an active interest in the continent, especially after the fifteenth century. One of the factors that determined the manner in which early European visitors to the continent related to the Africans they encountered, which was markedly different from their attitude toward, say, the Chinese and the Indians on their first contact with those peoples, was the absence of a writing system in African cultures; the Chinese and the Indians, by contrast, boasted a highly developed writing culture. Its absence in Africa signaled to Europeans a deficiency in all those attributes they associated with civilization (Adas 1989, 53), and, as Henry Louis Gates insists with particular reference to Africans transplanted to North America during the transatlantic slave trade, they regarded illiteracy in fact as an absence of an essential marker of humanity (Gates 1992, 57).

Among the European groups active in Africa early in the period of contact, the missionaries felt the most urgent need to correct the deficiency that nonliteracy supposedly represented, though their primary goal was the conversion of Africans to Christianity. Given the enormousness of the task and the paucity of their numbers, they saw the necessity of recruiting African helpers whom they would educate and train to serve a variety of functions. These included spreading the scriptures, teaching in mission schools, writing texts for school and church use, and preparing orthographies and dictionaries of the various languages. An exemplar of such helpers was the Reverend (later Bishop) Ajayi Crowther, who developed the Yoruba alphabet and compiled the first dictionary of the language in 1852. Other European interests in Africa took advantage of the services the Christians provided, especially through their educational institutions. Thus, European commercial establishments initially, and eventually the various colonial administrations, patronized the missionaries and relied on them to supply their needs for educated Africans to serve as clerks, agents, low-level civil servants, and messengers.

It would be wrong, though, to attribute the spread of Western education among Africans solely to its promotion by Europeans; quite early on, the value of such an education as a guarantor of access to the good life in the emerging economy became apparent to perceptive Africans. It opened the way for employment in commerce, in the colonial service, in the missions, and in the schools. Apart from the attractive remuneration it guaranteed, the association with Europeans (whatever the level) that went with such employment also carried considerable prestige; the more enlightened parents therefore sent their children to school, while some enterprising youths, lacking parental sponsorship, somehow attached themselves to European agents who in many cases enrolled them. As Chinua Achebe suggests through the actions and utterances of Ezeulu in *Arrow of God* (1964), even before the advantages of Western education became widely apparent, some well-placed and forward-looking Africans hedged their bets by acquiring a stake in it. Thus, Ezeulu enrolled his son Oduche in the white man's religion and school because he was impressed by the latter's power and wisdom, and because he saw the regime the Europeans had introduced as a new dance that prudent people would do well to learn, for those who failed to do so "will be saying *had we known* tomorrow."

In the British colonies, the Christian missions maintained a monopoly over the educational systems well into the colonial period, when the colonial government established a handful of high schools; neither provider of education, however, thought it necessary to educate Africans beyond the high-school level, apart from offering supplementary teacher education in teacher training colleges to staff elementary schools. Consequently, students who aspired to higher education had to go abroad, usually to Great Britain and (especially in the case of Liberia) the United States. If their parents lacked the funding to pay their way, they sometimes were fortunate to attract missionary sponsorship, as did J. J. Walters, the early Liberian educator and author of *Guanya Pau: A Story of an African Princess* (1891), who studied in the United States under missionary auspices in the waning years of the nineteenth century. Other strategies ambitious youngsters adopted included working on ships that plied the route between Britain and West Africa and terminating their employment on arrival at Liverpool, or simply stowing away, hiding in the holds while the ships were docked in West African ports and emerging from hiding when the vessels were well at sea. After the Second World War, many West Africans who had served in the British army and air force in European theaters during the war stayed on in Britain after demobilization to learn some profession, most training as lawyers. Fourah Bay College in Sierra Leone, founded as a teacher training institution in 1827, provided an alternative after it became affiliated with Durham University in 1876, and after 1945 university education became available elsewhere in West Africa—at university colleges in Nigeria (at Ibadan) and the Gold Coast, now Ghana (at Legon).

The foregoing overview of the early days of Western education explains a phenomenon that long characterized modern African literatures: the preponderance of men among the writers, and the corresponding underrepresentation of women. Just as Ezeulu would have thought it unthinkable to send a daughter to scout out the conditions in the bosom of the new thing the Christian missions represented, or to serve as his stake therein, so most parents at the time felt more comfortable sending their sons, and sometimes other male dependents, to school than committing their daughters. Other traditional factors were at work, too, of course, such as the pervasive belief (especially after the value of an education became obvious) that men had the greater need of equipping themselves with it than women had, since men bore the responsibility of providing for their families while women would be expected to mind the home and raise the family. Socialization certainly made women less adventurous than men, and thus less likely to embark on such ventures as stevedoring or stowing away. Furthermore, women were not offered the opportunity to enlist or be drafted to swell the ranks of the British troops engaged in the war against Germany.

Not surprisingly, therefore, the authors of the first African texts (literary and otherwise) in the modern tradition were African clients of the early Christian establishments, mainly clerics and teachers and almost invariably male, and people otherwise connected with the missions. For example, Carl Christian Reindorf (1844–1917) of the Gold Coast (now Ghana), who apart from collecting traditional tales also published *The History of the Gold Coast and Asante* (1877), was a catechist and later minister of the Evangelical Mission Society; and the Liberian Edward Wilmot Blyden (1832–1912), who apart from founding and editing the newspaper *The Negro* in Sierra Leone also published *Christianity, Islam and the Negro Race* (1887), was an ordained Presbyterian minister until his resignation from the ministry in 1886.

With the exception of the controversial Nigerian author Amos Tutuola (1920–97), practically all the dominant figures in post-1945 Anglophone West African literature benefited from extensive Western education and concomitant intensive westernization, experiences that inevitably manifest themselves in different guises in their works and careers. While authors with lower levels of education have produced and continue to produce a rich body of literature, their works are usually categorized as "popular," poor relations, that is, of the canonical—works that are issued by major international (or national) publishers, and that are likely to find their way into the reading lists of university literature courses. Tutuola's inclusion within the latter tradition results from fortuitous misunderstandings that initially placed him among the ranks of the cosmopolitan writers, and later kept him there long after his luster had become tarnished.[1]

The discussion of the African experience in the last five centuries bears witness to the European factor on the continent, as witness the adoption of colonialism as the major periodizing event—precolonial, colonial, postcolonial, or neocolonial. So, too, African literatures in general and the regional one under discussion in particular acknowledge in a number of ways the determining role of European activities: the delimitations and classifications of the literatures, their orientation and audience, and their themes and preoccupations. Moreover, the end of colonization has not resulted in emancipating African literatures from their dependence on the "European" (or American) factor, whose imprint remains as pronounced as during the days of high colonialism, and in some respects has even intensified. Understanding this phenomenon of persistent "coloniality" is therefore crucial for an understanding of the literatures themselves.

Delimiting the Subject

Identity in the modern or postmodern era has come under close scrutiny and has become a much less stable or reliable classificatory tool than it was thought to be even as late as the midpoint of the twentieth century, all its conceivable bases having since been exposed and discredited as inventions and social constructs. Speaking on the subject close to the turn of the century, Edward Said described the state as "the chief, most official, forceful, and coercive identity," and added that like other similar identities it needs to be scrutinized (Said 1992, 13). He was addressing the silver jubilee of the Association for Commonwealth

Language and Literature Studies in Canterbury, and his immediate target was the organizing rubrics of literature studies. Whatever identity might be attached to any of the various headings or subheadings into which literature and all aspects of the creative and scholarly enterprises involved in it are divided, he urged, it "need imply neither the ontologically given and eternally determined stability of that identity, nor its uniqueness, its utterly irreducible character, its privileged status as something total and complete in and of itself" (Said 1992, 13). His words serve as a reminder that the terms of reference used in constituting the subject of this book could be modified in any of a number of ways, thus significantly changing the area and scope of its coverage. One could adduce reasons, for example, to take the turn of the twentieth century as a starting point, or to substitute geography for language as the determining criterion (taking the whole of West Africa, the whole of Africa, or a single country as the subject), or focus on themes (such as protest and conflict), or take a generic approach (concentrating on fiction, drama, or poetry), and so forth.

Although there is some measure of arbitrariness in the definition of our present subject, there is also some sound justification for it. Said suggested in his speech that a way of destabilizing the rubrics in literature studies is "to look at the way a work … begins *as* a work, begins *from* a political, social, cultural situation, begins *to do* certain things and not others" (Said 1992, 14). If we apply the political and social criteria, the logic of the constitution of our subject is unimpeachable. As I asserted at the beginning, African literatures are a bequest of the interactions between Europe and Africa. The two most influential events in those interactions are the transatlantic slave trade, which raged from the sixteenth century to the nineteenth, and colonialism, which was essentially a feature of the twentieth century. Of the two, as far as the literature we are examining is concerned, colonialism has had the greater relevance and impact. In our geographical area, the dominant colonial powers were Britain and France, and the experience of the colonized subjects in the French sphere differed markedly from that of the people under British rule. France based its colonial practice on the policy of assimilation, that is, of absorbing colonized subjects as effectively as possible into French culture with the declared objective of transforming them into French citizens nominally on a par with the French of the *métropole*. Accordingly, the French designed the educational system in their colonies to wean their African subjects from their native cultures and instill into them French attitudes, habits, tastes, and manners. In order to make good on the promise of equal status as French citizens for the Africans, they provided for African representation in the French *parlement*, where African deputies from the colonized territories sat alongside their metropolitan compatriots. By contrast, the British colonial policy of indirect rule, devised by Frederick Lugard for Northern Nigeria initially in 1900 but extended in 1914 to Southern Nigeria and eventually adapted for the other West African colonies, was free of any desire to convert Africans to Englishmen and Englishwomen. The policy was predicated on the maintenance of traditional institutions, especially the administrative structures, but restructuring them to serve British colonial interests. Its approach to the education of the colonized peoples was also functional, mainly to provide low-level personnel for the bureaucracy. Far from attempting to inculcate any notion of Englishness in Africans, the educational system sought to encourage "love of tribe," and it was not until it became necessary to prepare Africans for independence, that is around the middle of the century, that the Indian model, based on Thomas B. Macaulay's famous "Minute on Indian Education" (1835), was adopted for West African countries as well.

The differences in the colonizers' policies and administration of their respective colonies spawned different approaches to, and processes of, decolonization in the two Europhone spheres, and, indeed, also different structures of postcoloniality, *francophonie* stressing a continuing linguistic and cultural bond with the *métropole*, while the commonwealth structure favored by Great Britain hinges on shared political interests and economic obligations.

The literary products of Anglophone West Africa (with the exception of Liberia) share a common political, social, and cultural basis, as well as a common purpose—namely shedding the debilitating heritage of colonization and forging a viable postcoloniality. We may attribute this common purpose to the authors' common experience of colonial education and the broader colonial elite formation process, and to their fashioning by the culture of colonialism, and to colonial institutions generally. Furthermore, since language is the heart and soul of literature, the use of English as the literary medium across the area is a powerful argument for taking a unitary view of its literature. It is precisely the common use of the English language that explains the inclusion of atypical subjects—a country that was not part of the British Empire (Liberia), and individuals from Francophone countries (Cameroon and Guinea) who opted to write in English.

A historical background for Liberia is provided later in this section, but a few words at this point will suffice to explain the interesting case of Cameroon. After the defeat of Germany in the First World War, the League of Nations split the German colony of Kamerun into two and mandated their administration respectively to the British (Cameroon) and the French (Cameroun). In 1961, at the height of the decolonization wave in Africa, the United Nations organized a plebiscite for the people of the two mandated territories to decide their political future. The southern part of the British mandate voted to join Francophone Cameroun as the Federal Republic of Cameroon, while the northern part opted to become a part of Nigeria. These developments account for the presence of a number of Anglophone writers in Francophone Cameroon, among them Mbella Sonne Dipoko and Bate Besong. Another notable Anglophone writer from a Francophone country is Prince Modupe (Paris) of Guinea, whose education and long residence in the United States resulted in his greater comfort with English and his preference for identity as an Anglophone writer.

The choice of the end of the Second World War as the starting point for this study has sound historical and political foundations. In an essay in *Decolonization and After* (1980), Dennis Austin explains that decolonization in the British empire was forced upon the colonizer by, among other factors, "the coercive costs of attempts to combat Asian or African or local nationalism of one kind or another," and the general weariness rife in the world after the First World War with the sort of imposed order that colonialism represents. "We may also add," he writes, "that, despite all the protestations of mutual esteem at numerous independence celebrations, there were beginnings of a strong undercurrent of cultural and racist resentment on the side of the colonised in respect of the history of the colonial part." Even though Africans resented being colonized right from the beginning and obliged the colonizers to mount "pacification" campaigns to enforce their rule, the Second World War proved to be a powerful catalyst for latent anticolonial sentiments in the colonies. Britain, like France, had enlisted its colonial subjects in its armed forces in the struggle to deny Adolf Hitler his goals of colonizing all of Europe, and those subjects had made the inevitable connection between the dispute in Europe and the reality in their own lands.

The explanations that the colonizing powers offered for waging war on Germany provoked a debate in West Africa and in colonies elsewhere about the rationales and legitimacy of European colonialism and imperialism. The most famous intellectual movement took place among West African and Antillean French subjects living in Paris and spread from there to the colonies. Negritude, as the movement was called, questioned both the claims of French culture to superiority over African ones and the logic of France's exercise of colonial authority over African territories that produced men like Léopold Sédar Senghor, reputedly an intellectual match for anyone the *métropole* could offer. The birth of *négritude* is usually dated to Senegalese Alioune Diop's inauguration of the journal *Présence Africaine* in Paris in 1947. According to Valentin Mudimbe, "What Diop's project represents is a questioning, not of the French culture *per se* but of the imperial ambition of the Western civilization." The magazine was thus a cultural enterprise whose purpose was to challenge the cultural basis of the "civilizing" mission, "to bring in the very center of the French power and culture what was being negated in the colonies, that is, the dignity of otherness" (Mudimbe 1992, xvii). Although the development took place in Paris, its application embraced all of Africa; as Mudimbe adds, "Diop's *Présence Africaine* claims to incarnate the voice of a silenced Africa" (1992, xviii). In fact its impact in time came to be felt, not in Africa only, but in the entire African diaspora.

The literature associated with *Présence Africaine*, in particular its poetry, defiantly embraced and celebrated the African heritage that the colonial project had decried as uncivilized and had sought to eradicate. Negritude turned the tables on the colonial doctrine by proclaiming the superiority of that heritage over European cultures, and although Anglophone intellectuals ridiculed what they saw as negritude's ostentatious negrism (as in the quip often attributed to Wole Soyinka to the effect that a tiger does not need to proclaim its tigritude), they were nevertheless affected by the movement. The title of Olumbe Bassir's *An Anthology of West African Verse* (1957), the first collection of poetry published in Anglophone West Africa, recalls that of Senghor's seminal negritude work, *An Anthology of New Black and Malgache Poetry* (1948), and it in fact contained mostly Francophone negritude poems in English translation. Early Anglophone poetry, like that of the Sierra Leonean Abioseh Nicol, the Ghanaian Kwesi Brew, and the Nigerian Sam Epelle, witnessed to the unmistakable influence of the movement; at least it shared negritude's impulses, specifically the embrace and celebration of nature. What it lacked was the sometimes anticolonial stridency of Francophone negritude, as exemplified by David Diop's verse.

Paradoxically, the Anglophone intellectuals, with their undeniable colonial fashioning, based their critique of negritude on the claim that whereas the French colonial philosophy of assimilation had radically alienated its clients from their culture the British policy of indirect rule had permitted British colonial subjects to remain in continuous contact with their roots and cultures. Yet, in reality there was little to choose between Francophone and Anglophone intellectuals and writers on this score: Francophone negritude writers flaunted their negrism in overcompensation for their earlier apostasy, and Anglophone writers flaunted theirs to demonstrate that they had never deserted their roots. In any case, both camps shared the postwar imperative of African assertion that propelled the drive for decolonization, and the concept of the African Personality, that driving force in Anglophone decolonization, is quite comparable to Francophone negritude.

In the genre of fiction, the earliest published work by an author from Anglophone West Africa was *Guanya Pau: A Story of an African Princess*, which was published in the United

States in 1891. On the African continent itself, Joseph E. Casely-Hayford's *Ethiopia Unbound: Studies in Race Emancipation* appeared in print in 1911, and quite a few other works followed before Chinua Achebe's *Things Fall Apart* came out in 1958. Yet historians of African literature credit Achebe's novel with inaugurating the modern tradition of Anglophone African fiction. The explanation is that Achebe's hugely popular first novel, an example par excellence of what Janheinz Jahn described as protest literature (1968, 90), was a resounding affirmation of African cultures, and a condemnation (although in a rather genteel tone) of colonialist arrogance toward and ignorance about the African world and its cultures. In a vein similar to that of Achebe's *Things Fall Apart*, the Sierra Leonean William Conton's *The African* (1960), an early anti-apartheid novel at a time when the pernicious system was at its most virulent in South Africa, offers a good illustration of the pan-African scope of the anticolonial sentiments rife on the continent. In this regard one can categorically state that modern African literatures began as a dialogue with history, specifically a discussion in some fashion of the fateful contact between Europe and Africa and its unfortunate consequences for Africa and Africans, and it has largely retained that quality in its transformations. The isolated earlier authors, even when they were critical of colonial unfairness (as some were towards the end of the nineteenth century), could not be considered as representing an anticolonialist tradition or a sustained movement in protest of European rule, and later writers such as Amos Tutuola, whose "ghost novel" *The Palm-Wine Drinkard and His Dead Tapster in the Dead's Town* was published in 1952, fall outside the mood and mainstream of the new West African literature.

Tutuola was not alone in deviating from the general movement to vindicate African cultures through literature and to celebrate the nations newly emergent out of colonialism. In contrast to the stance of their Francophone negritude counterpart, early Anglophone poetry and drama were as a rule also largely disengaged from political matters. In general the poetry of Abioseh Nicol, Ghana's Dei Anang and R. E. G. Armattoe, and even Nigeria's Christopher Okigbo and Wole Soyinka often dealt with private emotions or satirized fellow Africans for too glaringly aping European habits and manners. Similarly, early dramatists concentrated on domestic, familial relations and personal foibles, as did Soyinka in his *The Swamp Dwellers* (1957) and *The Lion and the Jewel* (1959), the Sierra Leonean Sarif Easmon in *Dear Parent and Ogre* (1965), and the Ghanaian Joe de Graft in *Sons and Daughters* (1963). Even so, a closer look reveals that the subject of these poems and plays was the unease Achebe referred to in the title of his second novel (1960), that is, the uncertainties and dislocations that the colonial experience had imposed on African lives.

To the extent that the authors' targets were, in one guise or another, habits that evinced imperfect assimilation of Western habits, and because the writers themselves emulated European models, the writers vindicate the description of their products (by Jahn and others) variously as "mission literature," "apprentice literature," and "tutelage literature," in addition to the already cited "protest literature." Missionary midwifery at the birth of African literacy (and therefore literature) explains the "missionary" epithet, while the understandable lack of mastery and sophistication in the earliest works, and the derivativeness of their styles, justify the charge of apprenticeship. Jahn rationalizes the seemingly incongruous coupling of "protest" and "tutelage" with the observation that protest writers used the glorification of their African heritage as a ruse to avoid the appearance of favoring tutelage, and that the coexistence of both strains merely reflected the nature of colonialism, "which gave with one hand and took away with the other" (1968, 91).

Historical and Political Context

The historical and political backdrops for post-1945 Anglophone West African literature are powerful as shaping forces for the literary works, and also as determinants of what and how writers choose to write, and even where they choose to live. Following are brief historical and political accounts for each of the applicable countries.

Cameroon

Because of Cameroon's colonial experience, its Anglophone literature, what there is of it, has always received only glancing attention as an appendage to Nigerian writing. It is necessary, therefore, to address it briefly at this point.

After Germany's defeat at the hands of the Allies in the First World War, the League of Nations divided its West African colony of German Kamerun between Great Britain and France as mandated territories, the much larger eastern part (now known as Cameroun) going to France and the western remainder (West Cameroon) going to Great Britain. In keeping with its colonizing policy of assimilation, which sought to absorb its colonized subjects into French culture, France inaugurated an educational system of rather respectable quality in its territory and introduced facilities such as publishing outlets. Great Britain on the other hand, whose colonizing policy was indirect rule (which one may fairly characterize as colonization on the cheap), treated educational and cultural matters with benign neglect. It in fact administered its mandated territory from Lagos as part of eastern Nigeria. The result as far as the literary arts were concerned was that while the newly Francophone Cameroonians were developing a literary culture, their Anglophone counterparts occupied themselves instead with cultivating a strong tradition in indigenous oral performances.

On February 11, 1961, after Nigeria's independence in October 1960, the people of West Cameroon held a plebiscite and decided to join their Francophone compatriots who had been granted their own independence on January 1, 1960. Thus came into being what Emmanuel Doh describes as the only country on the continent with "exo-glossic bilingualism," using French and English as its official languages (Doh 1993, 76). The Anglophone citizens of the unified country, being numerically inferior and relatively less westernized than Francophone Cameroonians, consider themselves (and are treated) as second-class citizens who are always suspect and under surveillance by the Francophone power structure. What Anglophone literature has developed therefore suffers from what Doh calls an "identity crisis" because of the strange context in which it has developed, a context in which the writer labors under the handicap of being colonized by his or her fellow Cameroonian (Doh 1993, 77).

Anglophone Cameroonians also confess to an inferiority complex in relation to their Francophone compatriots with regard to literary production. As Doh's title indicates, they are loath even to claim that they have produced anything that deserves to be designated as literature. Because they blame their backwardness in this regard on a lack of encouragement, especially in the form of publishing facilities, they find themselves in the paradoxical position of looking longingly back to colonial days when they at least had Nigeria's at their disposal. During the time of the mandate, the Cameroonian Mbella Sonne Dipoko lived and worked in Nigeria and achieved an international stature as a novelist and poet. Four decades after independence, no Anglophone writer has approached his level of accomplishment, although the playwright and poet Bate Besong and playwright Bole Butake have attracted some critical and scholarly notice. For the most part, these writers depend on Nigerian publishing outlets, and, as in Ephraim N. Ngwafor's *May Former Victoria Smile Again* (1989), lament their country's abandonment of Anglophone resources and infrastructures to ruin. It is no wonder, therefore, that they would contest the notion that they are experiencing postcoloniality, arguing instead that what exists in their part of Cameroon is a type of neocolonialism in which the colonizers are their nominally fellow Cameroonians.

The Gambia

The Gambia, whose population comprises Serer, Serahule, Jola, Fula, Mandinka, and Wolof elements, is demographically and culturally a part of Senegal, which is, however, Francophone, having been colonized by France. A former British colony called Gambia before independence, The Gambia became a sovereign nation on February 18, 1965. The country hugs the Gambia River, and for more than four hundred years the peoples settled along the river, who are said to have owed allegiance to the kingdom of Mali, maintained trading contact with the inhabitants of the Niger River's banks to the east. The various groupings also maintained close interactions, including trading and warring, among themselves.

The Portuguese began trading in the area in 1455, introducing groundnuts (peanuts) and cotton. In 1581 they relinquished their rights to the British, whose presence dated from 1587. The latter erected Fort James on an Island near the mouth of the Gambia River in 1661. Twenty years later, in 1681, the French built their own fort at nearby Albreda, and the two European powers thereafter became embroiled in frequent skirmishes from these bases, but in 1783 Britain secured the monopoly of trading up the Gambia River. The free hand enabled the British rather quickly to turn Fort James into one of the most active slaving establishments on the West African coast. After the abolition of slavery in 1807, they began to use the fort as a base for intercepting vessels that persisted in the traffic, in support of which activity they obtained a lease for Banjul Island from the King of Kombo in 1816. There they established the new settlement of Bathurst and later obtained permission from other neighboring rulers to build other settlements: MacCarthy Island in 1823, Barra Point in 1826, and Fatatenda in 1829. That same year they abandoned Fort James and for the next century and a half administered the territory from Sierra Leone. They intervened frequently in local conflicts, however, most often in response to invitation by one or the other of the warring parties in the dynastic wars that raged between the 1840s and 1890s, and received concessions in return for their help. One of these concessions was the right to build a fort in Lower Niani in 1844.

In 1894 Britain proclaimed a protectorate over the entire area and divided the land into districts under commissioners who exercised authority over the native rulers. Nationalistic and anticolonial agitation ensued, spearheaded by Edward Francis Small whose inspiration came from attending a meeting of the National Congress of British West Africa in 1920. He founded the Bathurst Trade Union in 1928 and called a general strike the following year. Other organizations he launched were the Rate Payers Association (whose slogan was "No Taxation Without Representation") and the Cooperative Union (which worked to give farmers some say in the pricing of their products).

The British response was cautious and tentative, in part because of doubts about the viability of the territory as an independent state. In 1930 they authorized the first representative institutions, the Bathurst Urban District Council and the Board of Health, and in 1959 convened the first of a series of constitutional conferences that would eventually lead to independence for the country. Also in 1959 Dawda Kairaba Jawara, a Mandinka veterinary surgeon, formed the People's Progressive Party. A constitutional conference produced a constitution in 1960, which, after another conference in 1961, was amended in 1962. Yet another conference in 1964 produced a new constitution under which the colony became the independent country of The Gambia in 1965. Five years later, in 1970, it proclaimed itself a republic.

In contrast to several African countries, The Gambia has largely retained a democratic tradition, holding elections every five years. This record was briefly interrupted in 1981 when a July coup by the paramilitary Field Force briefly deposed President Dawda Jawara. It eventually failed, though, thanks to intervention by Senegalese troops who reinstated Jawara. He showed his gratitude by leading his country into a confederation with Senegal, which adopted the name Senegambia, but it was short-lived: it was dissolved in September 1989 because of irreconcilable differences between the partners. Although relations between the two countries were strained for some time, they had improved enough by 1991 for them to enter into a treaty of friendship and cooperation.

In July 1994, junior officers of the Gambian military under the leadership of Lieutenant Yaya (also Yahya) Jammeh ousted Jawara's government in another coup. The international community roundly condemned the military takeover, especially because Jawara had managed in the almost thirty years of his rule to establish an international reputation for adherence to democratic rule and respect for human rights. Following intense pressure from both within The Gambia and outside, the military-led government announced a timetable for transferring power to civilians in 1996 after a review of the constitution, probes into the wealth of public servants, and elections.

A referendum on a new constitution took place on August 8, 1996, and a presidential election on September 26. A decree barred Jawara, his vice president, and all former ministers of the People's Progressive Party (PPP) from contesting the elections and from holding any political office in future. Following a strategy that has become familiar in West African politics, Yaya Jammeh resigned from the military to run for the presidency. Not surprisingly, he won the elections. He was reelected in 2001 and again in 2006.

Ghana

Farther to the south and east, the Portuguese had been trading along the coast from the late fifteenth century, exploiting the gold resources of the stretch known as the Gold Coast and building several forts to protect their interests. The British, the Danes, and the Dutch followed in the sixteenth century, also building their own forts. Intense rivalry was rife among them, especially after the commencement of the slave trade, which was so lucrative and whose volume was so huge that by the time the traffic came to an end early in the nineteenth century fully seventy-six slaving forts cluttered the coastline of modern-day Ghana alone. That heritage has left its mark on the psyche of Ghanaians, as well as on their literature (and cinema), as witness Kofi Awoonor's *Comes the Voyager at Last: A Tale of Return to Africa* (1992) and Ayi Kwei Armah's *Osiris Rising* (1995), both of which seek expiation for their authors' perceived African culpability for the heinous trade in human cargo. After the abolition of the trade the British concluded treaties with local chiefs in the area and continued to pursue "legitimate" trade. But in 1873 they devised a ruse to depose the most powerful of the rulers, the Asantehene of the Asante, and declared the British colony of the Gold Coast. They had little difficulty suppressing the local resistance, and the colony went on to prosper on the strength of an economy whose mainstay was cocoa; indeed in the 1920s the colony enjoyed the reputation of being the world's chief producer of the crop. The British pursued a policy of involving local people as much as possible in the colony's administration, and accordingly cultivated a well-educated elite, many of whom trained in the United Kingdom, and whose numbers were augmented by a University College that was established at Legon near Accra in 1948.

Ironically but predictably, it was from among this professional elite that the agitation for independence arose. Although he was not the initiator of the independence campaign, Kwame Nkrumah later came to personify it. He had studied and taught at Lincoln University in Pennsylvania between 1935 and 1945 before moving to London to study law. From there the United Gold Coast Convention recruited him to serve as its general secretary, a post he returned home to assume in 1947. Dissatisfied with the convention's lukewarm embrace of the idea of independence, he resigned the post and formed his own party, the Convention People's Party, in 1949. With the party as his base, he pressured the colonial administration by means of what he called "positive action campaigns" to grant self-government to the country. A successful general strike that he called landed him in jail, but from there he and his party won the general elections of 1951, and the authorities were obliged to release him and ask him to form a government. As chief minister, he succeeded in gaining the trust and respect of the British government, which had begun to make preparations to bring colonial rule in the Gold Coast to an end. Six years later, on March 6, 1957, the country became independent, with Nkrumah as its prime minister, and it renamed itself after the ancient Sahelian empire of Ghana.

Nkrumah's vision of a united Africa endeared him to many Africans, but what many saw as his megalomania, addiction to grandiose projects, and financial mismanagement resulted in his overthrow in a military coup in 1966. The sorry state of affairs in the country at the time of the coup and the disillusion that led to it constitute the subject of Ayi Kwei Armah's first novel, *The Beautyful Ones Are Not Yet Born* (1969).

After Nkrumah's fall, the country embarked upon a lengthy period of instability, replete with food shortages, military takeovers, and gross corruption. The government changed hands in rapid succession as the economy became a shambles and the currency, the cedi, became almost valueless. The crisis eventually led to the accession of Flight Lieutenant Jerry Rawlings in 1979 following another military coup. After executing several officers and politicians, he supervised a general election and in short order handed the reins of power to civilian politicians in the same year, a mere three months after he had seized control of the government. Shortly thereafter, however, he thought better of his action, and in 1981 he staged another coup to retake power and held on to it as a military dictator for twelve years. The country returned to a civilian constitution in January 1993, and Rawlings, running as a civilian, was elected president in 1996. He remained president until 2000, when he was obliged by the constitution to step aside. John Kofi Agyekum Kufuor succeeded him.

The years of military rule, including the early Rawlings years, were dangerous ones for opponents and critics of the government, some of whom were eliminated, and some of whom fled the country to seek safety abroad. But Rawlings is credited with returning some stability to the country's politics and economy, and for repairing the country's infrastructure. Under his leadership Ghana began to promote itself to tourists as the gateway to Africa, and to reach out to Africans in the diaspora, especially in the United States, to return to Ghana and invest in the country. The prominent African American scholar W. E. B. Du Bois had set an example by renouncing his U.S. citizenship in 1961 and emigrating to Ghana, where a cultural center in the capital, Accra, memorializes his life and achievements.

Liberia

Located on what was known as the Grain Coast, Liberia is bounded on the west by Sierra Leone, on the north by Guinea, and on the east by the Ivory Coast. Because of its history, it enjoys a special relationship with the United States.

Europeans made their appearance in the coastal areas in the 1400s, procuring such items as malagueta pepper, wood, fresh water, rice, palm oil, cassava, gold, ivory, camwood, local textiles, and later, of course, slaves. In exchange, they offered textiles, guns, gunpowder, knives, cutlasses, iron bars, brass basins, jewelry, and liquor. The manumission of slaves, combined with the abolition of the slave trade at the end of the eighteenth century and the beginning of the nineteenth, prompted certain people in the United States to seek territories in Africa for resettling unwanted freed slaves. They saw the Sierra Leone experiment as a promising example to emulate and envisaged their colony as an outpost of Christianity and Western civilization in Africa.

In collaboration with the U.S. government, which appropriated $100,000 for the venture, the American Colonization Society outfitted the ship *Elizabeth* and sent it off in 1820 with eighty-six freed slaves—men, women, and children—as the vanguard of the prospective colony's population. Under the tutelage of Samuel Bacon, John Bankson, and Samuel Crozer, all white men, the group made its first settlement on Sherbro Island and promptly fell victim to tropical diseases, shortages of supplies, lack of discipline, and hostile local populations. Those who survived soon abandoned the settlement and moved to Freetown, on the mainland in what is now Sierra Leone.

A new contingent of settlers sponsored by the American Colonization Society arrived in 1821. Their leaders initially failed to secure permission to settle at Grand Bassa, finally succeeded with some difficulty in persuading the local Dei, Gola, and Mahnbahn rulers to cede Cape Mesurado and its immediate environs to U.S. Navy Captain Robert Field Stockton and Eli Ayres, the official U.S. representative, for the purpose of resettling freed slaves from the Americas. From the start the settlers experienced difficulties because their negotiators failed to live up to the terms they agreed with the local rulers, and the local population refused on their part to ratify their chiefs' concessions. It was not until well into 1822 that the settlers were able to move from a temporary shelter on Dazoa (later named Providence), an island in the Mesurado River, to Cape Mesurado. The Society ran the settlement from 1822 to 1847 with the backing of the U.S. government, Ayres serving as the first agent. Jehudi Ashmun his successor named the settlement Christopolis in 1824, but the name was soon changed to Monrovia in honor of the U.S. president James Monroe. Later still, the name Liberia was adopted.

Other groups founded colonies nearby: colonization societies from New York and Pennsylvania established Edina in 1832; the Young Men's Colonization Society of Pennsylvania founded Bassa Cove in 1834; the same year the Maryland Colonization Society founded Maryland-in-Africa; and the following year the Mississippi Colonization Society, whose primary mover was Jefferson County Judge James Green, founded Greenville, also known as Mississippi-in-Africa.

In 1839 the Commonwealth of Liberia, comprising Montserado County and Grand Bassa, came into being, and Greenville joined in 1842. Friction resulting from, among other causes, differing conceptions about land tenure and supercilious paternalism toward Africans on the part of the settlers continued to mar relationships between the repatriates and the African population. The settlement also had to contend with European traders who did not recognize the authority of the colonization societies to impose duties or regulate trade. On consultation with the U.S. government about the best course to pursue, the American Colonization Society opted for independence for the territory. Accordingly, the country declared itself the independent Republic of Liberia on July 26, 1847, and Joseph Jenkins Roberts was elected its first president. By the turn of the century, Britain and France had recognized the republic.

Neither the external problems that suggested independence nor the local problems of "race" relations between repatriate and indigenous populations disappeared after the establishment of the republic. Furthermore, the hope that new immigrations would ease the country's economic slump was not realized. Poor race relations and the process of expanding the borders of the republic led to a series of conflicts between the settlers and the indigenous peoples, for example with the Grebo in 1875 and 1910, with the Kru in 1915 to 1916 and in the 1930s, and with the Gola in 1917. In an attempt to alleviate the internal problems, an Interior Department had been established in 1869, and in 1873 the authorities decided to extend limited representation in the legislature to indigenous peoples. Equal rights to all Liberians, at least nominally, became the official policy only in the 1940s, but that development did not disturb the repatriates' grip on power.

An anemic economy and the lack of an industrial base turned Liberia into a debtor country subsisting on a succession of loans, supplemented with high customs rates and the revenues from concessions (of lands and rights) to commercial enterprises, the most famous being the Firestone concession of 1926. It granted Firestone the rent of one million acres at about five cents an acre, and a tax rate of only 1 percent on its revenues from rubber production. The country's problems were complicated in the 1930s when a League of Nations investigation charged it with activities amounting to slave-raiding and slave-trading in connection with its supplying conscripted laborers to Spanish cocoa farmers in Equatorial Guinea. It was able to avoid, however, the fate some Europeans proposed: that the country be declared a mandated territory.

With the accession of William Tubman to the presidency in 1944, the country embarked on a more tranquil era, but when he died in 1971 and was succeeded by William R. Tolbert, his vice president for nineteen years, some discontent arose among people who wished for some fresh blood, especially because Tolbert was widely perceived as lacking in social and political acumen. He proved them right in their misgivings about him, as his gross inefficiency and ineffectiveness led to a political crisis to which he responded by becoming a recluse. His rule ended on April 12, 1980, when Master Sergeant Samuel K. Doe staged a military coup in which Tolbert was assassinated. Doe became the head of the ruling junta, the People's Redemption Council. Following the now familiar pattern, Doe stood for election for the presidency as a civilian in 1985, and after what was widely held to be a rigged election process he became the country's first indigenous president. His rule was marked by widespread corruption, heavy-handed repression, and abuse of human rights that forced many Liberians to flee to neighboring Guinea and Ivory Coast.

National Patriotic Front of Liberia (NPFL) rebels under the leadership of Charles Taylor invaded the country from Ivory Coast in 1989. When Taylor proclaimed himself president and threatened to seize hostages, the United States sent in troops to stop him. The chaos worsened when in the following year another pretender to the presidency surfaced in the person of Prince Yormie Johnson, whose men assassinated Doe. Under Nigeria's leadership, the Economic Community of West African States (ECOWAS) sent in a peacekeeping force and arranged negotiations among the contestants for power. It also installed an interim government under Amos Sawyer. Taylor, however, remained uncooperative; he besieged Monrovia with Libyan and Burkina Faso backing in 1992 and engaged ECOWAS forces in battles. The fighting went on in spite of several cease-fires until 1995, when a peace agreement signed in Abuja, Nigeria, led to the institution of a new government under Wilton Sankawulo, with the understanding that elections would be held in 1996. Fighting resumed in Monrovia toward the middle of the year, but the process of disarmament eventually began, and the war ended in 1997.

The legislative and presidential elections of that year saw Taylor assuming the presidency, whereupon he followed the familiar pattern most postindependence African leaders have established—enriching themselves and their cronies at the expense of the people. Taylor's questionable activities extended beyond Liberia's borders, inasmuch as he was known to have provided the main backing for Sierra Leone's Revolutionary United Front (RUF) rebels in return for diamonds. The exploitation of that country's gems to finance a civil disorder that was ugly even by African standards led the United Nations in 2000 to impose an eighteen-month ban on the international sale of diamonds in order to handicap the RUF; the UN also imposed sanctions on Liberia in May 2001.

Fighting between government forces and rebels had flared up around Voinjama in 2000, and the government had also to deal with Guinean forces on its border with that country. Soon the rebels were threatening Monrovia, and by July 2003 they were fighting within the capital, while peace talks were going on in Ghana. Taylor's position became more untenable when a United Nations court indicted him for crimes against humanity because of his sponsorship of the RUF and its atrocities in Sierra Leone. Under pressure from the rebels and the United Nations, and with the United States backing the ECOWAS forces in its effort to impose a peace, Taylor was finally persuaded to accept asylum in Nigeria, leaving the country to a caretaker government charged with its administration until 2006. An election that year saw the emergence of Ellen Johnson-Sirleaf as president, the first female head of state in Africa. The same year Charles Taylor was transferred to The Hague to stand trial for crimes against humanity.

Nigeria

Nigeria's history closely parallels that of Ghana. Its coastal area was heavily involved in the slave trade, a distinction that won it the designation Slave Coast. In 1861 the British took control of Lagos, proclaimed it a British colony, and set about interdicting the slave traffic from its waters. They also established themselves along the Niger River, and after the abolition of the slave trade shifted to commerce in commodities such as palm produce and ivory. In 1849 the British had appointed a consul with his seat in Fernando Po to assert and protect their interests in the Bight of Benin and the Bight of Biafra, and in 1885 they proclaimed the area the Oil River Protectorate. The following year the Royal Niger Company received a charter to administer the hinterland, which it did until in 1900 the crown proclaimed the area the Protectorate of Northern Nigeria. The three areas of British activity became unified as the Colony and Protectorate of Nigeria in 1914, the official, highly suggestive term for the process being amalgamation. As in the Gold Coast, the British went to considerable lengths to preserve the African character of their territory, involving local people in local administration (through the system of "indirect rule"), and keeping the number of British officials to a minimum. The establishment of University College in Ibadan in 1948 was part of the strategy of cultivating an African elite to collaborate with the colonizers and eventually take over the running of the country's affairs after independence.

The amalgamated regions were markedly different in their ethnic composition, religions, and traditional political structures. The northern region, the home of the Hausa, the Fulani, and other smaller groups, had been converted to Islam during the jihads of the nineteenth century, and its political structure was essentially feudal, with emirs and sultans at the helm. The forested hinterland of Lagos, the home of the Yoruba, was also characterized by a feudal political structure under *oba*s (kings). Because of their long interactions with both the Hausa-Fulani to the north and more recently the European traders from the coast, the Yoruba were partly Muslims and partly Christians, but overwhelmingly adherents of indigenous religions. The people of the eastern region, who were predominantly Igbo, had no well-defined political structure but practiced a sort of republicanism in which respected leaders formed deliberative councils to run the communities' affairs. Christianity was well established here also, along with a slight Islamic presence.

Through most of the colonial period the three regions were administered separately, and when political agitation for independence began in the 1930s the southern elite were united in the first political organization, the Nigerian Youth Movement, which came into being in 1934 but folded in 1941. The solidarity of the southern elite broke down thereafter, giving way to the formation of ethnically defined regional political parties. The first major party to emerge thereafter was the National Union of Nigeria and the Cameroons (NCNC) under the leadership of Nnamdi Azikiwe, an Igbo intellectual and politician. Originally national in membership, the party quickly became identified with the Igbo of the eastern region of the country, although it continued to have sizeable adherents among the Yoruba. The Action Group (AG), led by Obafemi Awolowo, was identified with the Yoruba and was predominant in the west, while in the north the Northern People's Congress under Ahmadu Bello held undisputed sway as the Hausa-Fulani party. The large number of ethnic groups in the country ensured the juxtaposition of large and small ones in the three regions, and thus the splintering of allegiances. That phenomenon has plagued Nigeria since before independence, and it may justifiably be blamed for the difficulties the country has experienced since.

After a number of constitutional conferences and constitutions, independence came amidst tremendous euphoria and great confidence that as the "giant of Africa" the country would embark on a role of leadership on the continent. But there was also pessimism, as Wole Soyinka dramatically showed in his play commemorating the country's attainment of independence, *A Dance of the Forests* (1960). It took a mere six years for the country's facade of unity to unravel, with the Igbo of the eastern region declaring their secession from the country to become the Republic of Biafra.

The causes of the war are complicated and still arouse passions on both sides, the Nigerian and the Biafran, as Chimamanda Ngozi's *Half of a Yellow Moon* (2006) demonstrates. In very brief summary, it resulted from the attempt, initially by the politicians of the three regions, to secure ultimate power in the federal administration, an attempt that British political and constitutional gerrymandering on the approach of independence made quite tricky. Disputed elections in 1964 and 1965, and political chaos in the Yoruba western region, made the country ungovernable, and the result was the first military coup led by Igbo officers on January 15, 1966. It delivered the government of the country to Major General Johnson Aguiyi-Ironsi, an Igbo and the highest-ranking officer in the Nigerian army. But the pattern of killings during the coup and the actions of Aguiyi-Ironsi on taking power aroused suspicions that an Igbo power grab was underway. The suspicions led to the killing of a large number of Igbos resident in the north, and thence to the exodus of Igbo refugees back to their heartland from all over the country. There, under their leader Colonel Odumegwu Ojukwu, they declared their secession from Nigeria and proclaimed the Republic of Biafra.

The war that followed, which lasted from July 3, 1967, to January 13, 1970, left indelible scars on the psyche of both the victors and the vanquished long after the reunification of the country. It also ushered in a prolonged period of rule by military regimes distinguished for their gross ineptitude and hardly imaginable venality: Aguiyi-Ironsi was succeeded by General Yakubu Gowon in 1966; Brigadier Murtala Mohammed took over in 1975, and on his assassination that same year was succeeded by Brigadier Olusegun Obasanjo. He returned power to the civilian regime of Alhaji Shehu Shagari (which proved a match for the military officers in graft and outright theft) in 1979, but the military retook control in 1983 under General Muhammad Buhari, who was himself overthrown in General Ibrahim Babangida's 1985 coup.

The huge wealth that the country derived from its oil resources beginning in the 1970s only pushed it deeper and deeper into economic ruin, as the soldiers and their civilian allies permitted the other sectors of the economy to atrophy while they secreted the revenues from petroleum into personal bank accounts in Switzerland and elsewhere.

The country's vigorous and outspoken press, as well as equally feisty intellectuals and writers, subjected the ruling cliques to ferocious criticism, for example in Festus Iyayi's *The Contract* (1982). The response, during the military regimes, was varying degrees of repression that forced several writers and academics into exile. During the regime of Sani Abacha (from 1993 to 1998), however, the country experienced the worst incidence of repression and government-sponsored murders in its history thus far. While inconveniences and hardships of varying degrees of severity at home, and better work and living prospects abroad, had always encouraged scholars and writers to migrate from the country to Europe, the United States, and even other African countries, the pace of exit accelerated considerably during the Abacha years. The arrest, trial, and conviction of the activist and playwright Ken Saro-Wiwa on a trumped-up charge of murder, and his execution despite worldwide objection in 1995, represented the lowest moment for the regime. Abacha's sudden and mysterious death in 1998 resulted in widespread jubilation, and his successor, General Abu-bakar, reading the clear signs of the depth of hatred for the military in the country, wisely arranged for elections preparatory to returning the country to civilian rule. The following year, Olusegun Obasanjo, a retired general who had headed the military junta from 1975 to 1979, won the presidential elections and took over the government. In 2003, the country made history when it went through a peaceful electoral exercise and change of government, even though Obasanjo was the president who emerged after the elections, and in spite of complaints that they were not free of shenanigans. He was reelected in the equally questionable general elections of 2005.

Sierra Leone

As was true for other parts of the West African coastline, the Portuguese were the first Europeans to arrive on the stretch of coastline they named Sierra Leone in 1462. The British came much later, but by the height of the transatlantic slave trade they had become the dominant power and the preeminent slave traders, with Bunce Island as their major trans-shipment port. As noted earlier, for a while they used Sierra Leone as the base from which they administered their Gambian interests.

During the war of American independence in the 1770s, a large number of American slaves fought on the British side and thus gained their freedom. After the war, fifteen thousand of them were transported to Britain, where they faced tremendous privations. These prompted some philanthropists under the influence of John Wesley to lease some land, named the Province of Freedom, in the vicinity of Bunce Island in 1787 to resettle the freed slaves. Three hundred among them, accompanied by a hundred whites, arrived to found Freetown later that year. Most of them soon succumbed to tropical illnesses, but a new infusion of fugitive American slaves from Nova Scotia and others from Jamaica arrived in 1792. Slaves from other parts of West Africa, liberated from slaving ships along the coast, added to their number. The result is that today Sierra Leone is home to more than a hundred ethnic groups, many of whom live in separate areas and continue to maintain their separate group identities.

Christian missionaries provided education to the settlers, and incidentally converted them to Christianity in the process. The result was the creation of a Creole elite class known locally as the Krio (who formed about 2 percent of the population); perennial conflict with the indigenous people became endemic, complicated by rivalries among the various indigenous groups. On the education front, in 1827 the Church Missionary Society (CMS) founded the Fourah Bay College, the first institution of higher learning in Anglophone West Africa. Initially intended as an institution for training clerics, it was upgraded in the 1870s to grant BAs in divinity and became affiliated with Durham University.

In 1895, Great Britain extended its control to the hinterland and imposed a hut tax, provoking a bloody riot in protest in which a large number of the Krio lost their lives as a consequence of their close identification with the colonial government. The intergroup tensions continued, but without major flare-ups, especially because the influence of the Krio had been somewhat weakened; an influx of Lebanese traders, who in many parts of colonial Africa served as a welcome buffer for the Europeans colonizers between themselves and their African subjects, had considerably weakened their economic clout. They maintained their monopoly on high civil-service posts among Africans, however. By 1924 tentative moves toward self-government were underway, in response to which the colonial administration established a legislative council with a membership that favored indigenous people. It was from among them that the leader of the independence movement emerged in the person of Wallace Johnson.

Independence came in 1961, by which time the country's mineral wealth, particularly in diamonds, had sown the seeds of the horrendous civil strife that has plagued its postcolonial history. Fueling the problem was the ethnic stratification of national politics, whereby the Sierra Leone People's Party (SLPP) was identified with the Mendes, while the All People's Congress (APC), formed by the trade unionist Siaka Stevens, was (in spite of its name) identified with the Temnes. It did not help either that both parties were on a par in terms of popularity among the general population.

The first prime minister of independent Sierra Leone was Milton Magai of the SLPP. When he died in 1964 he was succeeded by his brother Albert, who promptly set about replacing the top civil servants from other ethnic groups with Temnes. In the next election in 1967 the Krio threw their support behind APC, which won a slim majority in the parliament and made Siaka Stevens the new prime minister. The country's era of military coups began soon after, when Brigadier David Lansana deposed Stevens only to be arrested himself two days later by junior officers, who set up the National Reformation Council as the country's ruling body. Stevens went into exile in neighboring Guinea and began training a group in guerrilla warfare. His efforts however proved unnecessary, for another coup about a year later brought him back to head a new government. The political scene remained chaotic, though, enough so that in 1971 Stevens was forced to appeal to Guinea for a personal bodyguard after two assassination attempts on him in one day.

Political unrest, fiscal mismanagement, and cross-border conflicts with Liberia raged on. In 1985 Stevens turned eighty and nominated Major General Saidu Momoh to replace him as president. Momoh held the post until 1992, when a soldiers' uprising led by Captain Valentine Strasser forced him to flee the country, yielding control to Strasser and his National Provisional Ruling Council (NPRC). In the meantime, the infamous Foday Sankoh's Revolutionary United Front (RUF) had been raiding the country from Liberia since 1991; they continued to alienate more and more territory from government control and by 1995 were poised to take the capital, Freetown. The history of the conflict between the NPRC and RUF is complicated and bloody, and need not delay us. It suffices to say that despite numerous attempts at ending the bloodshed, fueled in large part by the lust for diamonds, it was not until the year 2000 that the prospect of a lasting solution seemed assured. Prompted by the increasing horror of the civil war, which was characterized by such atrocities as the chopping off of children's arms and legs, the United Nations assembled a large peacekeeping force of some seventeen thousand troops that succeeded in disarming the rebels in early 2002. The ensuing peace enabled the country to embark on the huge task of reconstruction, and of finding employment for the many thousands of combatants who roamed the country, many with no experience other than fighting.

Recurring Questions in Anglophone West African Literature

Students of African literature in general have at some point to confront such questions as: What comprises the literature? Who are the writers? What drew them to their calling? What is their conception of their role in society? And what *is* their relationship to the society? These would seem to be simple questions with obvious answers, as they might be in most other parts of the world, especially in Western countries, but with regard to Africa they are not so simple; neither are their answers so obvious.

The question as to what comprises *African* literature has no simple answer because there are in fact different contending literatures that could legitimately claim the title. The two major ones fall into two categories: literatures written in African languages, of which there are several, and literatures in the languages of the erstwhile colonizers, namely English, French, and Portuguese. Literature in English, which is what concerns us in this discussion, is itself divided into two types: the popular, and what we might call the elite. Typically, the popular literature is the product of people with a moderate level of education, and has a local clientele whose educational level (in the main) matches that of the writers. The elite literature is typically the product of university-educated writers from a variety of professions, and its clientele is international. I have used the word "typically" in the foregoing description because there are exceptions in both cases: some highly educated writers have addressed the popular market, for example Ghana's Asare Konadu and Nigeria's Cyprian Ekwensi, who is credited with inaugurating the famous Onitsha market literature. Perhaps the best example of a writer who had a modest education but took the international market by storm is the Nigerian Amos Tutuola.

Scholarly attention both within Africa and internationally has tended to favor the literature of the elite, which has a virtual monopoly of the African literary canon, although the popular literature has its own scholarly enthusiasts and has been the subject of a wealth of scholarship (see Obiechina 1972, 1973; Newell 2002).

The Writer's Role in Society

Inasmuch as our discussion will focus on the canonical literature and the canonical writers, we might now proceed to the question of their perception of their role in society. Fortunately, no less a person than the writer most often credited with pioneering modern African fiction has provided an explicit answer. In his view the writer champions his or her culture against external assaults and at the same time instills self-confidence in his or her people. Achebe's often-quoted statement of his aspiration limits itself to what impact he wished to have on his people: he would be pleased, he said, if he accomplished nothing more than convincing his readers that their past "was not one long night of savagery from which the first Europeans … delivered them." The essay in which he made the statement referred to the novelist as a teacher, and he obviously had his people in mind when he referred to his "readers." The work that best exemplifies his fulfillment of that role is his first novel, *Things Fall Apart* (1958), which eloquently proclaims the coherence and sufficiency of African cultures and societies, symbolized by Umuofia, and laid the blame for disrupting the life and history of the people on the colonizers' intrusion. The novel itself is a well-crafted rebuttal of the claims the colonizers and their apologists made against African traditional societies and cultures. For that reason, Edward Said, in taking issue with postcolonial writers who have been unduly critical of their own people for presiding over disordered climates, proffered Achebe as worthy of their emulation, for taking "the disorder back to the colonial intervention in the first place" in *Things Fall Apart* (Said 1994, 235).

Achebe's compatriot Wole Soyinka's early representation of what he perceived as the writer's function in society, as well as Ghanaian Ayi Kwei Armah's, is of a calling to be actively involved in leading society on the path of virtue. For Soyinka the writer is the embodiment of humanistic ideals in the society, "the record of the mores and experience of his people and … the voice of vision in his own time" (Soyinka 1968, 21). Lamenting what he saw as the "total collapse of ideals, the collapse of humanity itself" on the continent in the 1960s, he pointed out that the people at the helm of affairs were politicians, not writers, and asked, "Is this not a contradiction in a society whose great declaration of uniqueness to the outside world is that of a superabundant humanism?" (Soyinka 1968, 18). Armah made much the same point in 1979 when in a public lecture in Madison, Wisconsin, he claimed for African writers the mantle of the traditional bards destined to share power with traditional rulers, much as, he said, the artists of ancient Egypt ruled jointly with even the most powerful pharaohs. Because of this venerable tradition that invested the writer with political power, his exclusion from governance in independent African states, Armah claimed, represented a betrayal of African ethos.

A significant transformation (or evolution) is discernible in Achebe's perception of artistic roles on one hand and both Soyinka's and Armah's on the other. It is worth remarking that Achebe in his earliest work was doing battle with the colonizers on behalf of his people, broadly conceived, while Soyinka and Armah were more interested in confronting African inheritors of power and castigating them for their shortcomings. Achebe's position was that of a writer comfortable in his apparently unchallenged role as champion and teacher, whereas Soyinka's and Armah's testify to a sense of deprivation or marginalization by malfeasant usurpers. The implication of the development on the questions under discussion has been significant, but the transformation notwithstanding, the idea one comes away with is that the writer operates within his or her society and carries on a dialogue and relationship with it, whether they be harmonious or conflict-laden. One is not surprised, therefore, to read a scholar's contention that "one of the most important things for the Western reader of the African novel to remember is that the primary audience for most African novelists is not Western readers, but Africans" (Booker 1998, 14). While that would be the normal assumption, in fact the overwhelming weight of the evidence suggests quite the opposite. For example, what most readers of Achebe's early novels found irresistibly appealing was the access it gave them to hitherto unfamiliar African traditional practices and modes of expression. So generous was he in this regard that some among the readers and critics, especially Africans, wondered about the necessity to be so heavily anthropological. His diligence in translating Igbo terms into English—"*agadi-nwayi*, or old woman"; "the elders, or *ndichie*"; "hut, or *obi*"—and his painstaking explanations especially of the rationale for and significance of every cultural practice appeared to clearly indicate that the writer was not addressing himself to readers who shared his language and inside knowledge of such things. His incorporation of such traditional elements thus differed in its intention and effect from, for example, Efua Sutherland's use of folkloric material in such pieces as *The Marriage of Anansewa* (1971). Her intention was to indigenize the drama genre and enhance the possibilities for the growth of a traditional form by offering it a new vehicle.

Extraversion and Its Denials

Booker was able to make his contention because he took no account of the phenomenon that has been described as extraversion. The term refers to the outward direction of African efforts, in the realm of literature to the foreign publication of African works, the assumption of a foreign readership, and that foreign consumer's determining influence on the nature (and even content) of African writings. It also includes the physical gravitation of literary figures to North American and European domiciles.[2] Booker's contention would be quite valid if it referred to all the novelists on the continent, including the producers of the extensive body of popular literature. These are typically literary entrepreneurs who finance the printing and publication of their works or otherwise arrange to have them printed and published by local printers, and who also organize their marketing, sometimes peddling them personally in the streets. Rarely, however, do works in the popular genre travel beyond the limits of the local market. Furthermore, many of the authors (typified by the Onitsha market writers), because of their limited education and literary sophistication, are unlikely to be published by an outfit like Heinemann, say, or Grove.

It should come as no surprise that there is a far larger market for African writings in Western countries (Europe and North America mainly) than exists in Africa. Several factors account for the discrepancy. Unlike today when African writers have a choice of African publishers (for example, the East African Publishing House, Spectrum, and Afram) to patronize if they so choose, the pioneering Anglophone writers had to look to Europe and the United States for publishers. It is worth remembering that *Things Fall Apart* represented a new phenomenon, that African literature was still a new concept in 1958 (even though Amos Tutuola's sensational work had appeared five years earlier), and that consequently there was a paucity of publishers even in Europe or the United States that had any appreciable experience of it or with it. Heinemann, Achebe's publisher, set up the African Writers Series specifically in order to provide an outlet for the new phenomenon, and to that series (with Achebe as the founding editor) belongs the credit for nurturing Anglophone African writing from its infancy to maturity. Its success, and its authority, derived in large part from its being based in England, from where it could reach a wide market on the European continent, in North America, and in the countries of the British Empire and later Commonwealth. Other publishing houses in Europe and America soon followed Heinemann's lead, and the royalties that flowed in from those sources far surpassed anything the authors could have hoped for from local sales.

It was because of the small size of the African reading public that the writers had to depend, once they were published, on foreign readers for most of their sales. Those whose works the West African Examinations Council (WAEC) adopted as texts for high-school certificate examinations set throughout Anglophone West Africa were of course assured of a high level of sales for those particular works for as long as they remained on the examinations list. Other incentives to look outward for readers included the opportunity to take advantage of the many invitations that came from foreign universities and cultural bodies to attend conferences, give lectures, or be resident writers. They also enabled the authors to attract the attention of judges for such prestigious literature prizes as the Booker, the Commonwealth, and the Nobel.

Conflict with Rulers

The cultivation of markets outside Africa by many African writers soon became less important than a desire for residence in close proximity to those markets. The collapse of African economies evident as early as the end of the 1970s and the scuttling of the educational systems, especially at the tertiary level, were mainly responsible for inducing African intellectuals in general—and writers, of course—to seek better fortunes abroad. One other consideration, perhaps even more important, was that relations between the writers and the ruling authorities in most countries, as Soyinka's and Armah's complaints show, quickly soured after national independence. During the decolonization campaign the African side comprising the masses, the academic-intellectual elite, the politicians, and the traditional rulers generally presented a united front against the colonizers, but they were united only in the desire to see the end of colonial rule and replace the rulers in the exercise of power and enjoyment of its perquisites. Once independence became a fact, the united front disintegrated into competing factions united only in their hunger for power. Antagonisms were therefore unavoidable, especially when notions such as the rehabilitation of societies and cultures that colonialism had severely disrupted did not match individuals' appetite for self-aggrandizement and self-enrichment. The spate of literary works that lambasted the rulers and showed them up as ignorant, corrupt buffoons were the writers' weapon in the unequal battle against the authorities, civilian and later military, who had a monopoly of the means of coercion. The earliest of these include Achebe's *A Man of the People* (with Chief Nanga as the butt and villain), Armah's *The Beautyful Ones Are Not Yet Born* (featuring the corrupt Koomson), and Soyinka's much later play, *Madmen and Specialists* (with Dr. Bero as the sinister "specialist").

It is worth pointing out that the writers who have incurred the ire of the rulers and have therefore suffered persecution have often landed in trouble for activities not strictly related to their creative writing but rather for their political activities or political interventions. The question arises, though, as to the extent to which one can separate the two types of activity: is the aesthetic the political, or can the aesthetic be nonpolitical? Saro-Wiwa's *Sozaboy* is certainly political, as is Armah's *Two Thousand Seasons*, as is Soyinka's *Season of Anomy*. Yet, Armah did not suffer persecution because of *Two Thousand Seasons*; Saro-Wiwa was not executed for writing *Sozaboy*; and although Soyinka could have been in trouble for *The Open Sore of the Continent*, a broadside against Sani Abacha, he was persecuted for his politics rather than for his fiction, poetry, or drama. Whether the authorities would have paid any attention to the creative writers if they did not become involved in politics is an intriguing question, but the writers' professed activist calling precluded that option: they were obliged to live the role they had defined for themselves, in other words, to be "relevant," in order to legitimize themselves in the period immediately following independence. The rulers in postindependence Africa have for their part not proved tolerant of opposition or frontal criticism, and their reaction to challenges from writers who acted on their belief that the rulers were incompetent and ludicrous usurpers was predictable. The inevitable confrontation between writers and rulers has played a major role making canonical African literature in effect a largely exilic phenomenon, with more of its writers living abroad than on African soil.

But attributing the incidence of extraversion solely to writer-ruler conflict would be an erroneous and questionable generalization inasmuch as successive generations of writers, among them individuals who have had no run-in with the authorities, have opted for voluntary exile, most often for reasons of economy and self-fulfillment. Moreover, one must reiterate that writers have not been the only Africans who have pursued happiness outside the continent; to the dismay of developmental planners, more highly educated African professionals live and work away, principally in the United States and several European countries, than in Africa.

Criticism and Theory

Critical commentary on African literatures, whether formal or informal, accompanied the earliest publication of African creative works, but for our purposes it is fair to say that the earliest serious critical discussion of post-1945 Anglophone West African writing followed the gathering of writers from Africa and the African diaspora at Makerere in 1962. The main issues that engaged the attention of the participants at the Conference of African Writers of English Expression (so named even though it included Francophone African writers, as well as writers from the United States) of June 11–17, 1962 included how to define African literature, the problem of using the English language for African writing, and the need for good and enterprising publishers on the continent. With regard to the first, the Nigerian poet Christopher Okigbo raised the question whether African literature was to be understood as literature by black Africans, literature by people living in Africa, whatever their skin color, literature on African themes, or literature employing stylistic quirks that were peculiarly African. With regard to the use of English, the participants' concern was mainly with how to resolve the difficulty and anomaly of expressing African concepts in English. No definitive resolutions were forthcoming for any of the problems. The conference participants took notice of the Francophone negritude movement, which was predicated on a supposed black essence underlying African expression, but they did not adopt it as a model; it even came under some ridicule from Wole Soyinka, who to the annoyance of some of the Francophone participants composed a spontaneous poem parodying the poetry of Léopold Sédar Senghor, the president of Senegal and the writer most closely identified with negritude. At the same time, though, Anglophone writers and critics advanced the view that a work would be considered African so long as it expressed the "African personality."

On the language question, the farthest they went was to agree that writers would need to think their works in their own languages and then find effective means of translating or transliterating their thoughts into English. The problem assumed greater significance after the conference as a result of commentaries by the Nigerian scholar Obiajunwa Wali, who decried African creative writers' adoption of alien languages for their works. Their use of European languages, he predicted, would lead to a "dead end, which can only lead to sterility, uncreativity, and frustration" (Wali 1963, 9). That was the opening salvo in a critical debate that has since raged more or less unabated.

Defining African Literature

Another early issue in the critical discussion of African literatures was related to the question of quality—that is, what standards to apply in judging African writing. In those early years, Anglophone West African writers were keenly sensitive to the reception of their works by the international literary establishment, and they were ever watchful for signs of disparagement. One suspicious sign, many of them believed, was the relegation of their writing to an inferior African ghetto, a move they believed attaching the qualifier "African" to it represented. As a result they opted for what some referred to as "international" or "universal" standards. In a discussion of Wole Soyinka's drama, for example, Una Maclean attributed to the playwright the opinion that he preferred that his works be seen as international, in order, presumably, to discourage audiences and critics who might regard them as mere purveyors of exotica. Another example of the writers' sensitivity on this score was Christopher Okigbo's rejection of the Langston Hughes Award for poetry at the 1966 Dakar Festival of African arts, because it was designated for the best *African* poet, and he preferred not to be so pigeonholed. Soyinka, it is fair to note, has disputed the claim that he preferred the label "international" to "African" for his drama; indeed, in *Myth, Literature and the African World* (1976) he lashed out at European and American critics who would encourage him to reject his African self, or "the African world," arguing that such an invitation to Africans to deny "the reality of a cultural entity which we define as the African world … even to the extent of inviting the African world to sublimate its existence in *theirs*" (my emphasis), which, they assert all the while, arose out of suspicious motives.

The Impact of European and American Criticism

There was, to be sure, some justification for African writers' wariness about European (and American) valuation of their works. Certainly Edgar Wright's categorical assertion with regard to the quality of early African literature as a whole: "any literary value [was] often a bonus added to the political or social purpose which inspired much of the writing" (1966: 107), and Janheinz Jahn's description of the African writer as an " 'apprentice' learning to write" and the literature itself as "apprentice literature" (1969, 89), could not have been reassuring. It was to such attitudes that Chinua Achebe responded when, while expressing his disdain for the concept of universality, he told another Makerere gathering, this time that of the Association for Commonwealth Language and Literature Studies (ACLALS) in January 1974, "The latter-day colonialist critic … given to big-brother arrogance sees the African writer as a somewhat unfinished European who with patient guidance will grow up one day and write like every other European, but meanwhile must be humble, must learn all he can and, while at it, give due credit to his teachers in the form of either direct praise or, even better, since praise sometimes goes bad and becomes embarrassing, manifest self-contempt" (Achebe 1976, 3–4).

In addition to such complaints against what Achebe described as "colonialist criticism," there were objections to other attitudes toward African writers and writing, such as the tendency on the part of European and American critics to lump all of literary Africa together as an undifferentiated unity. As Nancy Schmidt observes, "a characteristic of critical works about African literature from the earliest to the most recent is generalizing about entire genres of African literature or the literature of large geographic areas, while providing little or no documentation in support of the generalizations."[3] The belief that African literary works reflected their societies and their cultures obviously renders such generalizations inappropriate, inasmuch as the writers came from distinct societies with discrete cultures and discrete social (and political) contexts. In this regard a pan-Africanist approach, which Frantz Fanon advocated with regard to decolonization because "for the colonialist, the Negro was neither an Angolan nor a Nigerian" (1968, 211), would not seem appropriate.

One other tendency in early criticism of African literature that deserves notice, and that has also met with some objection, is critics' predilection for finding affinities between canonical European writers and the new African authors. Observations such as Charles Larson's, "In his description of the village [of Umuofia], Achebe is not unlike Thomas Hardy in his creation of Wessex in his own novels" (1972, 39), were quite common, as were remarks pointing out Ayi Kwei Armah's closeness to existentialist writers such as Jean-Paul Sartre and Albert Camus. Furthermore, the quarrel that Chinweizu and other leftists (the *bolekaja* critics) had with poets like Soyinka, Christopher Okigbo, and John Pepper Clark-Beke-deremo stemmed from the critics' belief that the poets suffered from what they dubbed "Hopkins disease"—in other words, that they aped the opacity of Gerard Manley Hopkins. Janheinz Jahn's notion of "apprentice literature" (1968, 89–97) takes on a new significance in this regard; colonization, as Fanon has argued, succeeded because the colonized acquiesced in their being colonized, and African writers' emulation of Western masters can be construed as submission to tutelage, as, in a sense, acceptance of a particular form of colonization, at least as an embrace of one of its consequences.

African writers' preoccupation with European and American critics' assessment of their work made sense because the development of sophisticated African literary criticism (and literary theory) lagged well behind the development of creative writing, much as Aristotle's *Poetics* came well after Athenian tragedy had matured. The dominant literary critics of early African literatures were such figures as Judith Gleason (*This Africa: Novels by West Africans in English and French*, 1965), Janheinz Jahn (*Neo-African Literature: A History of Black Writing*, 1968), G. D. Killam (*The Novels of Chinua Achebe*, 1969), Margaret Laurence (*Long Drums and Cannons: Nigerian Dramatists and Novelists*, 1969), Charles Larson (*The Emergence of African Fiction*, 1971), and James Olney (*Tell Me Africa: An Approach to African Literature*, 1973). The appearance of monographs by African critics such as Oladele Taiwo's *An Introduction to West African Literature* in 1967 and Kofi Awoonor's *The Breast of the Earth: A Survey of the History, Culture and Literature of Africa South of the Sahara* in 1976 notwithstanding, the incontestable fact is that non-African critics defined the early debates (with exceptions represented by such commentators as Obi Wali) and called the shots. Not surprisingly, therefore, their views as to how African literatures should read and what African literatures should do were more or less magisterial. The same reasons that made early African literatures appeal to foreign readers at a time when most knew very little about the continent also dictated the literatures' focus on anthropological and sociological elements; the non-African critics expected African writing to reward the non-African reader by revealing the mind of Africa and the workings of African societies, both traditional and transitional. "Why do we (those of us who are not Africans) read African fiction?" Charles Larson asked, and he answered, "For certain critics the prime reason for their appreciation of African novels appears to lie in the cultural materials they are able to identify in a given book, ethnographical materials recorded by a writer about his own culture" (Larson 1972, 229–30).

This requirement, of course, has implications for the question of the language African writers should use, as attested to by Robert Plant Armstrong's statement in his discussion of Amos Tutuola: that his opting for English, even though he was somewhat incompetent in its use, was a boon for the foreign readers who did not understand Yoruba (1971, 151). Early African critics embraced those premises and assessed the writers' level of competence according to the extent to which they reliably revealed the realities of the African world.

Another measure of the tremendous influence foreign critics exerted was the embrace Amos Tutuola received from African critics after his huge success in Europe and America, even though the initial reaction to him on the continent, especially in Nigeria, had been quite negative.

Relevance

Relevance (or commitment) was another issue that preoccupied writers and critics. I have already alluded to the statements of writers like Achebe, Armah, and Soyinka on their understanding of what a writer's role and responsibility in society were and should be. The belief was widespread, for example, that the artist should not be preoccupied with form, and that the content of his or her work must not be narcissistic, solipsistic, or in any way self-indulgent, but must address the problems facing the society (or the nation, or the continent, or the African diaspora). Larson reported that relevance was one requirement that even African students expected of African literature. To be relevant, they told him, a literary work must "deal openly with a situation which can be comprehended by the average African reader" (Larson 1972, 227). It must not be too obscure, and it must deal with contemporary African problems. Moreover it must be "faithful to African life" and "depict the African way of life." He cites the elaboration of the requirement in Austin C. Clarke's Introduction to Peter Abrahams's *This Island, Now* (1971):

> Any work of fiction written these days by a black author is automatically inspected to see what the author's social commitment is to the problem, the people, or the country with which his work deals. There is a growing concern about the author's accountability to his people that is not strictly literary. This accountability is almost a prerequisite to any writing being done … by black authors, and it is certainly an essential dimension of the prevailing black consciousness in art, literature, and politics. (Larson 1972, 228)

The prevailing attitude, among writers and critics alike, was that art for art's sake was decadent, as Achebe put it, "just another piece of deodorized dog shit" (1976, 25), and that good art must have a utilitarian purpose. That belief was one reason for rejecting the notion of applying a "universal standard" to the evaluation of African literature. As Larson adds, the basis for evaluating African literature cannot be "universal," since the concept of universality is Western, white, and therefore irrelevant to the African literary tradition.

While by 1986 Soyinka had risen to the pinnacle of literary accomplishment by capturing the coveted Nobel Prize for literature, there was no African critic at the time who could claim to have made an *original* contribution nearly as significant to literary theory. With the exception of the occasional avant-garde critics such as Nigeria's Sunday Anozie, few African literary scholars went in for such "metropolitan" critical approaches as structuralism, deconstruction, phenomenology, or psychoanalysis. As late as 1990 the African philosopher Paulin Hountondji was lamenting the "theoretical vacuum" in Africa, and although he was primarily concerned with his own discipline, the vacuum characterized literature as well as philosophy. There was of course a great deal of discussion and writing in the areas of gender and literature (or feminist criticism), literature and social consciousness (Marxist criticism), and postcolonial literary theory, to which we now turn.

Gender

One of the major concerns in modern African life is the status of women in the society. The question embraces, among other things, their level of involvement in the public and intellectual life of the community, including, of course, literary activities. Compared to their female counterparts, African men were disproportionately and more deeply involved in all aspects of European colonization and conversion, including, of course, access to and acquisition of Western education. The development of modern African literature, to reiterate, was a direct consequence of the introduction of Western education and literacy; it follows, necessarily, that more men were in a position to produce literature early on. Some of the early writers received their education abroad, but most were educated in local institutions, as was Nigeria's Chinua Achebe, whom literary historians credit with the effective inauguration of Anglophone West African fiction. He was one of the earliest students of the University College, Ibadan (later the University of Ibadan), an institution established in 1948 to prepare the "leaders of tomorrow" to take over from the colonizers when their country attained its independence. Since the institution, with its sister college in Legon (Accra, Ghana), looms so large in the Anglophone West African literary culture, an understanding of the makeup and life of the student population will go a long way toward clarifying the gender aspect of the early writings.

Men predominated among the first intake of students—a mere handful and almost exclusively male—and for a long time women constituted only a small percentage of the student body. At the time of independence in 1960, the residential campus had four large dormitories for men (Mellamby Hall, Tedder Hall, Ransome-Kuti Hall, and Ahmadu Bello Hall) with another, even larger one, Independence Hall, to be added soon after, while the female students were housed in the much smaller Queen Elizabeth Hall. The weight of male presence by itself gave men an almost exclusive hand in running the affairs of the students, which they did through the Students' Representative Council, and also in setting the social agenda on campus. Even if the few women, jocularly dubbed "acadas" (academic women) and "queens" (after their residential hall), were inclined to participate actively in campus life the chauvinistic attitude of the men discouraged them; old habits of perceiving the action sphere as proper for men only died hard.

Socialization and dating between male and female students, while not unheard of, was quite uncommon, partly because the male students perceived their female counterpart as having (by virtue of their presence in a university) developed androgynous qualities, which the men did not quite know how to cope with; the male students preferred to socialize with the women in nearby trade and nursing schools rather than with their female fellow students. The general belief among the men, with some justification, was that the women felt (again with some justification) that they could do better by dating already well established, car-riding professional men instead of students whose only mode of transportation was "bus number eleven" (their two legs). The men also vindictively encouraged the speculation that the women had not actually passed the tough entrance examination but had been recruited to ensure a female presence on campus.

An eloquent illustration of the gender exclusiveness of campus life has to do with the foundation of what was to become the most exclusive and therefore most enticing social club on the campus, aptly named the Pyrates Confraternity. Consistent with their presumed role as leaders-in-preparation, in 1952 some students responded to the intrusion of ethnic pettiness into national politics, and even into student politics, at the height of the country's campaign for independence, by founding the Confraternity, whose declared purpose was to rid the country of ethnic particularism. Prominent among the original all-male membership of seven was the future Nobel laureate Wole Soyinka. The gender makeup of the Confraternity presaged a characteristic that has remained constant through the years of political activism and conflict in the country and other West African countries. As Soyinka's experience illustrates, the agitators (literary or otherwise) who have run afoul of the ruling authorities by challenging their rule and legitimacy have been men, women preferring to deal with the states of anomie in their different countries in less confrontational manners. The foregoing does not seek to minimize the significance of women's activism, as for example in the Aba antitaxation riots of 1929 to 1930 (Van Allen 1976), and the independence-era political careers of such women as Margaret Ekpo.

The preponderance of men among the "intellectuals" translated also into a predominantly male profile of the literary authorship. Many writers and critics have offered reasons other than the ones I have advanced for the relatively late emergence of female writers, mainly the demands of domestic chores, motherhood and its time-consuming responsibilities, and, not least, the hostility of husbands who threatened their wives with desertion if they persisted in writing. When the question was posed to Nwapa, she responded, "A Nigerian woman faces far too many problems in our society today. She goes to the university to get qualified, when she finishes she gets a job. Then she gets married. Within a short while she starts having children. Then she has to look after her children and her husband and she has a job to do ... the extended family comes in. She might be expected to send her younger brothers and sisters to school. How does she do all these?" Omolara Ogundipe-Leslie had a similar response: "Women have less time, less leisure and less preparation for writing. Women spend their time waiting on others and managing other people—their husband, their children and other relatives and visitors—in addition to managing their own lives. Where a man can withdraw into his study to write, a woman usually cannot."

Incidentally, though, Nwapa explained that she started writing because her job left her with too many idle hours that she needed to fill, and she filled them with writing. Her writing was interrupted, she said, only by the Nigerian civil war and her appointment after it as a cabinet minister.

Finally, such analyses assume that every potential female writer must be involved in a marriage or must be a mother, since they offer no explanations why women who have no such responsibilities have not proved an exception (until recently, of course), although they do suggest that publishers often denied female writers the attention and consideration they accorded their male counterparts. Some women have sought to circumvent that particular obstacle in recent years by starting their own publishing outlets—Nwapa founded the Tana publishing outlet, while Buchi Emecheta established Ogwugwu Afor. Emecheta has offered yet another possible reason that discouraged women from writing—the refusal of their menfolk to credit them with the brains to pull it off. The usual reaction from men on hearing that a woman has written something, she says, is "So she has written a book? I know who did it for her."

Time constraint is also the factor to which commentators attribute women's limited participation in theater and the production of dramatic literature, as well, of course, as the widespread belief that women who engage in theater (especially in acting) must be of loose morals. Without experiencing theater, commentators argue, women lack the opportunity to hone their skills in that genre. On the other hand, Ogundipe-Leslie believes that "African women have contributed quite substantially to African theatre and fiction," and wonders why "not so much to poetry?" As far as that genre is concerned, there have been few single-author volumes by women, with the exception of Ogundipe-Leslie's *Sew the Old Days and*

Other Poems (1985), and Abena P. A. Busia's *Testimonies of Exile and Other Poems* (1995). Given the complaint that the impediment to women's writing is time constraint, one would think that poetry would be their most abundant production, since unlike a novel, or a play, a poem does not require long sustained periods of writing at each sitting. Achebe turned to poetry during the Biafran War partly because it required less time than fiction (Obiechina 2002, 528).

Whatever the reasons, the gender imbalance of the early writers' community not surprisingly ensured that the preoccupation of the early literature would be with male experiences, social and otherwise, and male involvement in national affairs. Male writers created few female characters to match such male ones as, for example, peopled Achebe's first four novels—Okonkwo and Obierika in *Things Fall Apart*; Obi in *No Longer at Ease*; Ezeulu and Nwaka in *Arrow of God*; and Odili and Chief Nanga in *A Man of the People*. Only in *No Longer at Ease* does Achebe come close to creating a strong female presence in Clara, Obi's *osu* fiancée. The same male bias is evident in works by other early authors from Nigeria and elsewhere in Anglophone West Africa. The Sierra Leonean William Conton's *The African* (1960) is the story of Kisimi Kamara, who leads his country of Songhai to independence, and is set to unite all of Africa in a pan-African state, liberating South Africa from apartheid in the process; Onuora Nzekwu's *Wand of Noble Wood* (1961) is the story of Peter Obesie's ill-fated desire to marry Nneka, while his *Blade Among the Boys* (1962) concerns Patrick Ikenga, "a religious two-timer" juggling Catholic faith and traditional observances. The hero of Ayi Kwei Armah's *The Beautyful Ones Are Not Yet Born* (1968) is "the man," the other principal characters in that work and his next two works are men, and the hero of Kofi Awoonor's *This Earth, My Brother ...* (1971) is the lawyer Amamu, who goes berserk because of the morass his country is in. Cyprian Ekwensi's *Jagua Nana* (1961) is a notable exception, for it is more the story of the heroine Jagua Nana, a prostitute, than of her paramour Freddie, but the role in which she is cast is not without its stereotyping problems.

Indeed, the fact that the first woman to feature as the main character in a novel is a prostitute might be simply another manifestation of the attitude that limited the portrayal of women in significant roles. Newell writes that male writers (in Nigeria at least) use the figure of the prostitute or good-time girl to symbolize corruption in the society, and suggests that the usage may be an expression of male anxiety at the emergence of women outside patriarchal control. The unmarried woman, she says, is even more of a threat, because she poses a danger to the continuation of the lineage (Newell 2002, 6–7).

We might note at this point that the creative writers were not alone in paying scant attention to women, their activities, and their concerns. Early African scholars of African literature, also predominantly male in the early years, followed the lead of the creative writers in failing to acknowledge women's production long after they had begun to be published. M. Keith Booker, for instance, faults Emmanuel Obiechina for leaving women writers out of his discussion of Anglophone West African writing through the 1960s even though several women had produced works by then. Adeola James observes, "To say that the creative contribution of African women writers has not always been recognised is to put the case mildly. In fact, the woman's voice is generally subsumed under the massive humming and bustling of her male counterpart, who has been brought up to take women for granted" (1990, 1–2). In this regard, again, the lack of criticism by women, specifically single-author critical works on female writers, has also been blamed on the familiar explanation that writing such volumes demands long periods of time, which men can manage but women cannot.

Despite the foregoing, there were in fact published women writers in Anglophone West Africa even before the emergence of the now celebrated male figures. First on the scene among women was Mabel Dove Danquah, whose "Anticipation" (1947) is the first entry in Charlotte Bruner's anthology of West African women's writing (1984). The short story pokes fun at polygamy by depicting a chief paying dowry for a woman who is already his wife and marrying her a second time, because he has too many wives and does not know who they all are. The anthology also includes Adelaide Casely-Hayford's "Mista Courifer" (1961) about the collision of African and Western cultures. Although born in Sierra Leone, Casely-Hayford married Joseph Ephraim Casely-Hayford, a prominent Gold Coast (now Ghana) lawyer and lived in that country. Another Ghanaian writer, Ama Ata Aidoo, published her short play *The Dilemma of a Ghost* in 1965, and the following year she copyrighted the novel *Our Sister Killjoy*, although it did not appear in print until eleven years later. Her second play *Anowa* came out in 1970. Meanwhile, her compatriot Efua Sutherland's play *Edufa*, copyrighted in 1967, had been published in 1968.

When in 1966 Heinemann issued *Efuru* by Flora Nwapa of Nigeria in the African Writers Series, she became the first English-speaking West African woman to publish a novel. Her second novel, *Idu*, came out in the same series in 1970. An impressive stream of works by these and other women has since entered the canon, and through its dialogue with male-authored texts, it has dramatically altered the treatment of women in both African creative writing and critical commentaries. Unlike texts by male writers, those by women predictably deal with issues of primary concern to them, and portray women in decisive roles, sometimes depicting them as independent and complete outside of marriage (as is the case with Efuru, the eponymous protagonist of the first novel), and sometimes showing them as eternally faithful to their men (as with Idu, that of the second).

The female writer who has had the greatest impact on African literature in matters relating to women and gender, though, is the prolific Buchi Emecheta, whose provocative portrayal of African men in their relationships with women has endeared her to Western feminists and made her a hot ticket on the feminist lecture circuit. Her writing career began in London while she was undergoing traumatic hardship in an abusive marriage, and the bitter experience has left an indelible mark on her sensibility. In work after work, beginning with *In the Ditch* (1972) and through such later works as *Second-Class Citizen* (1974), *The Bride Price* (1976), *The Slave Girl* (1977), and the ironically titled *The Joys of Motherhood* (1979) among others, she has been unrelenting in chronicling the harsh lot African men have imposed on their women. In *The Family* (1990), which is about the Jamaican Brillianton family and was first published as *Gwendolen* (1989), she extends her castigation of misogyny to the African diaspora. Even though she sometimes seeks to distance herself from the Western feminist agenda, she has more wittingly than unwittingly vindicated the stereotype of the African man as an inveterate abuser of women.

In recent years Igbo women have displaced the Ghanaian and Sierra Leonean women who initially dominated the fiction scene. The disproportionately large number of Igbo women writers (prominent among them Flora Nwapa, Buchi Emecheta, Adaora Ulasi, Ifeoma Okoye, and Catherine Acholonu) has prompted some speculation about the reason for the phenomenon. Buchi Emecheta has attributed it to cultural peculiarities: she points out that the Yoruba language, for example, is well suited to drama because of its musicality, and that Yoruba rituals involve much singing, whereas Igbo rituals are more likely to involve extensive storytelling. Consequently, she concludes, theater is highly developed among the Yoruba, and fiction among the Igbo (James 1990, 36). A more plausible explanation, though, is the role Chinua Achebe played in promoting Igbo writers in his capacity as the pioneering editor of Heinemann's new African Writers Series beginning in 1962; the example he had set as an Igbo author, combined with his encouragement of John Munonye, Elechi Amadi, Cyprian Ekwensi, and Flora Nwapa resulted in the emergence and prominence of a crop of Igbo fiction writers, male and female, and an overrepresentation of them in comparison with writers from other ethnic groupings in the early years (see Griswold 2000, 62).

Themes and Strategies

As I observed earlier, women writers have tended to favor some themes that are not popular with male writers, as one would expect, and have adopted a different approach to their art from the one their male counterparts have followed. It is possible, though, to make too much of such differences. Undoubtedly, women's experiences in postwar West Africa differ from men's, but the conditions both sexes (or genders) share, in the private sphere as well as in the public, far outweigh the divergent ones. For that reason, among the themes Carole Davies and Elaine Fido list as favorites with women writers—"(1) the contradictions of motherhood; (2) the struggle for economic independence and success; (3) the precariousness of marital relationships; (4) tradition and modernity in relation to the role of women; (5) the politics of colonialism and neocolonialism and their effects on society in general and women in particular; and (6) the nature of power relationships in society" (Owomoyela 1993, 336)—only two can be considered to be of exclusive interest to women, and then not necessarily so. To the extent that the themes might suggest perennial lamentation and hand wringing, knowledgeable scholars will readily concede the traditional independence and feistiness of West African women, and therefore reject as preposterous any suggestion that their modern, educated daughters are "softies." That means that casting themselves as hapless victims whose only recourse against their male abusers is the putative mighty pen would be unappealing to most African women. It also means that one could argue that the self-conscious female West African writer, as I would describe the female West African writer who has not been co-opted into non-African-*ist* feminist sisterhoods, would acknowledge no gendered thematic exclusions.

I have cited the opinion that the prostitute is a device whose use by male writers betrays their anxiety about independent and uncontrollable women. But, as Newell also informs us, female writers themselves write about loose women in good-time-girl-and-sugar-daddy stories. Her explanation is that the female writers employ such figures to undermine traditional expectations, to question such things as arranged marriages, polygyny, and other established but objectionable practices that they would otherwise have no opportunities to question (Newell 2002, 5). The writers are in effect resorting to "existing repertoires of knowledge" akin to proverbs that may not be available to those not familiar with the culture.

This strategy is similar to what Valentin Mudimbe describes as "surreptitious speech" in his discussion of the journal *Présence Africaine* and its campaign against colonialism from a base in Paris, the capital of one of the colonizing powers. It is also what Brian Larkin suggests that the Hausa Muslim women authors of *littatafan soyayya* romantic fiction have adopted: the use of the discursive and performative models that Indian films provide to criticize arranged marriages and other practices objectionable to women (2002). By using the unfamiliar referents as a cover, they are able to protest the oppressive arrangements that parallel their own. Similarly, Anglophone women writers from Islamic areas question the role and place of women, at the same time taking precautions not to tear the social fabric, that is, balancing challenges to certain practices with preservation of the social harmony. "Alifa Rifaat's *Distant View of a Minaret* (1983)," observe Davies and Fido, "is powerful precisely because it gives us this balancing, a vision of a dissident womanhood within Islam … that nevertheless intends to remain within that culture" (Owomoyela 1993, 318).

Critics have also postulated a difference between the relationships of male and female writers to their subjects, and their ways of examining human experiences. According to this view, while men concentrate on individuals, women prefer to deal with communities. James Olney argues along this line in his discussion of the African autobiography using Noni Jabavu's *The Ochre People* (1963) as an example. But Ogundipe-Leslie suggests by contrast that the woman's individuality is of great importance. Among her list of complaints about "the male dominated African society" is indeed that it denies that there is any oppression of women while it glorifies the precolonial past, "claiming that 'the family' is more important than the fate of the individual woman" (Olney 1973, 68).

While Olney would interpret women's supposed privileging of the community over the individual in terms of identity, in other words as women's enhanced awareness of communality and its corresponding self-effacement, others see a distaste for self-exposure, especially when the issues women write about are delicate or potentially embarrassing. For the most part, they shun the confessional mode, the exposure of private lives, especially when these involve private or marital relationships, precisely the sort of thing that has earned Emecheta much criticism. They would much rather write about parallel experience by other women (Owomoyela 1993, 321–22).

Ama Ata Aidoo is one female writer who is not so sure that a woman necessarily sees things differently or writes about them differently from the way men do. "People have asked me," she says, "and I have heard other women writers say that because they are women, they relate to things or select their themes or treat things in a certain way.… I think, as a woman writer, you approach issues from your position in life, in society, in history as a *woman*. Now, as to whether the result of that position is saying things that are different from how a man would say or select them, that is a question that the critics ought to answer."

The attitude of African women writers to feminism is of considerable interest, because their opinions, and therefore their representations of women's experiences, differ widely. The writer whose works critics regard as the most uncompromising in their attack on misogyny, as I have mentioned, is Emecheta. Among literary critics, her compatriot Omolara Ogundipe-Leslie matches her militancy, dismissing with impatience those African women writers and critics who refuse to be labeled feminists because they identify it with Western women and their sometimes antimale predispositions. These would rather describe themselves as "womanist" (after Alice Walker) or "Africana womanist" (after Clenora Hudson-Weems), terms that signal a readiness to embrace men in the quest for women's empowerment. Even Emecheta, has expressed her uneasiness with the Western feminist embrace of her and her works, stressing that she does not perceive herself, or African women in general, as having the sort of problems Western women have in relation to men. In a 1986 paper, "Feminism with a Small f," she portrays Ibuza women as confident and able to assert their preferences over those of their husbands. Along the same lines, Ogundipe-Leslie pays homage to "so-called illiterate women" because they "have less of a mystique about marriage, the institution and the husband. They will divorce in a flash over practical things like money for food, clothes, sex etc. which they feel are their due from their husbands." She adds that they have a higher divorce rate and change partners more than do their elite sisters, "because for them, marriage is a pragmatic arrangement, and I think their attitude is much healthier." She has also praised Amos Tutuola's portrayal of the Drinkard's wife in *The Palm-Wine Drinkard* as "the best and most correct images of the Yoruba woman of all classes: a courageous, resourceful woman who dares situations with her husband, who works at anything and willingly changes roles with him, where the need arises" (Olney 1973, 70). One could logically infer from such statements that the downtrodden syndrome among modern African women is a new, nontraditional, condition.

Finally, Rhonda Cobham states the objection to Western feminism and its relation to the interests of African women in following terms:

> Liberal feminists in Western societies are notorious for the ease with which they invoke universal sisterhood as a means of achieving goals in their societies that are irrelevant to—not to say exploitative of women in other countries. Few feminist literary critics have found it necessary or even possible to include African-American writers in their canon of authors they consider essential reading for an understanding of their theories. Why then should anything they say be of greater relevance to the work of African women writers than the positions taken by male African writers or critics of African literature? (138)

One small note is in order to conclude this discussion of women and West African Anglophone literature: the huge step Achebe took in *Anthills of the Savannah* (1987) toward correcting what some commentators have criticized in his earlier works, namely, the representation of women as mere appendages to their men. The character of Beatrice, the high-ranking civil servant who is also an intellectual match for the male principals, including the head of state, and who single-handedly corrects a tradition of reserving certain important social functions for men, was designed to appeal to women, to acknowledge their equality with men in all important regards. His gesture is also an acknowledgment of the greater influence women now wield in literary matters compared to the early days of postwar Anglophone West African literature. The gesture notwithstanding, Ogundipe-Leslie's response to the question whether certain celebrated men in African literature could speak for women is instructive. "These men cannot speak for us," she said. "And they should not be expected to. Only rounded human beings who consciously seek wholeness in human society and life; who know that society can progress only with full recognition of men and women both, and not women ministering to men and living through men; only such whole men can speak for women" (Olney 1973, 72). The hopeful sign is her concession of the possibility that the right sort of men could.

Marxism, Theory, and the Colonization of the Mind

As a direct result of the Western presence on the continent and as a remote and indirect consequence of it, considerable turbulence has been a bane of African life, with an all too brief respite around the time of independence. For the most part today, as a result of what

Achille Mbembe has described as the prevalence of rule by *commandement*, definable as the grotesque and indiscriminate exercise of power and use of force on the part of rulers (Mbembe 2001), "an ordinary, comfortable everyday life, free of misery and harassment is the adventure. The opposite is the norm." Hardly anyone disputes the responsibility European intruders bear for initiating the disorder that still prevails, even though some commentators, African and non-African, are now saying that it is about time Africans took their own share of the blame.

The turbulence of life has imbued much of post-1945 Anglophone West African writing with a "spectacular" bent. I am borrowing the term "spectacular" from Njabulo Ndebele, who used it to describe South African writing during the apartheid period. "The spectacular," he writes, "documents; it indicts implicitly; it is demonstrative, preferring exteriority to interiority; it keeps the larger issues of society in our minds, obliterating the details.... It is the literature of the powerless identifying the key factor responsible for their powerlessness" (Newell 2002, 137). The explicit and graphic depiction of the more violent manifestations of official malfeasance, its tendency towards a naturalistic portrayal of life and living, is easily evident in Armah's novels *The Beautyful Ones Are Not Yet Born*, *Two Thousand Seasons*, *The Healers*, and *Osiris Rising*, and in Soyinka's *Season of Anomy* and his play *Madmen and Specialists*, to name only a few.

Another consequence is the preoccupation with exile, or apostasy, which has itself generated a variety of responses, from angst to passionate embrace of tradition. The writers' sensitivity on this score might have something to do with earlier vocal protestations about their role as teachers and champions, with their professed commitment to the amelioration of the conditions in their society, roles better carried out within the community (or society), than from abroad. How effective a teacher of Igbo, the exiled Achebe might ask himself, can one be from Annandale-on-Hudson? Griswold pointedly queries Nigerian writers' qualification for, and possible effectiveness in, the functions they would claim for themselves as witnesses or as teachers. While acknowledging that their "extraordinary level of education relative to their fellow Nigerians—relative to anyone!—supports their self-image as teachers," she wonders about their relevance since they are so unrepresentative of the populace (2000, 45). The comment would apply substantially across the board in the rest of Anglophone West Africa.

It is the writers' sensitivity about this issue, I believe, that explains the nostalgic, or "nativistic" dimension in some of their works, in the form of resort to traditional elements, proverbs, dirges, folktales, and the like. It often seems a device to compensate for the writers' alienated education and elitism, and to somewhat indigenize imported and adopted genres; Derek Wright describes them as "the artistic equivalents of the foreign luxury goods with which the ruling elites cut themselves off from the people" (1997, 9). He adds, "When the African writer, seduced by Western aestheticism, has to borrow the style and narrative techniques of the former colonial oppressor to bewail the continuing oppression of the African race, then writing itself becomes an act of betrayal, fashioning interesting art (for a primarily white audience) out of defeated revolution, aesthetic success from political failure" (1997, 16).

A contrasting treatment of apostasy has been to embrace it and represent it as the preferred mode of consciousness. It is in this guise that the challenge to identity and ethnicity, and the insistence on the constructedness and inventedness of such things, should be understood. Long before these issues came to prominence in the discourse of postcolonialism, West African writers, as we have seen, were already objecting to being identified as *African* artists, and their art as "African" art (as when Okigbo rejected the prize for African poetry at the 1966 Dakar Festival of African Arts). Like today's "cosmopolitans and celebrities" (Brennan 1989), they opted for unqualified membership of the multinational elite of letters.[4] They came under sharp rebuke in the 1980s when a group of Marxist critics and intellectuals took them to task on the issue, about which they already felt uncomfortable.

The social and political upheavals that descended on many parts of the continent, including Anglophone West Africa, soon after the attainment of independence, and that saw deadly confrontations between writers and rulers, contributed to the emergence and popularity of a school of criticism that demanded that writers use their writing to foster revolutionary change.

At the forefront of the movement were leftist academics at the Universities of Ibadan and Ife (Ile-Ife; now Obafemi Awolowo University), whose influence peaked in the 1980s. The leftists, including the so-called *bolekaja*[5] critics among whom Chinweizu was most prominent, lambasted writers such as Soyinka and Ayi Kwei Armah for what they considered those writers' ivory-tower preoccupation with style and their indifference to the problems of the masses in their societies—their slavish adoption of European forms and "Euro-modernism," clinging to the colonial tongue, and a particularly inaccessible version of it at that, and their hewing to subject matters that were of interest to their class only instead of championing the cause of the masses. Their preference for bourgeois Western approaches rather than radical social analyses, and for an "ethnic" rather than an "ethic" approach to social issues, all supposedly proved their lack of social consciousness.

Emmanuel Nara published his study *Art and Ideology in the African Novel* in 1985, the same year in which Georg Gugelberger's *Marxism and African Literature* (a collection of essays by some of the major leftist critics) appeared; and Chidi Amuta has contributed a representative monograph in *The Theory of African Literature* (1989). Gugelberger introduced the argument in his volume with a helpful categorization of the different schools of criticism (African and non-African) that had emerged in Africa up to that point. The "Larsonists" (after Charles Larson) were European critics who pontificated on African literature and compared it to European literature; the "African Euro-centrics" were African critics whose European training led them to apply European criteria to African works; the "*Bolekaja* critics" (nicknamed "Tarzanists" by "Ogunist critics") were those who resorted to polemics to rail against obscurantism and Eurocentrism, and who demanded an autonomous African aesthetic based on African "orature"; the "Ogunist critics" were "pseudo-traditionalists" like Soyinka, who, although they claimed to be traditionalists, were actually individualists writing in the European modernist tradition and were prone to "mythopoeic/Eurocentric formalism and neo-Negritudinist modes"; the "Marxist critics" (lampooned by Soyinka as "radical chick-ists") looked at literature's function in society and demanded social change and amelioration (Gugelberger 1985, 11–12).

Paradoxically, the Marxists, Chinweizu and company, shared everything—education, class, language, alienation, and apostasy—with the writers they lambasted, except that most of the critics taught in African universities while others worked in the media, and in those capacities they could give radical lectures to students and the public, join in demonstrations against the authorities, or write antiestablishment broadsides. For all that, however, their claim to have "*lost* and *found* themselves among the people" (Onoge 1985, 71; italics in the original) was unsustainable and unconvincing, since in their behavior and orientation they were just as extraverted as the ivory-tower writers.

They did get the attention of the writers, although the responses were not uniform. Poets such as Ghana's Atukwei Okai and novelists such as Nigeria's Festus Iyayi and Kole Omotoso, bona fide leftists themselves, needed no persuasion. But the activism the *bolekaja* critics urged probably shaped in some measure the stance of younger poets like Tanure Ojaide and Odia Ofeimun, who have positioned themselves on the side of the struggling masses and railed against official venality and rapaciousness. Isidore Okpewho's novels also, for example *Tides* (1993), along with the many works that the civil war spawned, have effectively done what the Marxists urged, but without announcing themselves as Marxist. Perhaps the most obviously and demonstrably responsive writer was Chinua Achebe, whose *Anthills of the Savanna* (1987) could easily have been written according to a Marxist blueprint, especially in its gambit of bringing together taxi drivers, trade unionists, students, and illiterate (or semiliterate) women traders as the combine that would shape the future, all under the guidance of an enlightened woman, Beatrice. Characteristically, rather than appease the leftists, Soyinka answered the attacks in kind in "The Autistic Hunt; Or, How to Marximise Mediocrity" (1988).

Among the groups the Marxists championed (or sought to champion) were women, who according to their ideology labored under patriarchal oppression, nowhere more debilitating than in Africa. Whether with their encouragement or with that of international feminism, the female writers (such as Ama Ata Aidoo, Buchi Emecheta, Flora Nwapa, and Ogundipe-Leslie) have for the most part concentrated on attacking the institutions of patriarchy. But the Marxist vogue lost much of its appeal after the fall of the Soviet Union and the collapse of East European economies, and with the ascendancy of postcolonialism.

The Language Question

Among the issues that have engaged critics' attention in discussions of Anglophone African literature, few have generated more animated debate than the question about the language proper for the literature. African literature as a whole is an exception to the convention of identifying literatures by the languages of the cultures from which they emanate. The presumption of a necessary relationship of identity among culture, language, and literature is so basic that Houston Baker, noting the anomaly in the African instance, posed the rhetorical question: "How ... does Tewa or Yoruba or Sotho thought achieve literary form in English? How, given the inseparability of thought and language, and the diversity of the world's language communities, should one approach the notion that English has global status as a literary language?" (1981, ix). It is a question that has dogged the literature since it began to attract worldwide attention in the early 1960s, and to which no satisfactory answer has emerged. It is the subject of intense debate between, on one side, so-called cultural nationalists (sometimes also dismissed as "nativists") who insist that by definition African literature must be literature in African languages, and on the other, (supposed) progressives and internationalists, who hold tenaciously to the notion Baker mentioned, and for whom insistence on African languages reflects all the worst tendencies of ethnic particularism and identity politics. The terms of the discussion become more specific, but before considering them it is well to revisit the developments that resulted in the present state of affairs.

The European colonizers who cobbled modern African countries together administered them during the colonial period for their own convenience and benefit, and in the process they trained a cadre among the colonized Africans to serve their colonizing purpose. The colonial governments encouraged the teaching of the colonial language at a very early stage in the education process in order to accelerate its acquisition by their colonial subjects, and thus to discourage their use of their mother tongues. French colonial policy enforced the sole use of French from the first days of schooling, while the British tolerated the use of the mother tongue for the first two years, after which instruction was mandated to be in English exclusively. In instances where church missions, who operated the great majority of the schools, were inclined for their own reasons to opt for mother-tongue education, government subventions sufficed to win their compliance with official policy.

The greater tolerance of the British for mother-tongue use did not indicate a higher regard for it than the French had, only the belief that its use for instruction in the first two years better prepared the pupils to learn English in later years, and thus to accelerate their availability for service in the colonial establishment (Bamgbose 1976, 13). As soon as pupils began to learn English, the school authorities, government and missionary alike, adopted drastic measures to impose English monolingualism on them, for example, by punishing them severely whenever they lapsed into their mother tongues on the residential school compounds where they lived most of their formative years. The students consequently emerged, after years of that sort of regimentation, fluent in the colonial language and leaden-tongued in their native languages, in which they characteristically could no longer converse without slipping into hilarious instances of code switching.

The same reasons for the colonial authorities' preference that their subjects abandon their own languages in favor of the colonizers' account for their wish that the independent countries retain the colonial languages for most significant purposes. Thus, although the French assiduously fight to prevent English borrowings from weakening French, and although they make every effort to promote the use of French in international forums, they nevertheless encourage their former colonies in Africa to use French rather than their own languages and praise African leaders and intellectuals for doing so. The British, for their part, have not gone out of their way to promote English worldwide, for the simple reason that English is already *the* hegemonic language against which others set up ramparts. They have thus relied on the efficacy of their management of decolonization as just another stage in the colonization process (Wallerstein 1973, 9). Accordingly, intellectuals in the independent Anglophone countries have taken up the task of arguing for maintaining the colonial regime with regard to language use, which many, or most, do not see as problematic in the postcolonial era. In a discussion of the prospects for the emergence of a national literature in The Gambia, poet Tijan Sallah expresses the opinion that the sort of literature he envisages "must intrinsically be a literature which, by virtue of the fact that English has become The Gambia's national lingua franca, must of necessity also be written in English." He adds in a footnote that indigenous languages need to be promoted, "because they are our children's first language, their natural language" ("Katchikali," n.d.). The acceptance of a "non-natural" language for the "national" literature could not be better demonstrated.

The so-called cultural nationalists believe that there are more compelling reasons for not only promoting indigenous languages, alongside colonial ones perhaps, but for working to substitute them eventually for the latter. Houston Baker's question has taxonomic, perhaps even existential, implications that the "nativists" would cite: the practice of identifying the cultural affinities of literary traditions with their languages makes sense because, as Baker's question implies (and as conventional wisdom and usage suggest), it is impossible to express one culture's thought *precisely and faithfully* in another culture's language. That is why "Chinese literature" is unequivocally literature in Chinese, and "Russian literature" unequivocally in Russian, and why the question Biodun Jeyifo once posed as to who would dispute the cultural (not so much demographic) affinity of those literatures, *is* rhetorical. Other arguments include the one the Nigerian linguistics scholar Ayo Bamgbose elaborated on the exclusionary effects of Anglophonism in independent African countries. The consequence, he argues, "is that two classes of citizens are immediately created, the class of the advantaged, and therefore, *included*, and the class of the disadvantaged, and therefore, *excluded*" (2000, 1; emphasis in the original). The included, he explains, have a vested interest in blocking the adoption of African languages as replacements for the colonial ones, and are quick to offer arguments in support of their opposition. Ngugi wa Thiong'o offers another argument: using a physiological analogy, he likens the exclusion Bamgbose describes to the detachment of the most essential part of the body from the rest. Equating the Western-educated intellectual elite to the head and the rest of the population to the body, he argues that inasmuch as the former's use of a language unintelligible to the latter precludes the possibility of meaningful communication between them, it in effect amounts to a sort of decapitation (1986, 28). For his part, Frantz Fanon denounces the intellectuals' insistence on holding on to the colonizer's languages, charging that their reason is the desire to "cheat the people and leave them out of things. The business of obscuring language," he continues, "is a mask behind which stands out the much greater business of plunder" (1968, 189).

The proponents of European language use of course have less sinister explanations. As Bamgbose has stated, they are "quick to point out that African languages are not yet well developed to be used in certain domains or that the standard of education is likely to fall, if the imported languages cease to be used as media of instruction at certain levels of education" (2000, 2). Typical of the proponents is Ali Mazrui, who contends that before the Europeans intervened in African affairs African minds were in a sort of captivity, and that "while formal [Western] education is an obvious factor in mental liberation, what is not obvious is precisely the role of foreign languages in releasing the African mind" (2000, 86). He cites Kwame Nkrumah's example to support the claim that Africans languages cannot express sophisticated thought, saying that Nkrumah could not have written *Consciencism* in his native Nzima. That opinion is one with which Achebe evidently concurs. Among the many reasons he has proffered for using English are: serious African writers like himself must address themselves to the world, not to the people around them, and only English is efficacious as a medium for that purpose; African languages are proper for "nondescript" writers only (1976, 82–83); in any case, English *is* an African language, because *any* language spoken on African soil is ipso facto an African language. This last recalls the words of a certain Mr. Meghani, a Kenyan who challenged the claim of the English to English and even urged that the name of the language be changed since it has become "a universal language belonging to all" (Mazrui 1975, 96–97).

The South African writer and critic Lewis Nkosi has also highlighted the benefits of the use of English for writing and other purposes in Anglophone independent African countries. Whereas Ngugi sees decapitation, or cleavage between segments of the community, as the consequence, Nkosi sees quite the opposite, representing the colonial language as a unifying force in multiethnic postcolonial "nations." Ironically, he comments, "colonialism not only delivered [Africans] unto themselves, but had delivered them unto each other, had provided them, so to speak, with a common language and an African consciousness." Achebe echoes the sentiment: "Let us give the devil his due: colonialism in Africa disrupted many things, but it did create big political units where there were small, scattered ones before.... And it gave them a language to talk to one another. If it failed to give them a song, it at least gave them a tongue for sighing" (1976, 77). Thus, he aligns himself with Prospero's self-serving claim that without him (or the colonizer) Caliban (or the colonized) would be forever condemned to speechlessness.

Even though Third World nationalists often react with some outrage to that particular rationalization of colonialism, it has a great deal of appeal for African intellectuals. For example, citing Caliban's vow (in response to Prospero's boast) to employ Prospero's language to curse Prospero, Awoonor concedes the colonizer's gift of voice to the colonized, but seeks to salvage some dignity by saying that he uses English in his writing for the purpose of cursing its donor (1976, 149).

Charles Larson's discussion of the language dilemma in effect acknowledges the consequences that Bamgbose, Fanon, and Ngugi have posited, but finds a positive construction for them, especially in the dangerous circumstances African writers have had to contend with. His point is that a writer's use of a language that is inaccessible to the people among whom he or she lives could be a wise, even lifesaving move. In Soyinka's case, he suggests, his use of a version of English that even ordinary English-speaking Nigerians cannot penetrate is an expedient to get his criticism of the authorities past them to the world at large without endangering the writer (Larson 1972, 24). There is also the economic argument, of course: African writers have to make a living, as Gerald Moore has pointed out, and only by writing in a "world language" such as English can they sell enough copies of their works to make a decent living from their vocation (1963, 9). Moore here refers to the reality Achebe addresses in his essay on African reading habits: that Africans read only for self-improvement, preferring to leisure reading materials instructional texts that would enable them to pass examinations or acquire marketable skills (1976, 50–54). In addition, internationalists such as Mazrui see Nirvana as the emergence of a "world culture," and the acquisition of a "world language" as an inevitable condition of possibility for it. Mazrui for one would not even countenance the development of technical vocabulary for African languages in order to remove the deficiencies some have claimed they have, because doing so would threaten the salutary hegemony that "world languages" currently enjoy on the continent (1975, 88). His goal being a world federation of cultures, he argues that "the spread of English and French as world languages is itself a great step toward a global system of federated cultures. A renunciation of the European imperial languages by African countries would [therefore] be a retrograde step" in his view (1975, 89).

The campaign in favor of African languages for African literature must, of course, come to grips with some legitimate questions. For example, can we expect every African writer to write in his or her mother tongue—Dagamba, Igala, Seres—given the multiplicity of languages on the continent, some of which are intelligible to only a few thousand people? As Sallah acknowledges, "Using an African language often involves uneasy or unpleasant political bargaining within a given African polity. Whose African language do you use? The language of the majority or of the plurality or of the powerful (economically or politically) or some combination of the three?" How, he implies, would we deal with those people whose mother tongues the chosen languages are not, and who might therefore object to the hegemony of even other African languages? It is because of such questions that Sallah endorses Achebe's view that each writer should write in the language he or she feels most comfortable with. Wole Soyinka once suggested that all African writers adopt Swahili as their medium, but nothing indicates the likelihood of that move, and it would not answer those questions.

In the meantime, Anglophone West African writers have sought different ways of reconciling their chosen medium with the imperatives of expressing African thought, and of producing literature that is tangibly and distinctively African. They have experimented with different ways of accomplishing what Achebe once recommended: "fashioning out an English which is at once universal and able to carry [the writer's] peculiar experience" (1976, 82). One expedient to which Achebe himself resorted, most prominently in *Things Fall Apart* (1958), is the copious use of proverbs as a distinctive mark of Igbo conversational convention. Another is what Niyi Osundare termed "cushioning" (1982), the attachment of sometimes lengthy parenthetical explanations to Igbo words or concepts in the text, a device that inevitably distracts attention from, and slows the flow of, narration and action. For his part, Gabriel Okara sought to invest his English in his one novel *The Voice* (1964) with the cadence and imagery of his native Ijo by maintaining Ijo syntax in his English sentences and by translating Ijo expressions literally into English. For example, "If you a bird of the sky take and in front of a fowl roast, the fowl's head aches" (69). In other words, if you roast a bird in front of a fowl, the fowl will certainly feel vulnerable. The result was fresh and engaging, but perhaps Okara suspected that the expedient might not have worked beyond one novel.

Another alternative has been the use of pidgin English, which has the appeal of being based on English and the additional one of being widely spoken and understood across West Africa, even by people with minimal English-language education. Its appeal accounts in large measure for the success of Saro-Wiwa's "rotten English" novel *Sozaboy* (1985). Earlier on in the 1960s, the Nigerian poet Frank Aig-Imoukhuede published a pidgin-English poem that demonstrated the medium's potential for humor:

> I done try go for church, I done go for court
> Dem all day talk about di 'new culture':
> Dem talk about 'equality', dem mention 'divorce'
> Dem holler am so-tay my ear nearly cut;
> One wife be for one man.

Apart from humor, though, writers have found another employment for pidgin or substandard English—as a means of stereotyping. In an extension of the postcolonial paradox according to which complete and effortless assimilation of westernisms serves as an index of good character, writers use substandard English, along with other evidence of imperfect westernization, as an indication of character flaws. Prime examples are, to name only a couple, Chief Nanga in Achebe's *A Man of the People*, and the timber contractor Amankwa in Ayi Kwei Armah's *The Beautyful Ones Are Not Yet Born* (1969, 21).

Postcolonialism

The phenomenon characterized as postcolonialism incorporates ideological, intellectual, and cultural aspects, all tending toward the reversal of the negative impact of colonialism on colonized peoples and societies. The "post" in the designation suggests that in terms of temporality it is posterior to colonialism, and the discourse associated with it presumes an orientation that is decidedly oppositional to colonialism and its supporting "library" and attitudes. In fact, inasmuch as challenges to the colonialist "library" and attitudes were rife even at the height of colonialism (negritude for example) the implication of posteriority must be qualified. Because even the most vocal champions of postcolonialism have opted to hold on to significant aspects of the colonial heritage (colonial languages for example), while others have adopted the colonialists' superciliousness toward non-Western cultural practices, its opposition to the colonial cannot be taken for granted.

Its designation also subjects it to the charge of acquiescence in the elevation of colonialism to so decisive a place in the lives of colonized peoples that it merits adoption for periodizing purposes—precolonial, postcolonial, and so forth—in spite of the fact that a country like Nigeria, for example, was a colony for only a mere half-century. The notion (implied in conferring such a privilege on colonialism) that the experience effected a sea change in the lives of Nigerian peoples, as some claim (Irele 2001, 12) has therefore met with serious challenge. Another objection of a more ideological nature questions the validity of the prefix "post," arguing that the result of the transformation that colonialism underwent during the process of decolonization was only a change in its tactics and public face, while its structures and impact on the colonized peoples and societies remain basically the same as before. Hence the preference in some quarters for neocolonialism over postcolonialism as the designation for the succeeding era.

Postcolonialism, as a concept, as an ideology, or as a practice, raises a host of intriguing issues, many of which are beyond the scope of this discussion. Its manifestation in recent West African Anglophone literature—how it has shaped literary production and discussion and how it is reflected in the lives of the literati—is, however, within our scope and pertinent. Perhaps as good a point of reference for its examination as any is Kwame Appiah's frank and astute representation of it in his discussion of its relationship to postmodernism. Leading off with a description of an instance illustrative of the commodification of African artistic productions in the West, and the equation of the right to speak for such art with access to negotiable capital, he deduces that postcolonialism is "the condition of what we might ungenerously call a comprador intelligentsia," which comprises a small class of Westernized intellectuals "who mediate the trade in cultural commodities of world capitalism at the periphery." They purvey their peculiar version of Africa for consumption in the center, and at the same time promote, in Africa and for Africans, both their own particular image of the West and their own preferred understanding of what Africa is or should be (Appiah 1992, 149). He might have added that they are resident in the West where they operate from well-endowed bases strategically located in academe. Postcolonialism would, in this view, represent simply a particular manifestation of postmodernism, which is characterized by the world capitalist economic system with its center-periphery structure or divide.

Emphasizing Cultural Production

Appiah's formulation usefully recognizes cultural production as just another negotiable commodity, and the intelligentsia as its merchants. As Robert Young asserts, the goal of the colonizers might have been "trade, economic exploitation and settlement," but the "transposition of cultural values" was an important byproduct (Young 24), for us the most important. To the extent that colonized peoples experienced colonization as a force militating against traditional (or native) mentalities and institutions, one would expect postcolonialism, coming in the wake of decolonization, to be a state (or condition) that reverses the effects of the cultural and institutional repressions associated with colonialism, and negates the major (or central) thematics of colonialism. One would expect that it would feature a rejection of the mentality that preferred all things Western to all things African, and a reexamination (and possible rehabilitation) of those traditional ways of knowledge that colonialism summarily and indiscriminately discredited. In fact and in practice, postcolonialism has been at best an ambivalent condition.

On one hand, it lives up to the suggestion of a move beyond mental and cultural colonization and retrieval of aspects of precolonial Africa that colonialism suppressed, but that persisted (surreptitiously or not). For example, under colonialist prompting it became de rigueur for "civilized" Africans to distance themselves from whatever seemed "superstitious" or irrational, to engage (as Marcien Towa more recently urged) in "revolutionary iconoclasm," the "destruction of traditional idols," in order to "welcome and assimilate the spirit of Europe" (Hountondji 1983, 172). That spirit is represented as positivistic, analytical, and rational, in contrast to its supposedly intuitive and irrational African counterpart. In the realm of literature the preference was for clearly expressive dialogue, and realistic plotting and characterization that allowed for denouements based on strict causality. One cannot deny that some writers flirted with experimentation and departure from directness, realism, and causality even during colonialism, but they did so at the risk of being charged with recidivism. Now, in the heyday of postcolonialism, writers such as Ben Okri, Syl Cheney-Coker, and Kojo Laing can revert back to what is in fact a characteristically African mode of perceiving the universe and expressing experience, a mode that acknowledges that there is more to reality than meets the civilized eye or is written in science books, and be hailed as exiting innovators. Of course, earlier writers such as Chinua Achebe and Soyinka also reached back to traditional modes of expression in their use of proverbs, but the "magical realists" do more than borrow rhetorical items from the traditional treasury; they adopt traditional ways of seeing and representing. And if one was in any doubt about the provenance of their form, one need only compare Ben Okri's short story "What the Tapster Saw" (1990) with Amos Tutuola's earlier work *The Palm-Wine Drinkard and His Dead Palm-Wine Tapster in the Dead's Town* (1953).

The opposite tendency (opposite to reconnecting with precolonial Africanity) is embodied in the various expressions of the wish for distance from Africa. A look at the tenets central to postcolonialism makes the point: a distrust of ethnic identity (or any identity at all); a preference for routes over roots, as in Paul Gilroy's formulation (1993, 19); a rejection of the reality of race and its usefulness as a basis for community formation; a preference for internationality over nationality; and a valorization of interstices, migrations, crossings, and so forth. One must point out that the items on the to-do-away-with side incidentally constitute the properties of the Other, the impediments in the path to an embrace of the spirit of Europe and reciprocal embrace by the West. The Westernized African philosophers' characterization of their abandonment as a "destruction of traditional idols" recalls a project at which the early missionaries, the clerical wing of the colonialist advance, were most adept. In this regard the philosophers share a weakness that plagued the aforementioned Marxists: the belief that there is no viable or responsible alternative to becoming "white," or at least mimicking whiteness.

The "post" in postcolonialism, like that in other "post" theories or ideologies (postcolonialism, poststructuralism, postmodernism), represents an emancipatory impulse, signaling a rejection (or transcendence) of disciplinary, ideological, theoretical, and other trammels embedded in the substantive. Postcolonialism's challenge to grand narratives, for example transcendent or exclusivist Westernism, is often described as a space-clearing gesture, one that would permit and legitimize the retrieval of a useful non-Western (precolonial) past. But its assertion (or practice) of freedom is equally directed against ethnic, racial, and national markers of Otherness, a project dear to the class Appiah described as "comprador intelligentsia" and Tim Brennan as "cosmopolitans and celebrities." The retrieval, therefore, is often less a matter of conviction than of expedience; and in the new economy the embrace of Africa or Africanity is fundamentally for the benefits derivable from it.

Appiah remarks on the silencing of a producer of African art, Baule artist and diviner Lela Kouakou, in the metropolitan marketplace for African art, while purchasers such as David Rockefeller and a number of intermediaries, African and non-African, are quite voluble. The arrangement symbolizes the extent to which the bulk of the African population is implicated in postcolonialism, and the nature of the implication. The observation that postcolonialism, equally with what it displaced (or succeeded), marginalizes and silences (not to say exploits) the people might prove difficult to dispute.

Postcolonialism, Self-Criticism, and African Modernity

In certain instances of self-criticism the writers (and intellectuals generally) have acknowledged the failings of their class, especially their failure to do much more than accept grooming as "leaders of tomorrow," especially in the lead-up to the attainment of national independence, without developing programs and strategies that would make them viable and credible alternatives to the corrupt, power-hungry postindependent rulers. They have acknowledged their own proneness to corruption (as Odili exhibits in Achebe's *No Longer at Ease*) and self-righteous fecklessness (as in Armah's hero the man in *The Beautyful Ones Are Not Yet Born*). They have also acknowledged how irrelevant they had become in the limbo to which their alienated education and socialization had delivered them: like Egbo in Soyinka's *The Interpreters*, they had been happy to cross the bridge of apostasy and eager to distance themselves from their peoples and cultures, and from their roots, heedless of the reality that, in Sekoni's words, instead of only leading away "a bridge also faces backwards."

After all is said and done, in discussing a subject such as post-1945 Anglophone West African literature, at some point we inevitably come again face-to-face with the determining and sustained impact of Western events and actions on African life. As Mbembe has remarked, we cannot make sense of events in or pertaining to Africa unless we pay attention to both internal developments and impinging international forces. African historicity, he urges, is "rooted in a multiplicity of times, trajectories, and rationalizations that, although particular and sometimes local, cannot be conceptualized outside a world that is, so to speak, globalized." From the fifteenth century, he adds, that historicity has been "embedded in times and rhythms heavily conditioned by European domination" (Mbembe 2001, 9). His observation is valid, even though we need also heed comments such as Brian Larkin's that neither the African experience as a whole nor African literature specifically has all been organized as a response to Western rule (Newell 2002, 19).

The topsy-turvy world of the African writer, which his or her writing reflects, is entirely consistent with the modern African condition, with African modernity in other words. Biodun Jeyifo applies the familiar postcolonial concepts "interstitial," "liminal," "diasporic," "exilic," "hybrid," "in-between," and "cosmopolitan" to postcolonial African writing (1990, 53), and they would serve equally for the writers' consciousness, cultural (and often physical) location, and identity. If one accepts the proposition that writers and their readers ideally belong in a coherent and cohesive community, that the writers reflect the values of their particular communities and speak both for and to them and in their languages, then one will have to concede that African canonical writers are largely more at home in their exile locations than they are, or would be, in any African community, where they would undoubtedly be misfits. Griswold makes the point with regard to Nigerian novelists (but a point applicable to the novelists in the entire area of our purview) when she observes that they are intellectuals, however one defines the term, fully 71 percent of whom have completed a university degree, in a country where only about 3 percent of the young adults go past secondary education (Griswold 209).

Irrelevance

The overriding issues that have preoccupied African writers and critics of African literature, to reiterate, are cultural affirmation—in refutation of the widespread opinion (disseminated by the intellectual apologists for colonialism) that African cultures, if any such thing existed, were not worthy of the human community; the propagation and vindication of the African personality—an adjunct of the project of cultural affirmation, but one with the additional goal of affirming a distinctive and coherent Africanity, which I have elsewhere described as an African *difference* (1996); and development (closing the gap between the new African states and the "developed" nations). In addition there was considerable attention to the exploration of acknowledged social problems, such as the clash between an older, tradition-bound generation and a younger, Western-influenced one, a problem that manifested itself, for example, in such guises as disagreement on the degree to which parents should be involved in choosing spouses or professions for their children, what rights wives should have vis-à-vis husbands and vice versa, and so forth. More serious were the virulent and socially debilitating problems such as official corruption, incompetence, and gross abuse of human rights. These were the issues that drove the confrontation between writers on one hand and intolerant rulers in some countries on the other, resulting in dissidence and exile on the part of the writers, and sometimes even incarceration, torture, and death.

One of the most profound questions this discussion has raised pertains to the relevance of the literature. Put succinctly, does the literature address itself to Africans or to the world outside Africa? Stephanie Newell makes a crucial point when she observes that although these writers are central to African fiction in the Western world, in Africa they account for only a small percentage of what the continent produces and what the readers read

(Newell 2002, 8). As for their cultural and existential location, one might suggest that they are poised, as it were, somewhere on a bridge that leads to the world away from Africa in one direction and the African world in the other, and there they have the privilege (or misfortune) of sharing with European and American modernist writers "the horror … the nightmare of history" (Ker 1997, 1).

NOTES

1. See my discussion of Tutuola's career in *Amos Tutuola Revisited* (New York: Twayne, 1999).
2. See Paulin Hountondji's discussion of the phenomenon in "Scientific Dependence in Africa Today" (1990).
3. The tendency was not confined to literature and literary criticism. The same objection Schmidt raised was leveled at Janheinz Jahn, who made this sweeping generalization: "Muntu … is a Bantu word and is usually translated as 'man.' But the concept of 'Muntu' embraces living and dead, ancestors and deified ancestors: gods. The unity expressed by the inclusive concept of Muntu is one of the characteristics of African culture, and further peculiarities are derived from it" (Jahn 1961, 18). *Muntu*, however, is a word that belongs only in certain languages of central Africa.
4. See challenges to African identities in such works as *In My Father's House* by Antony Kwame Appiah and *The Black Atlantic* by Paul Gilroy.
5. *Bólèkájà*, formed by contracting the Yoruba fighting invitation *Bó sílè ká jà* ("Come down and let's fight!"), is the name for passenger trucks whose touts are reputed for their bellicosity, a quality attractive to Chinweizu and company.

BIBLIOGRAPHY

Achebe, Chinua. *Things Fall Apart*. London: Heinemann, 1958.

———. *A Man of the People*. London: Heinemann, 1966.

———. *Morning Yet on Creation Day*. Garden City, NY: Anchor, 1976.

Adas, Michael. *Machines as the Measure of Men: Science, Technology, and Ideologies of Western Dominance*. Ithaca, NY: Cornell University Press, 1989.

Aig-Imoukhuede, Frank. "One Wife for One Man." In *Modern Poetry from Africa*, ed. Gerald Moore and Ulli Beier, 100–101. Harmondsworth, UK: Penguin, 1963.

Amuta, Chidi. *The Theory of African Literature: Implications for Practical Criticism*. London: Zed Books, 1989.

Anyidoho, Kofi, and James Gibbs, eds. *FonTonFrom: Contemporary Ghanaian Literature, Theater and Film*. Amsterdam: Rodopi, 2000.

Appiah, Anthony. *In My Father's House: Africa in the Philosophy of Culture*. New York: Oxford University Press, 1992.

Armah, Ayi Kwei. *The Beautyful Ones Are Not Yet Born*. London: Heinemann, 1969.

Armstrong, Robert Plant. *The Affecting Presence: An Essay in Humanistic Anthropology*. Urbana: University of Illinois Press, 1971.

Awoonor, Kofi. "Tradition and Continuity in African Literature." In *In Person: Achebe, Awoonor, and Soyinka*, ed. Karen L. Morell, 136–140. Seattle: African Studies Program, University of Washington, 1975.

———. *The Breast of the Earth: A Survey of the History, Culture and Literature of Africa South of the Sahara*. Garden City, NY: Anchor, 1976.

Baker, Houston A., Jr. "English as a World Language for Literature: A Session for the 1979 English Institute." In *English Literature: Opening Up the Canon*, ed. Leslie A Fiedler and Houston A. Baker Jr., ix–xiii. Baltimore: Johns Hopkins University Press, 1981.

Bamgbose, Ayo. *Mother Tongue Education: The West African Experience*. London: Hodder and Stoughton, 1976.

———. *Language and Exclusion: The Consequences of Language Policies in Africa*. Piscataway, NJ: Transaction, 2000.

Barber, Karin. "African-Language Literature and Postcolonial Criticism." *Research in African Literatures* 26, no. 4 (1995): 3–30.

Bishop, Rand. *African Literature, African Critics: The Forming of Critical Standards, 1947–1966*. New York: Greenwood Press, 1988.

Booker, Keith M. *The African Novel in English: An Introduction*. Portsmouth, NH: Heinemann, 1998.

Brennan, Tim. "Cosmopolitans and Celebrities." *Race and Class: A Journal for Black and Third World Liberation* 31, no. 1 (1989): 1–19.

Chinweizu, Onwuchekwa Jemie, and Ihechukwu Madubuike. *Toward the Decolonization of African Literature*. Washington, DC: Howard University Press, 1983.

Clarke, Austin C. Introduction to Peter Abrahams, *This Island, Now*. New York: Collier Books, 1971.

Cobham, Rhonda. Introduction. *Research in African Literatures* 19, no. 2 (Summer 1988): 137–42.

Davies, Carole Boyce, and Anne Adams Graves, eds. *Ngambika: Studies of Women in African Literature*. Trenton, NJ: Africa World Press, 1983.

Doh, Emmanuel Fru. "Anglophone Cameroon Literature: Is There Any Such Thing?" In *Anglophone Cameroon Writing*, ed. Nalova Lyonga, Eckhard Breitinger, and Bole Butake, 76–83. Bayreuth: Bayreuth University, 1993.

Fanon, Frantz. *The Wretched of the Earth*. Trans. Constance Farrington. New York: Grove, 1968.

Gates, Henry Louis, Jr. *Loose Canons: Notes on the Culture Wars*. New York: Oxford University Press, 1992.

Gilroy, Paul. *The Black Atlantic: Modernity and Double Consciousness*. Cambridge, MA: Harvard University Press, 1993.

Gleason, Judith Isley. *This Africa: Novels by West Africans in English and French*. Evanston, IL: Northwestern University Press, 1965.

Griswold, Wendy. *Bearing Witness: Readers, Writers, and the Novel in Nigeria*. Princeton: Princeton University Press, 2000.

Gugelberger, Georg M., ed. *Marxism and African Literature*. London: James Currey, 1985.

Hountondji, Paulin. *African Philosophy: Myth and Reality*. Bloomington: Indiana University Press, 1983.

———. "Scientific Dependence in African Today." *Research in African Literatures* 21, no. 3 (Fall 1990): 5–15.

Irele, Abiola. *In Praise of Alienation*. Ibadan: privately printed, 1987.

———. *The African Imagination: Literature in Africa and the Black Diaspora*. New York: Oxford University Press, 2001.

Jahn, Janheinz. *Muntu: An Outline of Neo-African Culture*. London: Faber & Faber, 1961.

———. *Neo-African Literature: A History of Black Writing*. New York: Grove Press, 1968.

James, Adeola. *In Their Own Voices: African Women Writers Talk*. London: James Currey, 1990.

Jeyifo, Biodun. "For Chinua Achebe: The Resilience and Predicament of Obierika." In *Chinua Achebe: A Celebration*, ed. Kirsten Holst Petersen and Anna Rutherford, 51–70. Portsmouth, NH: Heinemann, 1990.

———. "The Nature of Things: Arrested Decolonization and Critical Theory." *Research in African Literatures* 11, no. 3 (Spring 1990): 33–48.

———. *Wole Soyinka*. Cambridge: Cambridge University Press, 2004.

Ker, David I. *The African Novel and the Modernist Tradition*. New York: Peter Lang, 1997.

Killam, G. D. *The Novels of Chinua Achebe*. New York: Africana, 1969.

Kohrs-Amissah, Edith. *Aspects of Feminism and Gender in the Novels of Three West African Women Writers (Aidoo, Emecheta, Darko)*. Heidelberg: Books on African Studies, 2002.

Korang, Kwaku Larbi. *Writing Ghana, Imagining Africa: Nation and African Modernity*. Rochester, NY: University of Rochester Press, 2004.

Larkin, Brian. "Indian Films and Nigerian Lovers: Media and the Creation of Parallel Modernities." In *Readings in African Popular Fiction*, ed. Stephanie Newell, 18–32. Bloomington: Indiana University Press, 2002.

Larson, Charles. *The Emergence of African Fiction*. Bloomington: Indiana University Press, 1972.

———. "Wole Soyinka: Nigeria's Leading Social Critic." *New York Times Book Review*, December 24, 1972.

Laurence, Margaret. *Long Drums and Cannons: Nigerian Dramatists and Novelists*. New York: Praeger, 1969.

Mabuza, Lindiwe. "Wake." In *Contemporary African Short Stories*, ed. Chinua Achebe and C. L. Innes, 33–56. Oxford: Heinemann, 1992.

Maclean, Una. "Soyinka's International Drama." *Black Orpheus* 15 (August 1964): 46–51.

Mazrui, Ali. *The Political Sociology of the English Language*. The Hague: Mouton, 1975.

Mbembe, Achille. *On the Postcolony*. Berkeley: University of California Press, 2001.

Moore, Gerald. "Polemics: The Dead End of African Literature." *Transition* 3, no. 11 (1963): 7–9.

Mudimbe, Valentin Y. *The Surreptitious Speech: Présence Africaine and the Politics of Otherness*. Chicago: University of Chicago Press, 1992.

Ndebele, Njabulo. "Rediscovery of the Ordinary." In *Readings in African Popular Fiction*, ed. Stephanie Newell, 134–40. Bloomington: Indiana University Press, 2002.

Newell, Stephanie, ed. *Readings in African Popular Fiction*. Bloomington: Indiana University Press, 2002.

Nfah-Abbenyi, Juliana Makuchi. *Gender in African Women's Writing: Identity, Sexuality, and Difference*. Bloomington: Indiana University Press, 1997.

Ngara, Emmanuel. *Art and Ideology in the African Novel: A Study of the Influence of Marxism on African Writing*. London: Heinemann, 1985.

Ngugi wa Thiong'o. *Decolonising the Mind: The Politics of Language in African Literature*. London: James Currey, 1986.

Ngwafor, Ephraim N. *May Former Victoria Smile Again*. London: Institute of Third World Art and Literature, 1989.

Obiechina, Emmanuel. *Onitsha Market Literature*. New York: Africana, 1972.

———. *An African Popular Literature: A Study of Onitsha Market Pamphlets*. London: Cambridge University Press, 1973.

———. "Poetry as Therapy: Reflections on Achebe's *Christmas in Biafra and Other Poems*." *Callaloo* 25, no. 2 (2002): 527–58.

Ogunyemi, Chikwenye Okonjo. *Africa Wo/Man Palava: The Nigerian Novel by Women*. Chicago: University of Chicago Press, 1996.

Okara, Gabriel. *The Voice*. London: Heinemann, 1964.

Okri, Ben. "What the Tapster Saw." *Stars of the New Curfew*. New York: Penguin, 1988.

Olney, James. *Tell Me Africa: An Approach to African Literature*. Princeton: Princeton University Press, 1973.

Onoge, Omafume F. "The Crisis of Consciousness in Modern African Literature: A Survey (1974)." In *Marxism and African Literature*, ed. Georg M. Gugelberger, 21–49. London: James Currey, 1985.

———. "Towards a Marxist Sociology of African Literature." Ibid., 50–63.

Osundare, Niyi. "Caliban's Gamble: The Stylistic Repercussions of Writing African Literature in English." Paper presented at the 1982 Ibadan Annual Conference on Africa Literature, University of Ibadan.

Owomoyela, Oyekan. *A History of Twentieth-Century African Literatures*. Lincoln: University of Nebraska Press, 1993.

———. *The African Difference: Discourses on Africanity and the Relativity of Cultures*. New York: Peter Lang, 1996.

Parekh, Pushpa Naidu, and Siga Fatima Jagne, eds. *Postcolonial African Writers: A Bio-bibliographical Critical Sourcebook*. Westport, CT: Greenwood Press, 1998.

Petersen, Kirsten Holst, and Anna Rutherford, eds. *Chinua Achebe: A Celebration*. Portsmouth, NH: Heinemann, 1990.

Priebe, Richard K., ed. *Ghanaian Literatures*. Westport, CT: Greenwood Press, 1988.

Quayson, Ato. *Strategic Transformations in Nigerian Writing: Orality and History in the Works of Rev. Samuel Johnson, Amos Tutuola, Wole Soyinka, and Ben Okri*. Bloomington: Indiana University Press, 1997.

Rutherford, Anna, ed. *From Commonwealth to Postcolonial*. Sydney: Dangaroo Press, 1992.

Said, Edward W. "Figures, Configurations, Transfigurations." In *From Commonwealth to Postcolonial*, ed. Anna Rutherford, 3–17. Sydney: Dangaroo Press, 1992.

———. *Culture and Imperialism*. New York: Knopf, 1994.

Sallah, Tijan M. "The Dream of Katchikali: The Challenge of a Gambian National Literature." www.cx.unibe.ch/ens/cg/africanfiction/gambia/sallah/sallah.htm.

Saro-Wiwa, Ken. *Sozaboy: A Novel in Rotten English*. Port Harcourt: Saros International, 1985.

Schmidt, Nancy J. "Selective Introductions to African Literature." *Conch Review of Books* 1, no. 1 (1973): 6–12.

Soyinka, Wole. "The Autistic Hunt; Or, How to Marximise Mediocrity." In *Art, Dialogue & Outrage: Essays on Literature and Culture*, 279–314. Ibadan: New Horn Press, 1988.

Taiwo, Oladele. *An Introduction to West African Literature*. London: Nelson, 1967.

Tibble, Anne. *African/English Literature: A Survey and Anthology*. London: Peter Owen, 1965.

Tutuola, Amos. *The Palm-Wine Drinkard and His Dead Palm-Wine Tapster in the Dead's Town*. London: Faber & Faber, 1952.

Van Allen, Judith. "'Aba Riots' or Igbo 'Women's War'? Ideology, Stratification, and the Invisibility of Women." In *Women in Africa: Studies in Social and Economic Change*, ed. Nancy J. Harkin and Edna G. Bay, 59–85. Stanford: Stanford University Press, 1976.

Wali, Obiajunwa. "The Dead End of African Literature?" *Transition* 3, no. 10 (1963): 13–15.

Wallerstein, Immanuel. "Africa in a Capitalist World." *Issue: A Quarterly Journal of Opinion* 3, no. 3 (1973): 1–11.

Wright, Derek. *New Directions in African Fiction*. New York: Twayne, 1997.

Wright, Edgar. "African Literature I: Problems of Criticism." *Journal of Commonwealth Literature* 2 (1966): 103–12.

Young, Robert J. C. *Postcolonialism: An Historical Introduction*. Oxford: Blackwell, 2001.

PART TWO

West African Literature A–Z

Abani, Christopher (1966–) Chris Abani was born in Afikpo in southeastern Nigeria on December 27, 1966. He was raised Catholic and spent a brief period early in his youth in a seminary preparing to become a priest against the wishes of his family, but at twelve he was asked to leave because he did not seem to have a priestly aptitude. His early education was in Nigeria, and in its course Abani repeatedly ran afoul of the military regimes that were in power at the time, getting arrested and thrown in jail, once even on death row, for his politically charged literary activism. After having received his BA from Imo State University in 1991 with a specialization in English and literary studies, he moved to London and studied for an MA in gender, society, and culture, which he received in 1995. He then came to the United States, living first in New York and then in California. He earned another MA in English from UCLA in 2002, and a

PhD in literature and creative writing from the same university in 2004. Abani teaches in the creative writing program at the University of California, Riverside, and is much sought as a reader on campuses, where his performances often include demonstrations of his expertise as a jazz saxophonist.

Abani wrote his first book, *Masters of the Board*, a political thriller about a fascist coup, when he was only sixteen. It won the Delta Fiction Award for 1983, but when he published it in Nigeria in 1985 it earned him his first arrest and six-month imprisonment by General Ibrahim Babangida's regime, which claimed that the play had prompted General Mamman Vatsa's attempted coup. He was arrested twice more for his writing and theatrical activities, once for the play *Song of a Broken Flute*, which he had written for his university's convocation in 1990. His prison experiences provided the material for his first poetry collection, *Kalakuta Republic* (2001).

Abani's most celebrated successes are the novels *GraceLand* (2004) and *The Virgin of Flames* (2007). Set in Lagos, *Grace-*

Land chronicles the life of a teenage Elvis impersonator whose destitution and parental abuse draw him into the underworld and eventually prompt him to emigrate to the United States. It serves as a vehicle for Abani to show the vibrancy and squalor of the sprawling metropolis, with its assorted characters and hybrid cultures. The plot of *The Virgin of Flames*, in which Abani explores the complex issue of identity, takes place in Los Angeles and centers on the experiences of Black (born Obinna), a mural artist whose father is Nigerian and mother Salvadoran. His father's death in Vietnam is the trauma responsible for the loss of his sense of connection to Africa and of identity generally. His confusion transcends culture and nationality to embrace gender and sexuality as well. Black is fond of cross-dressing in his friend Iggy's wedding dress, in which garb a crowd mistakes him as an apparition of the Virgin Mary.

Abani's other works include the novellas *Becoming Abigail* (2006) and *Song for Night* (2007), the poetry collections *Daphne's Lot* (2003), *Dog Woman* (2004), and *Hands Washing Water* (2006), and the plays *Room at the Top* (1983) and *Song of a Broken Flute* (1990). The ambitiousness of the projects Abani undertakes in his writings, the vivid characterization and keen observation of individual lives and social conditions, as well as his humor and often arresting visual imagery, combine to offset the sometimes uneven sprawl of his plots and occasionally labored language. He has deservedly been the recipient of numerous awards: *GraceLand* won the 2004 Barnes and Noble Discover New Writers award, the 2005 PEN Hemingway Book Prize, and the 2005 Hurston / Wright Legacy Award for Debut Fiction, among others; and *Becoming Abigail* was honored as a *New York Times* Editor's Choice as well as a *Chicago Reader* Critic's Choice for 2006, and was also a selection of both the *Essence* Magazine Book Club and the Black Expression Book Club for the same year.

Abdallah, Mohammed Ben (1944–) Mohammed Ben Abdallah was born in Kumasi, Ghana. He studied theater at the University of Georgia, where he received his MFA, and at the University of Texas, Austin, where he earned his PhD in 1982. After his studies he returned to Ghana and joined the staff of the School of Performing Arts at the University of Ghana in Legon. He served in J. J. Rawlings's government as minister of education and culture and minister of culture and tourism. He has also been the chair of the newly formed National Commission on Culture, of the Panafest Foundation, and of the National Theatre of Ghana. In 2002–2003, while serving as the chair of the theater department of the University of Ghana, he was a Fulbright scholar-in-residence in the College of Arts and Sciences and the Center for the Study of Global Diasporas at California State University, Dominguez Hills.

As a playwright, Abdallah has focused his interests on issues ranging from history and politics to the supernatural. *The Slaves*, written in 1972, was his contribution to the quest for a new African theater. It is set in a dungeon in one of Ghana's slave castles and based on an incident in the transatlantic slave traffic. It saw its first performance at the National Culture Center in Kumasi and was subsequently filmed for television. It was entered in competition organized by the National Association for Speech and Dramatic Arts (USA) and won the first prize as well as the Randolph Edmonds Award for playwriting. Abdallah revised the play in 2004, and is part of the official program commemorating the fiftieth anniversary of Ghana's independence in March 2007.

In *The Trial of Mallam Ilya* (1987) he deals with Ghanaian history, while in *The*

Fall of Kumbi (1989) he tackles that of the Asante nation. Political tensions are the subject of *The Verdict of the Cobra* (1987), developmental strategies are explored in *Land of a Million Magicians* (1993), while the Asante trickster's antics feature in *Ananse and the Golden Drum: A Play for Children* (1994).

Although he writes in English, Abdallah is an advocate of the literary use of African languages; he also demonstrates his commitment to African culture by incorporating folkloric elements as well as traditional rituals, dance, and music into his works.

Abruquah, Joseph Wilfred (1921–) Joseph Wilfred Abruquah, a Ghanaian novelist, received his early education at the Mfantsipim Methodist School in Cape Coast, Gold Coast (now Ghana), and later studied at the Wesley College in Kumasi. From there we went on to King's College and Westminster College, both in London, there receiving a BA degree with honors and a diploma in education. On returning to Ghana he taught at Keta Secondary School and served as its headmaster before moving on to take the same position at his alma mater. He remained at that post until 1972, when on the fall of the Busia regime he was relieved of his duties.

Abruquah's short literary career began with the publication of *The Catechist* (1965), which Donald Herdeck described as "probably the first autobiography written in Ghana." It is believed to be closely based on his father's ill treatment by the missionaries he served in the early days of Christian proselytizing in the country. The narrative in the first person uses the real names of recognizable personalities and discloses details that some critics found embarrassing. He followed it with *The Torrent* (1968), a work thematically typical of the Anglophone West African fiction of

the era of independencies. It is the story of Josiah Afful, a young boy caught up in the rapid social change engulfing his society. Tracing the boy's progress from the shelter of the family hearth and village school to a grammar school run by British missionaries, where he experiences the problems of adolescence and is introduced to sex, Abruquah offers an expose of the trauma attendant on the collision of African and European worlds, of the traditional and the alien, the old and the new, and also a critique of the new educational system in which barely qualified teachers in effect miseducated their young African charges.

Abruquah was reportedly working on a third novel when he lost his job in 1972. He thereafter apparently lost all interest in fiction writing.

Achebe, Chinua (1930–) Although Achebe was not the first African, West African, or Anglophone West African to be published in the post–Second World War era, historians of the subject nonetheless refer to him as the father of modern African literature. The description acknowledges his importance in setting the tone and direction of modern African writing, as well as his role in nurturing the developing literature in his capacity as general editor for the Heinemann African Writers Series on its inauguration in 1962. His contribution to African letters extends from the genre of fiction, for which he is most famous, to essays on issues ranging from the role of the artist in society to the choice of language proper for an African writer and to matters of leadership and responsibility in national politics.

Born into the Igbo community of what was the Eastern Region of Nigeria in 1930, Achebe grew up in a strict Christian home; his great-grandfather had granted the first Christian missionaries to arrive in their village permission to operate from his compound, eventually expelling them, however, for fear their funereal singing might give people the wrong impression that his household was plagued by incessant bereavement. Achebe's father was a church leader, and so seriously did his parents take their Christianity that they forbade their children from associating with non-Christians, whom they characterized as "the people of nothing" as opposed to "the people of the church."

His primary education was in a Christian school, and his secondary education at Government College, Umuahia. He enrolled in the newly established University College, Ibadan (later University of Ibadan) in 1948 and earned his BA in 1953. After graduating, Achebe worked at the Nigerian Broadcasting Corporation in Lagos, rising from the rank of a producer to become the director of external broadcasting by the time the Nigerian Civil War, also known as the Biafran War, broke out in 1966.

In the course of his studies he had become familiar with the literature of the colonial narrative in such works as Joseph Conrad's *Heart of Darkness* and Joyce Cary's *Mister Johnson*, a narrative that depicted Africans as incapable of self-governance and therefore justified European colonization of their continent, but in whose literature Achebe was unable to recognize the Africa and Africans he knew. He consequently assumed the responsibility of representing a more credible and more authentic portrayal of the African world, as much for the benefit of the world at large as for that of colonized Africans themselves. In an oft-quoted declaration of intent in the essay "The Novelist as Teacher," he stated that his goal was to persuade his people that their past "was not one long night of savagery from which the first Europeans acting on God's behalf delivered them."

Accordingly, he set *Things Fall Apart* (1958), his first novel, in the traditional Igbo village of Umuofia and in it depicts the moment of contact between Europeans and Africans on African soil and the unfortunate attitudes that would plague future relations between the two for the duration of the colonial period. In particular, he dramatizes the failure of the colonizers to concede any rhyme or reason to African traditional institutions and practices, a failure that led to their insistence on forcing their will and ways on their African hosts. Charged though the subject is, Achebe's handling of it is nevertheless relatively balanced, showing that the Igbo side, represented by the well-meaning but irascible and misguided Okonkwo, shares some of the blame for the rocky relationship and its traumatic outcome.

The book has remained spectacularly popular, partly because it came at a time when African nations were emerging from colonial status, while Europeans were becoming increasingly interested in learning about the continent (preferably from Africans rather than Europeans as before), and partly because of what has been described as its anthropological features—careful descriptions of Igbo cultural institutions and social protocols and demonstration of traditional rhetorical habits, especially the copious use of proverbs. One measure of the work's success is its widespread use in schools and universities in the United States, in disciplines and courses as diverse as anthropology, history, and literature. When Heinemann (a publisher that had up until that time published only textbooks written by European authors for sale in African schools) undertook to publish the work it took a gamble, cautiously publishing only two thousand copies, but the work went on to sell over three million copies in the UK edition alone. Furthermore, it inaugurated the highly successful Heinemann African Writers Series, which came into being in 1962 as an outlet for more books by African authors in an affordable paperback format. Alan Hill of Heinemann Educational Books came up with the idea of the series in 1959 in conjunction with Van Milne, whom he had persuaded to join him in the venture, and they prevailed on Achebe to assume the role of general editor.

In four other novels, Achebe traces the troubled history of Nigeria from the establishment of colonial rule to the period of military dictatorships that set in shortly after the country's independence. Each successive novel deals with the generation that constitutes the subject of the preceding book, with the exception that the second and third works, *No Longer at Ease* (1960) and *Arrow of God* (1964), are out of sequence: *Arrow of God*, the third to be published, focuses on the generation between those of *Things Fall Apart* and *No Longer at Ease*, both of which Achebe had written as one work but split in two for publication. Apparently dissatisfied with the extent to which he had compressed history in those two books, he doubled back to a period bracketed by the two as the subject of *Arrow of God*, which he considers his best work. A careful look at its subject and structure reveals that it is essentially a more complex treatment of issues almost identical with those he had addressed in *Things Fall Apart*. In *No Longer at Ease* and the works that deal with subsequent generations, Achebe turns away from blaming the Europeans as the source of Africa's problems and dwells instead on the failings of Africans themselves—moral disorientation in *No Longer at Ease*, political ineptness and official corruption in *A Man of the People* (1966), and megalomaniacal oppressiveness on the part of military dictators in *Anthills of the Savannah* (1987).

Between the publication of *No Longer at Ease* and the appearance of *Anthills of the Savannah*, twenty-one years elapsed, during which period Achebe's Igbo people at-tempted to secede from Nigeria and were forcibly thwarted. Achebe was intimately involved in the secessionist struggle, acting as a roving ambassador and spokesperson for the Republic of Biafra; the trauma of the war and the responsibilities of his office robbed him of any inclination to write novels, he has said. He therefore turned to poetry and short fiction, which are collected in *Beware, Soul Brother* (1971) and *Girls at War and Other Stories* (1972) respectively. In addition he has published collections of essays, like *Morning Yet on Creation Day* (1975) and *Hopes and Impediments* (1988), the monograph *The Trouble with Nigeria* (1983), and the autobiographical *Home and Exile* (2000). He has also written stories for children.

Achebe evidently regards his Christian upbringing and westernization as apostasy, for he wrote in an essay that *Things Fall Apart* was "an act of atonement with my past, the ritual return and homage of a prodigal son." And although his latest works focus more on the failure of African leadership than on European disruption of African cultures and history, he has nevertheless been tireless, especially in numerous public presentations, in lambasting the latter, his favorite (and persistent) target being Conrad and *Heart of Darkness*. Yet, he has also enthusiastically embraced some consequences of colonization, especially its displacement of indigenous languages and imposition of (in his case) English, which in his view is a valuable inheritance that enables an author like him to reach a worldwide audience.

Alan Hill credits Achebe with much of the success for the African Writers Series; he asserts that Achebe's name "was the magnet that brought everything in, and his critical judgement was the decisive factor in what we published. And in addition to that, the fantastic sales of his own books selling by the million provided the economic basis for the rest of the series. I did a calculation in 1984, by which time we had published getting on for three hundred titles, and one third of the sales revenue from the entire list came from Achebe's four novels" (1990, 152).

Achebe lives with his family in Annandale, New York, where he is the Charles P. Stevenson Jr. Professor of Languages and Literature at Bard College.

FURTHER READING

Booker, M. Keith, ed. *The Chinua Achebe Encyclopedia*. Westport, CT: Greenwood, 2003.

Currey, James, Alan Hill, Keith Sambrook, and Kirsten Holst Petersen. "Working with Chinua Achebe: The African Writers Series." In *Chinua Achebe: A Celebration*, ed. Kirsten Holst Petersen and Anna Rutherford, 149–59. Oxford: Heinemann, 1990.

Emenyonu, Ernest N., ed. *Emerging Perspectives on China Achebe*. Trenton, NJ: Africa World Press, 2004.

Ohaeto, Ezenwa. *Chinua Achebe: A Biography*. Bloomington: Indiana University Press, 1997.

Sallah, Tijan M., and Ngozi Okonjo-Iweala. *Chinua Achebe, Teacher of Light: A Biography*. Trenton, NJ: Africa World Press, 2003.

Acholonu, Catherine Obianuju (1951–)
Catherine Acholonu was born on October 26, 1951, in Orlu, Imo State, in the Igbo-speaking area of eastern Nigeria. Her father, Chief Lazarus Emejuru Olumba, was a trader, as was her mother Josephine. She recalls growing up in an affluent home that housed the families of her father and his three brothers, and consequently being constantly surrounded by those she loved.

Her devout Catholic Christian parents sent her to local mission schools for her education, first to the Holy Rosary School in Orlu and thence to the Holy Rosary Secondary School, Ihioma, also in Orlu. Immediately after her secondary education she married Brendan Douglas Acholonu. On the completion of his studies in West Germany, Catherine joined him there in 1973. Soon thereafter she enrolled at the University of Düsseldorf to study English and American language and literature and Germanic linguistics, receiving her MA in 1977. The following year the family returned to Nigeria and she took up employment as a lecturer in the English Department of the Alvan Ikoku College of Education in Owerri. While thus employed, she worked for a doctorate in Igbo studies from her German alma mater; she received the degree in 1982. In 1986 she participated in the United Nations Expert Group Meeting on Women, Population and Sustainable Development, which took place in the Dominican Republic. Awarded a Fulbright Residency Scholarship in 1990, she was a visiting professor at Manhattanville College, Purchase, New York, and lectured at colleges of the Westchester Consortium for International studies in the state. In 1999, President Olusegun Obasanjo appointed her as his special advisor on arts and culture, a post she held until 2002. She later became her country's sole representative at the global Forum of Arts and Culture for the Implementation of the UN Convention to Combat Desertification (UNFAC).

Acholonu, who in the prefatory matter in *The Igbo Roots of Olaudah Equiano* (1989) describes herself as "a serious poet and dramatist," had a banner year in 1985, when she came out with two volumes of poetry, *The Spring's Last Drop* and *Nigeria in the Year 1999*, and two plays, *Trial of the Beautiful Ones* and *Into the Heart of Biafra*. The following year she wrote another play, *The Deal and Who is the Head of State* (1986). *Nigeria in the Year 1999*, as the title of suggests, is a critical commentary on the unedifying state of the country's affairs—social, political, moral—a state she attributes to the effects of the Nigerian Civil War, which is the subject of the play *Into the Heart of Biafra*.

Besides politics, culture and tradition have occupied an important place in Acholonu's consciousness. Her insistent message, especially spelled out in *The Spring's Last Drop*, is that one should be anchored in one's tradition, including its folklore and folkways, and acknowledge supernatural forces or risk cultural loss and social death. She also uses her poetry to intervene in the discussion of gender, in which regard she urges the importance of motherhood, stressing that mothers must be treated with respect, and that mothers for their part must exhibit motherly responsibility. She spells out her thesis in *Motherism: The Afrocentric Alternative to Feminism* (1995), in which she argues that "the matrix of *motherhood* ... is central to African metaphysics and has been the basis of the survival and unity of the black race through the ages." Her study of African traditional ways of life, art, and prehistoric cave paintings, she reports, revealed that traditionally the African woman was essentially a matriarch and social nurturer who sometimes exercised royal authority and was often a goddess, a priestess, a soldier, and always a quintessential partner to the man.

Acholonu attracted considerable interest in 1989 when she published the result of her investigations into the real identity of Olaudah Equiano in *The Igbo Roots of Olaudah Equiano*. In that work she details her biographical sleuthing, which involved interviewing several people around Isseke. Her discovery that Olaudah Equiano was in fact Olaude Ekwealuo of Isseke in Nigeria's Anambra State has convinced hardly anyone.

Acholonu's other publications include *The Earth Unchained: A Quantum Leap in Consciousness (A Reply to Al Gore)* (1995), her Southern Hemisphere reply to Al Gore's *Earth In The Balance*, and *Africa the New Frontier: Towards a Truly Global Literary Theory for the 21st Century* (2002). These locally published works are not widely known outside Nigeria.

FURTHER READING

Ogede, O.S. "Exile and the Female Imagination: The Nigerian Civil War, Western Ideology (Feminism), and the Poetry of Catherine Acholonu." *Neohelicon* 26, no. 1 (1999): 125–34.

Acquah, Kobena Eyi (1952–) Born in Winneba in the Central Region of Ghana, Acquah attended the University of Ghana, Legon, and studied law at the Ghana Law School. He combines his practice as a lawyer and investment counselor with active involvement in the programs of the W.E.B. Du Bois Center for Pan-African Culture in Accra, and he has served on the Ghana Book Development Council and the Ghana Copyright Board.

Although he has published short stories and essays, Acquah is best known for his poetry, which has been widely anthologized. Among his works are *The Man Who Died: Poems 1974–1979* (1984), *Music for a Dream Dance* (1989), *Rivers Must Flow*, and *No Time for a Masterpiece: Poems* (1995). *The Man Who Died* earned honorable mention in the 1985 competition for the Noma Award for Publishing in Africa.

Acquah's works testify to his appreciation of traditional artistic and rhetorical resources such as like folktales, riddles, and proverbs, as well as to his conversance with his people's history. Thematically they are preoccupied with the difficult realities of postindependence Africa, as well as the oppression and indignity to which all black people are subjected wherever they may be. Critics attribute to his strong Christian faith the measured and cautious tone in which he exhorts oppressed peoples to strive for their rights.

Adichie, Chimamanda Ngozi (1977–) Chimamanda Ngozi Adichie, an Igbo, was born on September 15, 1977, in Enugu, Anambra State, in eastern Nigeria. Her father, James Adichie, was vice chancellor at the University of Nigeria, Nsukka, where her mother Grace was also a lecturer. She received her secondary-school education at the school set up on the university campus for the children of the staff, there distinguishing herself by winning several academic prizes. After her secondary education she gained admission to the university's school of medicine to study to be a doctor, and combined her studies with editing *The Compass*, the magazine of the Catholic students in the medical school. She stuck with her medical studies for a year, enough time to realize that the calling was not for her, inasmuch as she could not stomach dissecting even frogs, and then switched to pharmacy.

By 1998, when she left Nigeria for Drexel University, she had undergone another transformation in her career interest. She had in the meantime published a collection of poems, *Decisions* (1998), and a play on the traumatic civil war, *For Love of Biafra* (1998), and she enrolled at Drexel to pursue a course in communication. From there she went on to Eastern Connecticut State University to study communication and political science, graduating summa cum laude in 2001. She had begun the novel *Purple Hibiscus* (2003) while in her senior year at Eastern, and she continued to work on it while working for her master's degree in creative writing at Johns Hopkins University in Baltimore.

Purple Hibiscus is the story of fifteen-year-old Kambili Achike and her difficult childhood growing up with her brother Jaja under the stern care of their father Eugene. Eugene is a fanatically devout Catholic who will have no dealings with his own father because he has not abandoned his tradition-

al religion for his son's imported one, and who sternly punishes his children for any lapses (like failure to attend communion or earn good grades) and beats his wife when she crosses him. The work is set in the dysfunctional Nigeria of the 1990s, during the military dictatorship of Ibrahim Babangida, and because of its subject matter and some intertextual reference to Chinua Achebe's *Things Fall Apart*, as well of course as its Igbo authorship and setting, some critics have concluded that it is a deliberate update of Achebe's earlier novel.

Readers and critics have been greatly impressed by *Purple Hibiscus*, which was short-listed for the Orange Prize for Fiction in 2004, listed for the Booker Prize the same year, and won the Hurston / Wright Legacy award in the Best Debut Fiction category also in 2004, the Commonwealth Writers' Prize in the Best First Book (Africa Region) category in 2005, and the Commonwealth Writers' Prize as the Best First Book (overall) for the same year. These awards were preceded by one for the short story "That Harmattan Morning" in the 2002 BBC Short Story Competition (in which she was a joint winner), the O. Henry Prize in 2003 for "The American Embassy," and the Pen Center International Short Story Prize in 2003 for "Half of a Yellow Sun." The novel has also been translated into several languages, including Spanish, Dutch, French, German, Greek, Italian, Polish, and Turkish.

Adichie's second novel is also entitled *Half of a Yellow Sun* (2006). She takes her title from the emblem on the flag of the short-lived secessionist state of Biafra, and she tells her story against the backdrop of the secessionist war. The heroines are the twin sisters Olanna and Kainene; the other characters include Odenigbo (Master), a mathematics professor and Olanna's lover; his houseboy Ugwu; and Richard, a British writer and Kainene's lover. The impending and then raging war with its many instances of human suffering offers the author opportunities to explore the unstable relationship between the two sisters, and men's inconstancy in their commitment to the women in their lives.

The civil war over Biafra's attempted secession ended several years before Adichie was born, but its impact on her is evident in those vignettes in which she documents the horrors the Igbo experienced. She avoids any simplistic assignment of guilt or innocence to the major players (or ethnic groups) in the conflict, and, indeed, many critics have described the sophistication of her characterization and thematic explorations quite justifiably as "astonishing" and "stunning" in a only the second novel by a still developing writer.

FURTHER READING

Hewett, Heather. "Coming of Age: Chimamanda Ngozi Adichie and the Voice of the Third Generation." *English in Africa* 32, no. 1 (May 1, 2005): 73–97.

African Literature Association The African Literature Association (ALA) is an independent nonprofit organization open to scholars, teachers, and writers from every country. It exists primarily to facilitate the attempts of a worldwide audience to appreciate the efforts of African writers and artists. The organization welcomes the participation of all who produce the object of its study and hopes for a constructive interaction between scholars and artists. The ALA as an organization affirms the primacy of the African peoples in shaping the future of African literature and actively supports the African peoples in their struggle for liberation.

The ALA defines the qualifier "African" in diasporic terms; that is, it embraces all people of African descent everywhere and their scholarly or creative productions.

Its commitment to support the liberation struggle of African peoples has often been on view in resolutions it has passed to advocate better treatment of writers in Africa and the release of those held in detention, often for their criticism of the regimes in their countries. Its ambit has occasionally been expanded, though, to include non-Africans, especially writers, for example, when it passed a resolution in support and defense of the writer Salman Rushdie against the *fatwa* the Ayatollah Ruhollah Khomeini pronounced on him in 1989 for his novel *The Satanic Verses* (1988).

Like the African Studies Association (ASA), it is the premier professional association internationally in its field, and thus shares with the older and larger association (out of which it grew) the anomaly of being located outside Africa even though it is the primary forum for discussions on an African subject. Unlike the ASA, though, it strives to minimize the anomaly by holding occasional annual meetings around the diaspora. Thus, it has met in Canada, Martinique, Ghana, Senegal, and Egypt.

It justifiable enjoys a reputation as the most feminist-friendly of any professional association with anything to do with Africa. The argument can be sustained that its women's caucus, WOCALA, more than any other group, has the first say in the policies and activities of the organization.

African Personality The African personality was for Anglophone Africans what negritude was for their Francophone counterparts during the decolonization campaign. The latter doctrine (or philosophy) is in fact believed to have derived from the former concept, which originated with Edward Wilmot Blyden, the nineteenth-century black nationalist who migrated from the West Indies to West Africa and lived in Liberia and later Sierra Leone. J. E. Casely

Hayford, the early writer from the Gold Coast (now Ghana) and an admirer of Blyden, furthered the notion of the African personality in his book *Ethiopia Unbound* (1911), which was largely a vindication of African cultures. Hayford also credited his inspiration to the Nigerian Mojola Agbebi, a cultural nationalist who in 1888 reacted against Europeans' ill treatment and humiliation of Africans in the established Christian denominations in Lagos by founding an independent African Church. After Ghana became independent in 1957, Kwame Nkrumah became its most eloquent proponent and elaborated it at the All-African People's Conference, which took place in Accra in December 1958. It has a practical aim of unifying Africa and offering Africans a means of expressing their yearnings while countering the slander they had long endured from the West.

Negritude and the African Personality, however, differed in two important regards: the former concerned itself with black people everywhere, while the latter focused specifically on Africans on the African continent; while negritude was primarily elaborated in the realms of the arts (poetry especially) and had something mystical about blackness associated with it, too, the African Personality was concerned with sociological and political matters mainly, or, with human relationships and political independence. The Organization of African Unity was its political expression, an organization that political leaders such as Kwame Nkrumah of Ghana and Julius Nyerere of Tanzania saw as a precursor for an eventual United States of Africa. Since both ideologies were formulated within the framework of the struggle by black people around the world to free themselves from oppression at the hands of white people—Europeans and Americans—and in response to their claims of African subhumanity and cul-

tural depravity, they both articulated what their proponents perceived as the unique traits that distinguish Africans from other peoples, white people in particular, and went further to assert not simply the worth of the African and African cultures, but indeed their superiority to Westerners and their cultures. For both, the West is a world of artificiality rather than humanity; it is, as a commentator observed, a world in which people would rather move around in vehicles than on their feet, and in which they would rather eat with iron cutlery than with their fingers. Africans differed from Westerners, as another observer noted, in that they do not explore or climb mountains just for the conquest; they do not develop game parks to entertain themselves; when they go on vacation they do not go to lonely out-of-the-way places but to visit other people; and they do not seek out lonely streams to go fishing. Furthermore, despite being close to nature and respectful of all forms of life, they would not shed tears over the extinction of a species of lions or elephants (Mphahlele 1962, 71–72).

The proponents of the African Personality were realistic enough to acknowledge the fact that it had to account for the complexity of the continent and the variety of its peoples. It also had to acknowledge the undeniable influence the West had had on the African world, an influence that has been greater in some parts (like South Africa) than in others, and that has provoked resistance commensurate with its intensity. They frowned on those Africans who had sought to remake themselves in the image of the West, Africans who on moving into the new cities "begin to visit by invitation or permission through the phone" (Mphahlele 1962, 71). In his discussion of the African Personality, Robert July used the main characters in four novels, among them Cheikh Amidou Kane's *L'Aventure Ambiguë* (1961;

Ambiguous Adventure, 1963), to illustrate the various manifestations of the phenomenon. In all cases the characters were caught in the necessity of reconciling traditional ways and values with Western ones, and of negotiating the move from traditional village life to westernized urbanism, with results that were sometimes fatal and sometimes promising.

The ideal among African thinkers was an African personality that would, rather than uncritically adopt Western ideas or habits, be discriminating, accepting them more as means of survival than as replacements for traditional precepts. It would seek to achieve development, or modernization, but not at the expense of the sort of apostasy that would abort the possibility that Africans might make a uniquely African contribution to world civilization. It would, therefore, make the necessary modernizing moves while at the same time insisting on perpetuating the humanity and communion that characterized traditional African communities, and it would not be defeated by the problems that currently beset the continent during colonization and immediately afterward, but recognize them as temporary setbacks that cannot block the glorious future in store for the continent and its peoples.

FURTHER READING

July, Robert W. "The African Personality in the African Novel: Alex la Guma; Cyprian Ekwensi; Onuora Nzekwu; Cheikh Amidou Kane." In *Introduction to African Literature*, ed. Ulli Beier, 228–43. London: Longman, 1967.

Mphahlele, Ezekiel. "The African Personality." In *The African Image*, 67–78. London: Faber & Faber, 1962.

African Writers Series (1962–2003) Chinua Achebe's career as a writer and the history of the Heinemann Educational Publishers'

African Writers Series are closely linked, inasmuch as the series came into being as a result of the publication of Achebe's *Things Fall Apart* in 1958, and as his subsequent involvement with the series significantly contributed to its success.

Until the publication of *Things Fall Apart*, Heinemann's commercial involvement with Africa was limited to publishing and marketing schoolbooks on the continent. It had otherwise never published a book written by an African, nor was it in the business of selling fiction to the African public. At the time that Achebe's manuscript came to the attention of Alan Hill, however, a great deal of excitement was abroad in Great Britain, for Nigeria was approaching independence as the famous "wind of change" swept over the continent. On the enthusiastic report of Donald MacRae, a professor who had just returned from West Africa, that Achebe's manuscript was excellent, Hill took a gamble and published the work, but cautiously ordered a run of only two thousand copies.

Respectable reviews and good sales encouraged Hill to look for more works by new writers from Africa, like the manuscript he knew Kenneth Kaunda was working on (eventually *Zambia Shall Be Free*, 1965), Cyprian Ekwensi's already completed manuscript for *Burning Grass* (1962), and another manuscript that Achebe had written (*No Longer at Ease*, 1960). These he intended to publish along with a new edition of *Things Fall Apart* in cheap paperback editions that would sell more readily in Africa. Hill persuaded Van Milne, who had just had a row at Nelson, to join him on the project. It was Milne who came up with the idea of a series in 1961, and the following year it became a reality.

In the meantime Chinua Achebe, who was attending a writers' conference at Makerere in 1962, had met James Ngugi and read his unfinished manuscript for *Weep*

Not Child. He recommended it to Hill and Milne who accepted it for publication. Realizing that Achebe would be a valuable asset to the series, Hill met with Achebe in Lagos later that year and offered him the general editorship of the series. Achebe accepted it immediately.

At about the same time Milne left Heinemann to return to "the big time" at Nelson, and Keith Sambrook replaced him in 1963. From 1962 until 1972 Achebe remained the general editor, not only reading all submitted manuscripts and making recommendations (which Hill and Sambrook invariably accepted) but also doing substantial editorial work on many of them. When the war over Biafra's secession attempt broke out, Achebe's preoccupation with it considerably reduced his capacity to participate in editorial duties, but he maintained his interest in the series and contacts with the publishers. At this time (in 1967) James Currey took charge of the series, and in 1972 Achebe recommended Ngugi to Currey as his successor as general editor.

In all the years that Achebe served as the general editor he received no payment for his services. Moreover, Hill credits the profits from the sale of Achebe's books for sustaining the series, as they accounted for fully a third of its revenue. The adoption of its titles as school texts by the West African Examinations Council and its East African counterpart in the 1960s also helped the series along. One key factor in its success, though, was its publication in paperback, although a few titles were also issued in cloth in order to attract reviews in British newspapers.

The series continued to prosper after Achebe ended his official connection with it. From 1972 to 1984 it published 270 titles, and by then it had established itself, in the words of Becky Clarke, the series acquisitions editor at the turn of the millennium,

as "the canonical series of African literature, an internationally recognized classic series for African study." And during the celebration of its thirtieth anniversary in 1992 James Currey praised it as a series for Africa by Africans, noting that 80 percent of its sales was on the continent.

It should be mentioned that the editors did not confine themselves to fiction written originally in English, or exclusively to writers from Anglophone Africa. They published in English translation the fictional works of the Francophone Cameroonians Ferdinand Oyono and Mongo Beti and the Senegalese writers Sembene Ousmane and Mariama Bâ, among others, and they also published, poetry anthologies, collections of plays, works of folklore, and so forth, some of them in translation from other languages.

But already by the 1980s the series was experiencing some difficulties. The imposition of restrictions on foreign exchange by governments like Nigeria's made the importation of books in the series virtually impossible. Then Heinemann itself became caught up in the big-business takeover of the publishing industry: British Tyre and Rubber (BTR) bought the publishing house and imposed a limit of no more than two new books per annum on the series. The development prompted James Currey's departure from the series in 1984 to start his own imprint.

Heinemann changed hands several times, and changed the series' direction as many times, but with Adewale Maja-Pearce and Abdulrazak Gurnah serving as series editor and series consultant respectively, it limped along. In October 2002 Becky Clarke gave a paper at Wellesley College in Massachusetts lauding the successes of the series, but at the end of January the following year Heinemann announced its demise.

At a gala dinner held in July 2002 in Cape Town, South Africa to celebrate Africa's 100

Best Books of the Twentieth Century, Heinemann won a prize for the top twelve books, and it was the only publisher with that many titles on the list. It also has the distinction of having published all three African winners of the Nobel Prize in Literature to date: Wole Soyinka in 1986, Naguib Mahfouz in 1988, and Nadine Gordimer in 1991. It also emphatically gave countless African writers an outlet that many of them would never have had, and by maintaining local branches in Africa itself (at Ibadan, Nigeria; Nairobi, Kenya; Lilongwe, Malawi; and Cape Town, South Africa, the local editors being Aig Higo, Henry Chakawa, Simon Gikandi, and Laban Erapu respectively) it ensured that the series would be in close touch with developments on the continent. Furthermore, in 1993 Heinemann took an important step toward promoting African independence in publishing. It established an Alan Hill scholarship to sponsor an African student to study for an MA in publishing at Oxford Brookes University.

By any account the Heinemann African Writers series had a glorious run, although it was not without its critics. These have faulted it, however, for having propagated a particular type of literature as authentic for Africa, a literature that carries the imprint of writers such as Achebe (supposedly meaning literature with anthropological overtones), or that was Afrocentric, meaning combatively anticolonial, anti-imperialistic, and Europhobic. Others have argued that toward the end it was publishing works that were not up to expectations, the same charge that, ironically, was leveled against it in the early years when it was somewhat lax with its standards in its effort to build up its list. Yet the end of the series made some African scholars apprehensive about the vacuum it was leaving, while others saw it as an opportunity for Africans to assert their ability to found their own canonical literary arbiter instead of relying on others.

FURTHER READING

Clarke, Becky. "The African Writers Series—Celebrating Forty Years of Publishing." *Research in African Literatures* 34, no. 2 (Summer 2003): 163–74.

Currey, James, Alan Hill, and Keith Sambrook in Conversation with Kirsten Holst Petersen. "Working with Chinua Achebe: The African Writers Series." In *Chinua Achebe: A Celebration*, ed. Kirsten Holst Petersen and Anna Rutherford, 149–59. Oxford: Heinemann, 1990.

Aidoo, Ama Ata (1942–) A novelist, playwright, and activist in the women's cause, Ama Ata Aidoo comes from a lineage accustomed to social and political activism, her paternal grandfather having been tortured to death in a colonial prison for his anticolonial agitation. Aidoo is an artist whose work testifies to the hybrid of experiences that characterizes many Africans who were born around the middle of the twentieth century. Born in 1940 in Abeadzi Kyiakor in Ghana's central region, she was one of a mixed set of twins of which the male partner was stillborn. Her father, Yaw Fama, alias Manu IV, was a chief, *ohene* (a kingmaker) of his village. Aidoo consequently grew up experiencing at first hand the traditional ceremonies that were a constant feature of Fante court life while also living through the interaction of tradition with modernity in the years leading up to Ghana's attainment of independence. The mix of experiences would later assert itself in the form of a juxtaposition of indigenous and modern elements in her consciousness and her writings.

Her early schooling was at the prestigious Wesley Girls High School in Cape Coast, where she benefited from the friendship and encouragement of her Yorkshire teacher, Barbara Bowman. The latter materially encouraged Aidoo's ambition as a writer by giving her an Olivetti typewriter.

In 1958 she won a Christmas story competition sponsored by the national newspaper, *The Daily Graphic*, with her short story "To Us a Child Is Born."

On completing her high school education, Aidoo entered the University of Ghana at Legon in 1961 to do a course in Honors English. The following year, on the strength of her second short story, "No Sweetness Here," she was invited to participate in the African Writers' Workshop at the University of Ibadan in Nigeria. Also attending the workshop were Langston Hughes, Chinua Achebe, Ezekiel Mphahlele, Wole Soyinka, and Christopher Okigbo, whose presence further inspired Aidoo.

At the university she was an active participant in the school of drama and the writers' workshop, over which her compatriot Efua Sutherland was already exerting considerable influence. In March 1964, when she was in her final year and just a few months before her graduation, the university's school of drama produced her first play, *The Dilemma of a Ghost* (pub. 1965). Concurrently, she gained recognition beyond Ghana's borders by winning a short-story competition organized by the Mbari Club, Ibadan.

On graduation Aidoo received a Junior Research Fellowship at the Institute of African Studies of the University and did research into Fante folklore until she relinquished the position in 1966. She has subsequently been variously employed: she coordinated the African literature program at Cape Coast University from 1972 to 1982. During the same period she was also a visiting professor in the ethnic-studies program at Xavier University, New Orleans, from 1974 to 1975, and from 1972 to 1979 she held the directorships of the Ghana Broadcasting Corporation, the Arts Council, and the Medical and Dental Council. She also served as a consultant to the Phelps-Stokes Fund's Ethnic Studies Program, and from 1983 to 1984 she was minister of education in Jerry Rawlings's administration. After relinquishing that position she lived briefly in France before moving to Zimbabwe, where she taught and worked with the Zimbabwean Women's Writers' Union as well as the Ministry of Education, and where she wrote the novel *Changes* (1991).

In her writings Aidoo combines outspoken advocacy for women's rights and their emancipation from patriarchal oppression. She dramatizes the difficulties new generations of Africans confront in negotiating the interface between tradition and modernity, and encourages her compatriots, and Africans as a whole, to rid themselves of the mentally debilitating effects of their colonial experience. In *The Dilemma of a Ghost*, the character most affected by the conflict is the diaspora African Eulalie, the African American wife whom Ato Yawson has brought home with him from the United States. Eulalie's American upbringing has not prepared her for African patterns of relationship, and what therefore seem to her the intrusion of Ato's family into their private affairs, and the members of the Yawson family are unable to understand what to them are Eulalie's strange ways. Ato is, of course, caught in the middle, but in the end, thanks to the reasonableness of her mother-in-law, Eulalie and her new family arrive at a rapprochement, and all ends well.

Anowa (1970) is more focused on women's rights; the eponymous character goes against tradition by choosing her own spouse in defiance of her parents, and she later refuses to countenance or support what she regarded as her husband Kofi Ako's questionable business practices. She insists on his humane treatment of their servants, whom she sees as slaves, and accuses him of engaging in slavery, which, the audience is left to infer, caused him his potency. There is no happy ending here, for Kofi shoots himself offstage after Anowa publicizes his erectile dysfunction, while Anowa sits giggling onstage.

In her other works, such as the novels *Our Sister Killjoy, or Reflections From a Black-Eyed Squint* (1977) and *Changes: A Love Story* (1991), the short-story collection *No Sweetness Here* (1970), and the poetry collections *Someone Talking to Sometime* (1985) and *An Angry Letter in January* (1991), she continues to explore the problems women face in African societies, although in the process she seems to undermine some standard feminist positions. For instance, the claim that patriarchal tyranny robbed the traditional African woman of autonomy of action can hardly be sustained with Anowa's example. She defies tradition and parental authority to marry who she pleases, and her self-assertion in her marriage results in her husband's destruction, not hers. Nor can the supposition that polygynous marriages are unthinkable for the modern educated African woman be supported with Esi's case in *Changes*. The university-educated Esi, a senior civil servant, leaves her monogamous marriage and eventually enters into a polygamous union as a junior wife. It is true, though, that she finds satisfaction in neither.

In addition to Aidoo's focus on issues affecting women, she also devotes some attention to the effects of mental colonization on contemporary Africans, and to political corruption in African countries. She has also written works that are meant for children and that explore their world, such as the short-story collections *The Eagle and the Chicken and Other Stories* (1987), *Birds and Other Stories* (1987), and *The Girl Who Can and Other Stories* (1997).

Whatever her subject, Aidoo engages in some measure of stylistic experimentation that she says has earned her the reputation of writing like a man. In *Our Sister Killjoy*, for example, she freely combines prose and poetry, while in *Changes* (which won the Africa section of the Commonwealth Writers' Prize for 1992) she mixes straight prose narration with dramatic presentation. In all cases, moreover, her expository and descriptive passages as well as the dialogue she writes for her characters bear witness to the sensitivity of her ears to indigenous languages and their discourse strategies, and to her familiarity with traditional storytelling conventions and strategies.

Apart from being one of Africa's favorite writers, Aidoo continues to be in high demand as a visiting scholar and artist on university campuses both in Africa and abroad. She was a fellow at Stanford University's Advanced Creative Writing Program, and has taught at Mount Holyoke College, Smith College, Oberlin College, Hamilton College, Brandeis University, and Brown University.

In 2005, she received the Millennium Award for Literary Excellence from Ghana's Excellence Awards Foundation. She is the founder and executive director of Mbassem (which means "women's words, women's affairs"), an Accra foundation set up to provide a haven and writing space for women. African women writers, she told a BBC 4 interviewer in March 2006, more than any women writers anywhere else, need what Virginia Woolf called "a room of one's own," because she believes that writers are more important in a developing society than even food or agriculture.

FURTHER READING

Azodo, Ada Uzoamaka, and Gay Wilentz, eds. *Emerging Perspectives on Ama Ata Aidoo.* Trenton, NJ: Africa World Press, 1999.
Berrian, Brenda F. "African Women as Seen in the Works of Flora Nwapa and Ama Ata Aidoo." *College Language Association Journal* 25, no. 3 (1982): 331–39.

Booth, James. "Sexual Politics in the Fiction of Ama Ata Aidoo." *Commonwealth Essays and Studies* 15, no. 2 (1993): 80–96.

Elder, Arlene. "Ama Ata Aidoo and the Oral Tradition: A Paradox of Form and Substance." *African Literature Today* 15 (1987): 109–18.

Kohrs-Amissah, Edith. *Aspects of Feminism and Gender in the Novels of Three West African Women Writers (Aidoo, Emecheta, Darko)*. Heidelberg: Books on African Studies, 2002.

Odamtten, Vincent O. *The Art of Ama Ata Aidoo: Polylectics and Reading Against Colonialism*. Gainesville: University Press of Florida, 1994.

Aig-Imoukhuede, Frank Abiodun (1935–)
Born in the small town of Edunabon near Ile-Ife in 1935, Aig-Imoukhuede received his secondary education at Igbobi College, Lagos, and his university education at the University of Ibadan, where he joined Wole Soyinka and five other students in forming the famous Pyrates Confraternity in 1952. His publishing career as a poet began while he was at the university, when John Pepper Clark published some of his poems in *The Horn*, a student literary journal. After graduation he embarked on a journalism career, working for the Nigerian Broadcasting Corporation in Lagos and later for the Lagos newspaper *Daily Express*. He also worked for the Nigerian Ministry of Information, and served on the Nigeria Arts Council.

Aig-Imoukhuede has been published in *Black Orpheus* and included in Austin J. Shelton's anthology *The African Assertion* (1968). What most set his verse apart from the start was his use of pidgin English—for example, in his celebrated humorous poem "One Wife for One Man," a tongue-in-cheek ribbing of the idea of monogamy. The use of pidgin English, he later explained in the title poem of the poetry collection *Pidgin Stew and Sufferhead* (1982), also made pos-sible a critical and humorous subversion of a repressive and authoritarian establishment. (The late antiestablishment musician Fela Anikulapo Kuti popularized the term *sufferhead*, and Aig-Imoukhuede's use of it aligns him with the musician's political outlook.) It is also not irrelevant that pidgin is the lingua franca of the "common person."

Aig-Imoukhuede has also written plays and made films, but he has not kept up in his later years his early interest in poetry. He has however made his mark in other cultural areas, especially that of cinema. He headed the Nigerian contingent to the 1984 Film Week in London, and was later named chairman of the Federal Government Committee for the Review of the 1992 National Film Policy. In 1999 he chaired UNESCO's Scientific Committee on "The Iron Roads in Africa," a multidisciplinary traveling exhibition designed to foster intercultural dialogue. The Nigerian government rewarded his service to Nigerian culture by including him in President Olusegun Obasanjo's National Honour Awards list for 2006.

Aiyejina, Funso (1949–) Funso Aiyejina was born in Ososo, in the state of Edo, southwestern Nigeria. He studied for his BA at the University of Ife and his MA at Acadia University in Nova Scotia, Canada, and he earned his PhD from the University of the West Indies, Trinidad. He taught at the University of Ife (now Obafemi Awolowo University) before emigrating in 1986, and he has been on the literature staff of the University of the West Indies in Trinidad since 1990. He spent the 1995–1996 academic year at Lincoln University in Jefferson City, Missouri, as a visiting Fulbright lecturer in creative writing. A poet, short-story writer, and playwright, he has had his works published in such journals as *Okike*, *Opon Ifa*, *West Africa*, *Greenfield Review*, and *Trinidad and Tobago Review* and broadcast on radio in both Nigeria and Great Britain. He has also been widely anthologized. *A Letter to Lynda and Other Poems* (1989), his first collection of poems, won the Association of Nigerian Authors Prize in 1989, and *The Legend of the Rockhills and Other Stories* (1999), a collection of ten short stories that humorously satirize corrupt public officials and reflect the mess that is Nigerian life, was shortlisted for the Commonwealth Writers Prize in 2000.

As a writer, Aiyejina aligns himself with the new generation of activists who find the confrontation between black and black more engrossing than that between black and white, which was the preoccupation of predecessors such as Chinua Achebe and Wole Soyinka. While colonialism undoubtedly damaged the African psyche, he argues, more important is what Africans have done (or left undone) to repair the damage since they attained their independence. His horizon is not limited to the African space, however, for he is keenly interested in connections between Africa and the black diaspora. His work is thus consciously political and critical.

Aiyejina, whose maternal grandfather was an Ifa priest, reaches back to traditional cultural resources, like the ritual songs he remembers or has recorded in his native village, to make his points. The effect is best exemplified in his poetry collection, *I, The Supreme and Other Poems* (2004). Although a product of his residence in the Caribbean, the work remains rooted in Africa, specifically Nigeria, and is devoted to its seemingly intractable difficulties.

Aiyejina has also published works on Caribbean literature and writers, including *Self-Portraits: Interviews with Ten West Indian Writers and Two Critics* (2003).

FURTHER READING

Fox, Robert Elliot. Review of *The Legend of the Rockhills and Other Stories*, *The Remains of the Last Emperor*, and *Bulletin from the Land of the Living Ghosts: Romance in the Reign of Commander Cobra. Research in African Literatures* 34, no. 3 (Fall 2003): 208–12.

Kundu, Vedabhyas. "The new generation of African writers are no longer pre-occupied with colonialism." www.meghdutam.com/index.php.

Aké: The Years of Childhood (1981) *Aké: The Years of Childhood* (1981), the first autobiographical work by Wole Soyinka—the second is *The Man Died: Prison Notes of Wole Soyinka* (1972), the third is *Ibadan: the Penkelemes Years: A Memoir, 1946–1965* (1994), and the fourth is *You Must Set Forth at Dawn* (2006)—spans the first decade of his life. It is a chronicle of a mandarin upbringing in the cloistered parsonage of Aké, where his father lived and worked as the headmaster of the mission school, St Peters Primary School. Soyinka recollects his eventful life as an irrepressible, inquisitive, and precocious child up to the time of his departure for high school education at Government College, Ibadan, at the unusually young age of ten.

The Aké of his childhood was a self-contained world closed off from the surrounding community by a high wall. It housed both the living and the resident ghosts of such long-dead personalities as the pioneering missionary Bishop Ajayi Crowther, whose "gnomic" face the young Wole saw peering at him from behind the parsonage's shrubs, and with whom he held imaginary conversations. From the safety of the parsonage the inhabitants could hear the sounds of life outside; sometimes they were those of the traditional cults *orò* and *egúngún*, and sometimes sounds connected with the modern life that jostled the traditional in Abeokuta. One such sound, that of the marching music of a passing police parade, lured the young Wole out of the parsonage, unnoticed by the marchers or residents of Aké, to join the parade until it arrived at the police barracks. Stranded there, he came to the notice of the white police officer and astounded the latter with his perfect command of English. He was only four and a half years old at the time.

The early upbringing and socialization the book documents benefited from the liberalism of the author's parents and their enlightened and activist relatives and colleagues. It testifies to his parents' encouragement of his inquisitiveness and his father's insistence that a headmaster's son does not prostrate himself, as tradition would demand, in greeting his elders; it also documents his exposure to the intellectual disputations his father engaged in with his friends in their customary visits to the parsonage after Sunday worship. Also noteworthy is his early experience of political activism in the form of the rebellion by the Egba Women's Union against the colonial administration's imposition of taxation on market women. Wole's account places him in the thick of the action in the role of courier between the spearhead of the rebellion, his aunt Beere (Mrs. Funmilayo Ransome-Kuti) assisted by her husband Daodu (the Rev. A. O. Ransome-Kuti), and Wole's mother Eniola, whom he calls "Wild Christian."

In addition to the foregoing, another significant element of the upbringing, which later events have proved crucial for the author's career, was the mixture of both traditional and modern practices. The mother might be a "Wild Christian" and the father a modern "progressive" who would not permit traditional forms of obeisance; they however could not prevent his grandfather from administering traditional fortification to him in the form of traditional juju incisions on his ankles, fortification that rendered him immune to bullying by bigger schoolmates, and to the effects of any evil charms.

This first installment of Soyinka's life ends with his preparation to depart for Government College, Ibadan, for his secondary education, a school that was extremely sparing in its resort to caning as a form of discipline, and that permitted no pockets in students' shorts either, but, most disconcerting to Wole, allowed no shoes!

FURTHER READING

Lindeborg, Ruth H. "Is This Guerilla Warfare? The Nature and Strategies of the Political Subject in Wole Soyinka's Ake." *Research in African Literatures* 21, no. 4 (1990): 55–69.
Ogundipe-Leslie, Molara. "The Representation of Women: The Example of Soyinka's *Ake*." In *Re-Creating Ourselves: African Women and Critical Transformations*, 102–10. Trenton, NJ: Africa World Press, 1994.

Alkali, Zaynab (1950–) Zaynab Alkali was born in 1950 to Borno parents in Garkida, Adamawa State, in northern Nigeria. Her father was a Christian who converted from Islam. She accordingly received a Christian upbringing, but she converted to Islam when she was in her teens. The atmosphere in the home in which she grew up was artistic: her grandfather was a drummer and her grandmother a singer and composer of songs. She enjoyed listening to her grandmother's evening storytelling sessions, from which, along with her ordinary conversations, she learned the proverbs that she would later incorporate into her own writings.

Alkali's early education was at Waka Girls Boarding School in Biu, Borno State. Later she attended the Queen Elizabeth Secondary School, Ilorin, in Kwara State. She studied for a BA in English at Bayero University, and after graduation she became the principal of Shekara Girls' School, Kano, serving at that post until 1976. She then took a position as an assistant lecturer at Bayero

University, Kano, and she has also taught at Madibbo Adama College in Yola and at the University of Maiduguri.

Her first novel, *The Stillborn* (1984), is about the struggles of an adolescent village woman named Li to find her place in the face of the competing pulls of traditional expectations and modernity, and her eventual symbolic option to free herself from the village and move to the city. The novel won the Association of Nigerian Authors (ANA) literature prize for 1985. In some views, Alkali is a writer in favor of change, but only incremental change. She has said that her motivation for writing was to correct the inadequate representation of women in writings by African men, but she has also expressed some impatience with "the women's movement," which she believes interferes with women's writing. She nevertheless admits to being concerned with the condition of women in general in the modern world. Those views would explain the quality of moderation evident in her works.

Her second novel, *The Virtuous Woman*, was published in 1987; she wrote it, she told an interviewer, as a moralistic address to the youth, to give them role models in the spirit of the War Against Indiscipline that the country was waging at the time. Her collection of short stories, *The Cobwebs and Other Stories*, was published in 1997, the same year in which she won the ANA prize for the best short story of the year.

Other honors that Alkali has received include the Merit Award of the National Council for Women's Societies for 2000, and also the Merit Award of the National Council for Arts and Culture for 2001, for what the council described as the strongest voice north of the Niger, which spoke loudly on behalf of both Islamic culture and its voiceless women. In the same year Adamawa State named her Magiran Garkida, its highest title (with both secular and Islamic significance) for women, which was last awarded before the Second World War.

Alkali holds a readership at Bayero University.

FURTHER READING

Azuike, Macpherson N. "Language and Style in Zaynab Alkali's *The Stillborn*." *Humanities Review Journal* 3, no. 1 (2003): 21–28.

Johnson, Rotimi. "The Social Vision of Zaynab Alkali." *Canadian Journal of African Studies / Revue Canadienne des Études Africaines* 22, no. 3 (1988): 649–55.

Koroye, Seiyefa. "The Ascetic Feminist Vision of Zaynab Alkali." In *Nigerian Female Writers: A Critical Perspective*, ed. Henrietta Otokunefor and Obiageli Nwodo. Ikeja, Nigeria: Malthouse Press, 1989.

Ogunyemi, Chikwenye Okonjo. *Africa Wo/Man Palava: The Nigerian Novel by Women*. Chicago: University of Chicago Press, 1995.

Aluko, T. M. (1918–) A member of the first generation of modern African writers, Timothy Mofolorunso Aluko was born in Ilesa in Nigeria's modern-day Osun State on June 14, 1918. After his primary education in his hometown he went to Yaba Higher College (near Lagos) and then to Government College, Ibadan, for his secondary education. From 1946 to 1950 he studied civil engineering and town planning, first in Lagos and later at London University. After returning from London in 1950 he worked as the town engineer for Lagos from 1956 to 1960, at which time he moved to Ibadan as director of public works in the civil service of the Western Region of Nigeria. He remained in the public service until 1966, when he left to teach engineering at the University of Lagos. Much later, he worked for a doctorate in municipal engineering, which he received in 1976. He retired in 1978.

Aluko's early short stories appeared in *West Africa Review* in the 1940s and were also broadcast on the BBC program "Calling

Africa." It was the publication of his first novel, *One Man, One Wife* (1959), though, that propelled him into the literary limelight. It is a satirical account in which fanatical Christians in Isolo are pitted against crotchety guardians of tradition over marital conventions, while the common people went about their lives as usual. The success of the novel, which Aluko had had printed himself, won him enough credibility for Heinemann to accept the publication of his second novel, *One Man, One Matchet* (1964), another humorous work in which Udo Akan, an Igbo district officer stationed in the Yoruba area during colonial times, attempts to persuade the recalcitrant people of Ipaja to cut down their diseased cocoa trees in order to save their economic base. As usual, the British colonial officers forcibly carry out their will and imprison the local ruler in the process. The whole mess forces the well-meaning Akpan to resign.

Aluko continued writing about social issues in his third novel, *Kinsman and Foreman* (1966), set in the colonial period (in 1950). Titus Oti, an engineer trained in England, has to contend with pressures from his relatives in his effort to effect the improvement of local conditions. His fourth work, *Chief the Honorable Minister* (1970), which came out after the postcolonial pattern of official corruption, violence, and military coups had established itself, is devoted to a criticism of the trend. The hero is a man very much like Aluko himself, Alade Moses, a school headmaster who becomes the minister of works in the newly independent state of Afromarcoland. Although virtuous at first, he soon joins his colleagues in the widespread practice of graft and corruption. Soon, the country becomes engrossed in violence, which eventually leads to a military coup. Aluko has written several other works in the same vein: *His Worshipful Majesty* (1973), *Wrong Ones in the Dock* (1982),

A State of Our Own (1986), and *Conduct Unbecoming* (1993). His autobiography, *My Years of Service*, appeared in 1994.

Aluko was awarded the Order of the British Empire (OBE) in 1963 and the Order of the Niger (OON) the following year. Critics praise him, with good reason, for his close knowledge of the people he writes about and for his sense of fun, although he has never been able to impress them as a prose stylist or, for that matter, as a plot craftsman. He however deserves approbation for his consistent criticism of corruption in public life and of fanaticism of any sort. He has also been equally critical of both the colonial project and the failure of African postcoloniality.

FURTHER READING

Adamolekun, Ladipo. "T. M. Aluko." *Afriscope* 5, no. 2 (1975): 57–59.

Dzeagu, S. A. "T. M. Aluko as Social Critic." *Legon Journal of the Humanities* 2 (1976): 28–41.

Lindfors, Bernth. "T. M. Aluko: Nigerian Satirist." *African Literature Today* 5 (1971): 41–53.

Ngwaba, Francis-E. "From the Artifice to Art: The Development of T. M. Aluko's Technique." *Literary Half Yearly* 23, no. 1 (1982): 3–11.

Palmer, Eustace Taiwo. "Development and Change in the Novels of T. M. Aluko." *World Literature Written in English* 15 (1975): 279–96.

Amadi, Elechi (1934–) Elechi Amadi is an Ijo who was born on May 13, 1934, in Aluu (near Port Harcourt), in the Delta region of eastern Nigeria. He received his high-school education at Government College in Umuahia and went on to University College, Ibadan (now the University of Ibadan), to study physics and mathematics, receiving his BSc in 1959. He worked briefly as a land surveyor and later as a science teacher in Oba and Ahoada before enlisting in the Nigerian army in 1963. He was commissioned as a captain and assigned to teach at the military school in Zaria. He resigned two years later and went back to teaching at the Anglican Grammar School in Port Harcourt. During the Nigerian civil war the Biafran authorities twice arrested and released him, because they rightly suspected him of sympathies with the federal cause. He eventually reenlisted in the Nigerian army, and when the war ended he joined the public service of the new Rivers State, heading the ministry of information and then of education.

Amadi took a detour into academia from 1984 to 1987, when he joined the College of Education in Port Harcourt as writer-in-residence and dean of the faculty of arts. From 1989 to 1990 he served the Rivers State government as commissioner for land and housing and was honored with the state's Silver Jubilee Merit award in 1992.

Amadi's first novel, *The Concubine* (1966), followed the pattern Achebe had set earlier, focusing on traditional life and beliefs in the Igbo world before the arrival of the Europeans. It explores the misfortunes of the beautiful Ihuoma, who, because the sea god has chosen her as his bride, is destined to be no more than a concubine to any man and to bring disaster to any man who marries her. *The Great Ponds*, which followed in 1969, and *The Slave* (1978), are usually considered as forming a trilogy with *The Concubine*, since all deal with traditional society without acknowledging European activities, colonization, or their disruption of African lives. The former has as its subject a war between two villages over the ownership of some ponds, while the latter is about a hapless man who seeks to better his lot by becoming a cult slave. While some might fault him for being indifferent to the forces that have had such tremendous consequences on African societies, others see

his discountenancing them as evidence of a conviction that traditional Africa was sufficient unto itself, even to the extent of creating its own dramas.

The war experience affected him as an artist as colonialism did not, for after the conflict he recorded his experiences in *Sunset in Biafra* (1973), and later, in the novel *Estrangement* (1986), he wrote of the disruption that war causes in society as well as in personal lives. He has also written plays, notably *Dancer of Johannesburg*, which was performed in 1979, a drama in which a Nigerian diplomat becomes involved with a nightclub dancer who, unbeknownst to him, is a spy for the apartheid government of South Africa.

FURTHER READING

Eko, Ebele. *Elechi Amadi: The Man and His Work*. Lagos: Kraft Books, 1991.

Finch, Geoffrey J. "Tragic Design in the Novels of Elechi Amadi." *Critique: Studies in Modern Fiction* 17, no. 2 (1975): 5–16.

Gikandi, Simon. *Reading the African Novel*. London: Heinemann, 1987.

Ivker, Barry. "Elechi Amadi: An African Writer Between Two Worlds." *Phylon: The Atlanta University Review of Race and Culture* 33 (1972): 290–93.

Kiema, Alfred. "The Fantastic Narrative in Elechi Amadi's Works: Narrating and Narrator." *Commonwealth Essays and Studies* 12, no. 2 (1990): 86–90.

McLuckie, Craig. "Aesthetic Reversal: Historical Fact in Selected Writings of Elechi Amadi." In *Salutes: Selected Essays*, ed. Monica Idehen, 84–100. Evanston, IL: Troubadour Press / Whirlwind Press, 1994.

Niven, Alastair. *A Critical View on Elechi Amadi's* The Concubine. London: Rex Collins, 1981.

Nyamndi, George. *The West African Village Novel, with Particular Reference to Elechi Amadi's* The Concubine. Berne: Peter Lang, 1982.

Palmer, Eustace. *An Introduction to the African Novel*. New York: Africana, 1972.

Taiwo, Oladele. *Culture and the Nigerian Novel.* New York: St. Martin's Press, 1976.

Aniebo, I. N. C. (1939–) I. N. C. Aniebo was born in 1939 in Awka, in the present Anambra State of eastern Nigeria, and received his high school education at Government College, Umuahia. In 1959 he enlisted in the Nigerian army, which sent him for officer training in Ghana and later in the United Kingdom. In the early 1960s he served as an officer in the United Nations peacekeeping force in the Congo and afterward underwent further officer training at the U.S. Army Command and General Staff College at Fort Leavenworth, Kansas. When the Nigerian civil war broke out he joined the rebel forces and served as an officer, and on the conclusion of the war he was discharged from the Nigerian army (which had reabsorbed alienated Biafran soldiers). On his discharge he went to the University of California, Los Angeles, to study English and history. He returned to Nigeria to take up a teaching position at the University of Port Harcourt, where he has taught literature and creative writing since 1979.

He began his writing career while still in the army, and his first novel, *The Anonymity of Sacrifice* (1974), is set during the war. Its action spans three days in the war and features the horrors of the conflict as well as disagreements between two Biafran officers on military matters. His next work, *The Journey Within* (1978), explores marital problems such as estrangement, infidelity, and rape, while his third, *Of Wives, Talismans and the Dead* (1983), is a collection of sixteen short stories, some of which are set against the background of the civil war, about the problems of adolescence and the difficulties of interpersonal relationships. He has published two other collections of short stories, *Man of the Market* (1994) and *Rearguard Action* (1998), the latter of which

comprises eight stories that testify to the horrors of war and its debilitating effects on people and their morals.

Hardly what one would describe as a cultural nationalist, in particular with regard to the persistent question of the proper language for African writing, Aniebo has categorically asserted in a 1995 interview with Ugochukwu Ejinkeonye that any work written by an African in any language, and anything written by anybody who has lived in Africa and knows Africa, qualifies as African literature. He also chides African critics for their lack of independence of thought, for taking their cue from European and American critics about which African writers to acclaim, and for being afraid to disagree with them.

FURTHER READING

Ejinkeonye, Ugochukwu. "Interview with I. N. C. Aniebo." *Chicken Bones: A Journal for Literary and Artistic African and African American Themes,* 2006. www.nathanielturner.com/ interviewwithincaniebougchukwu.htm.
McLuckie, Craig. "Chapter 2: The War Within Biafra: Communal Schisms in S. O. Mezu's *Behind the Rising Sun* and I. N. C. Aniebo's *The Anonymity of Sacrifice.*" *Nigerian Civil War Literature: Seeking an "Imagined Community."* Lewiston, NY: E. Mellen Press, 1990.

Anowa (1970) Ama Ata Aidoo's *Anowa* (1970) followed after the success of *The Dilemma of a Ghost* (1965) and confirmed her as a playwright to reckon with. It also established her, even more than the earlier play, as a champion of women's autonomy and of social rectitude. The action centers on slavery and the slave trade, but it also encompasses a woman's right to choose her own spouse and to have a say in her family's affairs. The premises the play asserts through the heroine Anowa include the following: the institution of slavery was an integral part of African society before the arrival of the white man; it served the interests of men, who therefore persisted in the traffic and practice despite the strenuous objection of the women; and men ("the lords of our Houses") were responsible for delivering the continent to white marauders ("those-that-came-from-beyond-the-horizon"). The explanation, as it is offered in the prologue, is that men "will always go where the rumbling hunger in their bowels shall be stilled."

Anowa is an independent-minded woman, so resistant to her mother's control that the latter contemplates assigning her care and control to a priestess. True to her character, she chooses Kofi Ako as her spouse over the objections of her mother who considers Kofi a poor catch. Upon marrying, the two move away from their village of Yebi and become traders, doing business with white men. When the business prospers and requires more hands, Kofi proposes to hire a few men to help, but Anowa objects to "buying" men. Kofi does as he proposes, and their marriage falls apart. Anowa's rebellion continues in the form of railing against the evils of Kofi and men in general, and shaming Kofi by going about in rags even though the family business continues to prosper. Her opportunity to avenge herself arrives when she finds out that Kofi has become impotent. She broadcasts the news to the entire household, and, unable to bear the shame and ridicule, Kofi commits suicide by shooting himself.

The play, among other things, recalls the argument about the propriety of describing the sort of domestic or commercial servitude that existed in traditional societies as slavery. Anowa construes it as such, whereas Kofi describes his helpers as "bonded men," argues that they eat out of the same dishes as the freeborn members of the community from whom they are indistinguishable, and asserts that among them "those who have

brains are more listened to than are babbling nobility." Besides, he continues, they are eligible to attain the highest military ranks through valorous service and may even become respected patriarchs in the community. It is also unabashed in sharply distinguishing men from women with regard to ethics, suggesting that men are essentially depraved and women virtuous.

The foregoing summary however also indicates a degree of even-handedness on the part of the playwright, inasmuch as she gives Kofi counterarguments that are actually sound, not simply asinine babbling.

FURTHER READING

Ekpong, Monique O. "Feminist Tendencies in West African Drama: An Analysis of Ama Ata Aidoo's *Anowa.*" In *Current Trends in Literature and Language Studies in West Africa*, ed. Ernest N. Emenyonu and Charles E. Nnolim, 20–33. Ibadan: Kraft Books, 1994.

Anthills of the Savannah (1987) Chinua Achebe's *Anthills of the Savannah* (1987), his fifth novel, came a full twenty-one years after its immediate predecessor, *A Man of the People*. In the intervening years Achebe had been fully involved in his Igbo people's bid to secede from Nigeria, during which he made the secessionist case before audiences abroad and also raised funds for the war effort. The trauma of the conflict and its aftermath, Achebe has said, were not conducive to the production of full-length fictional works; he therefore occupied himself with writing poetry, short stories, and essays. In all three genres he gave vent to his reflections on the troubled history of Nigeria and its effects on the lives of its citizens. The most substantial work in this regard is his political essay, *The Trouble with Nigeria* (1983), in which he declared that the country's woes had all resulted from a plague of bad leadership. Having made the declaration in an essay, Achebe went on to repeat it in a fictional form. Hence, *Anthills of the Savannah*.

Sam, Chris Oriko, and Ikem Osodi were colleagues and friends in school, who had chosen different career paths. Sam, acting on the advice of his British schoolteacher, had enrolled in military school to train as an officer in the colonial army, while Chris and Ikem had become journalists. Political upheavals in the country resulted in a military coup, as a result of which Sam became the military dictator. He persuaded his friend Chris to join his ruling council as the Commissioner for Information, and Chris in turn appointed Ikem to the editorship of the nation's chief newspaper, the *Gazette*. Perhaps inevitably, Sam soon began to deviate from the idealistic expectations of his friends, as he became increasingly megalomaniacal and autocratic, insisting on abject worship and obedience even from his commissioners and his long-term friends, and set machineries in motion to make himself dictator-for-life. When first Ikem and then Chris defy him, Sam orders their elimination and Ikem is killed. Chris goes into hiding, but ironically, just as the forces Sam had unleashed recoil against him and he is killed in a coup, Chris is also killed in a roadside scuffle with a drunken soldier.

Apart from the male principals, the story also features Beatrice Okoh, a high-ranking bureaucrat in the civil service who had studied with Chris and Ikem in Britain and had become engaged to Chris. She is therefore drawn into the affairs of the men because of her social involvement with them. The author makes his major political statements through his male surrogates—through Chris, who because of his vantage point as a member of Sam's cabinet is like the anthill that survives seasonal fires to report on last season's events to the grass of the new season, and through Ikem, the self-effacing intellectual who turns his back on his privileged class to champion the cause of the downtrodden, and who is, pointedly, engaged to the illiterate Elewa. Beatrice's presence in the story enables Achebe to lash out against men's abuse of women (Beatrice hates the memory of her father who grossly abused her mother), and their use of women as social props (as Sam once used Beatrice while entertaining a visiting American journalist). Achebe also makes the case (through Ikem), though, that men should involve women in state affairs from the start, instead of waiting until they have made a mess of things before inviting them in as rectifiers.

Achebe attempts in the novel to position himself on the right side of the socialist discourse that was rampant in academic and literary circles in Nigeria at the time of its writing, an objective he pursues through set speeches (most typically Ikem's before a university audience and his "love letter" to Beatrice) and lengthy essays, like the ones identifying Beatrice with the goddess Idemili. It might not be unfair to surmise that the novel bears the traces of its origins as an essay.

FURTHER READING

Boehmer, Elleke. "Of Goddesses and Stories: Gender and a New Politics in Achebe's *Anthills of the Savannah*." In *Chinua Achebe: A Celebration*, ed. Kirsten Holst Petersen and Anna Rutherford, 102–12. Oxford: Heinemann, 1990.

Anyidoho, Kofi (1947–) Born Kofi Kpodo in Wheta in the Volta Region of Ghana, Kofi Anyidoho grew up learning firsthand about the traditional poetry of his Ewe people from his mother, who was a practitioner of the performance art form. He dropped his father's name and took on that of his uncle, Kojovi Anyidoho, out of anger that his father would not raise the money to send him to middle school. Because of his father's refusal he was forced to interrupt his schooling for a year, which he spent weaving Kente cloth. After completing his primary education he entered the Accra Teacher Training College to train for a career in teaching. While there he discovered his interest in literature and became a member of the Creative Writers Club. After a two-year stint teaching in Brong Ahafo's Wenchi District, he went on to the Advanced Teacher Training College, Winneba. After graduating from there he took a job teaching English at Achimota Secondary School. In 1974 he entered the University of Ghana and studied English and linguistics, graduating with a BA in 1977. After teaching for a year he left Ghana for Indiana University, where he studied folklore. In 1980, after he had obtained his MA from Indiana, he went on to the University of Texas at Austin and earned his PhD in comparative literature in 1983. He returned to Ghana and began to teach at the University of Ghana, Legon. He has served for many years as head of the English Department, director of the School of Performing Arts, and director of the African Humanities Institute.

Anyidoho is a poet who believes that poetry should be a living art, a "full drama" art, not something fossilized on the printed page and thus distanced from potential audiences. Arresting though his poetry is in print, it achieves its full impact when the poet himself performs before an audience, with the skill and assurance of a traditional master artist. He told his hosts at Barnard College, where he was spending the 2005–2006 academic year as a distinguished visiting scholar, that for him poetry has ceased to be a textual art subject to the distancing that writing and printing impose, and has been liberated, presumably by aural technology and dramatic presentation. His foray in the direction of performance poetry began, he recalls, when in 1984 Efua Sutherland as chair of the Ghana National Commission on Children invited him to put together a literary-dramatic

program to be performed by Accra school-children to mark OAU day. That was for him the beginning of the process of returning the drama of orality to African poetry.

Anyidoho's fellow Ghanaian, Kofi Awoonor (also born in Wheta), once described him as a poet whose work is marked by "a depth of lyricism and a fundamental grasp of imagery as an element of general and particular statement." He also acknowledges Anyidoho's deep understanding of the Ewe dirge, an understanding that has benefited his poetry.

His published volumes of poetry include *Elegy for the Revolution* (1978), *A Harvest of Our Dreams* and *Earth Child* (1985), *The Fate of Vultures* (1989), and *Ancestral Logic and Caribbean Blues* (1993). In them he comments on such issues as the ill use Africans have experienced at the hands of the colonizers and Africans' own mismanagement of their own affairs. He is not a doleful poet, however, for he has found room in his works for humor as well as optimism. The edited volume *The Word Behind Bars and the Paradox of Exile* (1997) grew out of a workshop held at Northwestern University under his direction in November 1994, which brought together a group of African writers.

Anyidoho has won several awards both for the writing and the performance of his poetry, including the Langston Hughes Prize, the BBC Arts for Africa Poetry Award, the Fania Kruger Fellowship for Poetry of Social Vision, and the Ghana Book Award. He has also been Ghana's Poet of the Year and has served as president of the African Literature Association.

FURTHER READING

Anyidoho, Kofi. *Earthchild*. Accra: Woeli Publishing, 1985.
Fraser, Robert. *West African Poetry: A Critical History*. Cambridge: Cambridge University Press, 1986.

Armah, Ayi Kwei (1939–) Ayi Kwei Armah was born in Sekondi Takoradi, on the coast of western Ghana, in 1939. His secondary education was at Achimota College, Accra, the premier high school in the country. In 1959 he received a scholarship to study at the Groton School in Groton, Massachusetts. From there he went on to Harvard University, from where he received a degree in sociology in 1963. He worked in Algeria for a short while as a translator for the magazine *Révolution Africaine*, and returned to Ghana in 1964. Back home, he was employed at Ghana Television as a scriptwriter, but, frustrated in that job, he left to teach English at the Navarongo School. In 1967 he left Ghana for Paris and took a job as editor with the magazine *Jeune Afrique*, a job he held for one year. In 1968 he left for Columbia University to study creative writing, and graduated with his MFA in 1970. He taught for a while at the University of Massachusetts before leaving for East Africa, going first to Kenya and then to Tanzania, where he taught until 1976 at the College of National Education, Chamg'omge. He used his stay in Tanzania to learn Swahili and also to do some writing, before leaving the country for Lesotho, where he taught at the National University. He has been a visiting scholar at the University of Wisconsin at Madison, and he now makes his home in the village of Popenguine in Senegal.

Armah has devoted his career to registering his disillusionment with a society in which the birth of the "beautiful ones" has been indefinitely deferred, if not entirely aborted. Like many youthful Ghanaians he shared in the great expectations of the country's attainment of independence in 1957, and in its promise that Ghana under Kwame Nkrumah's leadership would spearhead the unification of Africa and the closing of the development gap between the continent and the industrialized West. The failure of the Nkrumah regime, which fell in a 1966 coup, has left an indelible mark on Armah's consciousness, but that was not his only disappointment. When he returned to Ghana in 1964 it was with an idealist's sense of mission, but he met with frustration at the hands of incompetent, self-important bureaucrats who for their part had no patience with his type.

His creative career began with the publication of poems and short stories in such journals as *Okyeame*, *Harper's*, and *The Atlantic Monthly*; it was the fall of the Nkrumah government, however, that provided the impetus and furnished the material for his first novel, *The Beautyful Ones Are Not Yet Born* (1969). It depicts a nation in pursuit of "the gleam" at the expense of the country, fellow citizens, and even close relatives, and a country in which the good people, like the nameless hero (the man), have become paralyzed with ennui. *Fragments* (1970), his second novel, has much in it that is autobiographical: Kofi Baako, an artistic and naively idealistic young man, returns home from studying in the United States only to find himself in the stultifying embrace of an appetitive family who see him as the supplier of all their wants and the answer to all their prayers; their demands and the resultant pressure on him eventually drive him insane. His third novel, *Why Are We So Blest?* (1972), focuses on the characters Modin Dofu and Solo, who are Africans, and Aimee, who is Modin's white American girlfriend. It is set against the background of the Algerian revolution, to serve in which Modin has abandoned his education at Harvard, but for which his association with Aimee makes him ineffectual and unwelcome. Solo, another failed revolutionary, is the keeper of Modin's diary through which his story unfolds. The book's title refers to the annual self-commemorative ritual of Thanksgiving in the United States.

Two Thousand Seasons (1973) is an epic historical reconstruction that, in poetic cadence, lambastes the "white predators from the desert" and the "white destroyers from the sea," but no less their African collaborators and stooges (the kings who sell their own peoples to the Europeans and the *askaris* who work as bloody hired guns for the foreign exploiters) for the thousand-year suffering Africa has experienced after its people lost "the way." *The Healers* (1979) cites disunity as the bane of African history and posits unity as the salvation of the continent and its people. Armah completed both novels while living in Tanzania.

In *Osiris Rising* (1995), which is based on the Egyptian Isis-Osiris myth and in which the major characters bear such names as Ast, Nwt, Set, Asar, and so forth, Armah returns to the theme of corruption, moral and physical, past and present. Modern-day state security functionaries employ the most sophisticated machinery to keep the virtuous people in subjugation. While the immigrant African American Ras Jomo Cinque Equiano, the conniving progeny of a slave and collaborator with slavers, plays lackey to the corrupt rulers, another African American, the irresistibly beautiful and formidably intelligent Ast, brings the promise of redemption and regeneration. His next work of fiction also hacks back to the Afrocentric claim to the heritage (now lost) of ancient Egypt. *KMT: In the House of Life* (2002) is a quest to discover how and why Africa missed the way after enjoying the glory that was Kemet. The heroine Lindela (echo of Mandela), is, like Ast, an Egyptologist with rare fluency in hieroglyphics. She comes upon millennia-old Egyptian texts whose message pose such questions as: "How best can Africa's multimillennial history be envisioned as one continuous stream? Why did the society that invented literacy sink into the misery of illiteracy, ignorance and religion? … And why did the ancient scribes call the concept of Maat our best promise of regeneration?"

Armah's style is impressive in its technical sophistication, and varies as does the subject from novel to novel. For example, he matches the moral corruption of *The Beautyful Ones* with scatological language and images that are capable of turning the reader's stomach, while in *Two Thousand Seasons* the language is dignified and ornate, even though the author here, too, indulges in graphic descriptions of gruesome scenes.

At his Popenguine hideout, Armah operates his own publishing establishment, Per Ankh: The African Publication Collective, and is constructing a retreat there for writers who need a place to write in solitude.

FURTHER READING

Fraser, Robert. *The Novels of Ayi Kwei Armah: A Study in Polemical Fiction*. London: Heinemann, 1980.

———. *Critical Perspectives on Ayi Kwei Armah*. Washington, DC: Three Continents Press, 1992.

Jackson, Tommie L. *The Existential Fiction of Ayi Kwei Armah, Albert Camus, and Jean-Paul Sartre*. Lanham, MD: University Press of America, 1997.

Lorentzon, Leif. "*An African Focus*": A Study of Ayi Kwei Armah's Narrative Africanization. Stockholm: Almqvist & Wiksell International, 1998.

Ogee, Ode. *Ayi Kwei Armah, Radical Iconoclast: Pitting Imaginary Worlds Against the Actual*. Athens: Ohio University Press, 2000.

Wright, Derek. *Ayi Kwei Armah's Africa: The Sources of His Fiction*. London: H. Zell, 1989.

Yankson, K. E. *The Rot of the Land and the Birth of the Beautyful Ones: The World of Ayi Kwei Armah's Novels*. Legon: Ghana University Press, 2000.

Arrow of God **(1964)** Chinua Achebe's third novel, *Arrow of God*, is set, like *Things Fall Apart*, in the Igbo area of Nigeria in the years 1921 to 1922. While the earlier novel documents the first arrival of Europeans in the area and the conflict that resulted from the contact of two radically different cultures, the latter novel is about events that take place several years later, when the Europeans are firmly established and have fully colonized the territory. It comes after *No Longer at Ease*, which skips a generation after that of *Things Fall Apart*, moving to the mid-1950s to deal with the disorientation of the new African elite class with its Western tastes and habits, and with the dilemma of reconciling traditional expectations with modern realities in the multiethnic Lagos, capital of a multiethnic Nigeria. In *Arrow of God*, Achebe doubles back in time to the in-between generation he had omitted.

Achebe has acknowledged that *Arrow of God* is his favorite among his writings, one that he is likely to go back and reread. He feels so strongly about it that he has taken the trouble to rewrite it and make revisions in order, as it were, to satisfy himself that it definitively says what he wishes to say about the nature of the encounter between Africa and the West and its consequences. In his words, "Although maybe to a lesser degree than *Things Fall Apart*, the novel was inspired in part by my desire to revaluate my culture. Like many others, it had been branded as inferior and bad by British oppressors, when they did not say it was nonexistent. It appeared to be a vital cultural necessity to fight and rebel against that view." The strong thematic affinity with *Things Fall Apart* is therefore both explicit and intentional, and the attentive reader will find that the later novel recalls the earlier in several significant regards.

As in *Things Fall Apart*, the central action is the destruction of a proud and forceful champion of tradition as he understands it, but whose vision is clouded and flawed by hubris. In his zealous obeisance to his distorted perception of his community's ethos, the hero Ezeulu violates what he claims he is protecting, and contravenes a fundamental principle—the primacy of the communal will. Ezeulu, the Chief Priest of Ulu (the symbol of the collective aspirations of the composite six villages of Umuaro), precipitates his own destruction by appropriating the authority of his god for use against the community in order to avenge an injury to his ego, with the consequence that both the community and his god abandon him. After his destruction the people conclude that "their god had taken sides with them against his headstrong and ambitious priest and thus upheld the wisdom of their ancestors—that no man however great was greater than his people; that no man ever won judgement against his clan."

Because the imposed authority of the white man contributes significantly to the falling out between Ezeulu and Umuaro, and because the alternative that the white man's religion offers to the community enables it to successfully defy Ezeulu, Achebe reiterates the thesis he pronounced in the earlier novel, namely, that the coming of the white man provided the means for weakening traditional bonds, that it placed a knife on what bound the community together, the result being that things fell apart.

According to Achebe, his intention in this novel was to demonstrate that action and reflection are crucial for solving Nigeria's problems. *Things Fall Apart* had not adequately made the point, for Okonkwo its hero was not a man of thought but of action, and therefore not the sort of person to serve as a vehicle for demonstrating the necessity of combining action and reflection. "In Ezeulu," Achebe told an interviewer, "I tried to combine the two [qualities] in one person" (Wilkinson 1997, 142), and he consistently insists on the intellectual quality of the man, whom he describes variously as "a great intellectual," "an intelligent man ... a clever intellectual," "that magnificent man," and so forth.

Apart from adding an intellectual dimension to his hero, Achebe seizes the opportunity of revisiting his earlier theme to add to its complexity, as well as that of his characters. For example, Achebe repeats scenes in *Arrow of God* that recall some in *Things Fall Apart*—the abuse of a sacred python in both, and the Pumpkin Leaf ceremony in the latter novel, which can be compared to such ceremonies as *iyi uwa* and *isa ifi* in the previous one. In all cases Achebe devotes more time to the later instances and makes them yield more significance, both thematic and philosophic.

His characterization is also more sophisticated; apart from enhancing the hero's character by combining in him the will to act and the capability to reflect, he also corrects the weakness some critics had cited with regard to *Things Fall Apart*: the caricaturing of the European characters, especially the Reverend James Smith, the single-minded and overzealous successor to the cautious, if equally single-minded, Mr. Brown. In *Arrow of God*, Achebe invests his white men with some humanity: he gives Captain Winterbottom a history—his military service, the loss of his wife, and his principled disagreement with official policy, for example. He even gives his readers opportunities to see the Europeans at home as they entertain one another to dinner and discuss their mission. With regard to style, whereas Achebe painstakingly glossed Igbo expressions in the earlier novel, in the latter he lets the context do the job, and its use of proverbs is also more sparing.

The instances of intertextuality in the novel, wherein events in *Things Fall Apart* are recalled, include the destruction of Abame, and Mr. Clarke's reading—*The Pacification of the Primitive Tribes of the Lower Niger* by George Allen—the book that the district commissioner in *Things Fall Apart* contemplates writing, and whose title provides the concluding words in that novel.

FURTHER READING

Gikandi, Simon. *Reading Chinua Achebe*. London: James Currey, 1991.

Innes, C. L. *Chinua Achebe*. Cambridge: Cambridge University Press, 1990.

Lindfors, Bernth, ed. *Conversations with Chinua Achebe*. Jackson: University Press of Mississippi, 1997.

Association of Nigerian Authors (ANA)
The Association of Nigerian Authors was the brainchild of Chinua Achebe. It was formally inaugurated at a meeting of the country's authors held at the University of Nigeria, Nsukka, from June 26 to 28, 1980. The formal opening took place on June 27, with Ngugi wa Thiong'o in attendance as an honored guest, along with most writers of any consequence in the country. At this inaugural meeting Achebe was elected president, and he occupied that position until he relinquished it in 1986.

The association's aims and objectives are quite ambitious: it seeks to encourage Nigerian literature, both written and spoken, including the performance and transcription of the latter, and its translation into other languages, Nigerian and non-Nigerian, for wider dissemination. It further aims to nurture indigenous talent and champion the causes of writers in all matters pertaining to their well-being and rights as writers, to promote solidarity among writers and encourage them to commit themselves to the ideals of a humane and egalitarian society. It also seeks to cooperate with other organizations that share its ideas, and to coordinate with groups throughout the world for the promotion of the book.

In practical pursuit of its objectives, ANA works to remove constraints on writers whether these be in the form of scarcity of materials for writing or publishing, difficulty in finding publication outlets, or restrictions on the freedom of writers to express themselves without fear of persecution. It encourages new writers by publishing their works in anthologies of prose and poetry, and also in single-author volumes. It also publishes an annual journal, the *ANA Review*, which it hopes eventually to upgrade to a quarterly. Another way in which it promotes its objectives is by holding annual competitions in various categories: poetry, prose, drama, and children's literature, and awarding several prizes. Four of the prizes are sponsored by the Niger Delta Development Corporation (NNDC): for drama (named for John Pepper Clark-Bekederemo); for prose (named for Ken Saro-Wiwa); for poetry (named for Gabriel Okara); and for women's writing (named for Flora Nwapa). It also awards the Cadbury Poetry Prize, the Spectrum Prize, and the Atiku Abubakar Prize for Children's Literature. The All-Africa Okigbo Prize for poetry, which Wole Soyinka instituted in 1987, has since been "suspended."

The ANA also recognizes lifetime achievements with awards; it honored its founder Achebe with its Triple Eminence Award in 1990. In 1988, with the support of the federal government, the French embassy, and UNESCO, the ANA organized an international symposium and a book exhibition in honor of Wole Soyinka's Nobel award of 1986. It also collaborated with several other organizations to organize an elaborate commemoration of the author's seventieth birthday in 2004.

The ANA, which maintains a chapter in every state of the federation and the Federal Territory of Abuja, takes pride in the contributions Nigerian writers have made to the enhancement of the international image of their country, not least through the long list of literary prizes they have won—prizes at the 1962 All-Negro Festival of the Arts, several Commonwealth Prose and Literary Prize, BBC Drama, Poetry, Short Story and Folklore Prizes, Noma Awards, the Booker Prize, and the Nobel Prize. The ANA points out with pride that in the case of the last two Nigerian writers were the first black Africans to win them.

One of the association's unrealized hopes is the establishment of a pan-African library of creative works by people of African descent, published or unpublished, from the beginning of time to the present. Another is the construction of Writers' Village, which it envisages to be the heart of the "home for literary culture at the heart of the nation's prime metropolis," Abuja. It in fact succeeded in getting the government to grant it a secretariat in Abuja and some prime property for the village in 1985. It has yet to develop the property, though, and the Capital Development Authority has found other uses for the secretariat.

True to the activist impulse evident in the statement of its aims and objectives, the Association also makes pronouncements on issues that, while not strictly literary, indirectly affect writers as citizens. Thus, for example, at its annual convention in November 2003, whose theme was "Literature, Democracy and World Peace," in addition to expressing its concern at the high cost of publishing materials and asking for an increase in the amount of funds available to the libraries in the country's educational institutions, it urged the government to: accelerate the pace of work on a petrochemical industry under construction; reverse its decision on not repairing the existing oil refineries and building new ones; and abandon its privatization and deregulation policy, which is proving a hardship to the people.

Atta, Sefi (1964–) The granddaughter of a traditional ruler, the Atta of Igbira, Sefi Atta was born in Lagos, Nigeria, in 1964 into what she describes as a neo-Nigerian family. Her parents were Igbira and Yoruba, northern and southern, Moslem and Christian. Her father had studied at Achimota College in Ghana and Oxford University. Her mother had worked as a model and as a secretary in the United Nations. The Atta home was open to culture and people of all cultures and Sefi had an idyllic childhood during which she traveled within Nigeria and West Africa.

Tragedy struck when in 1972, her father, who was then the head of the Nigerian civil service, died of cancer. Their mother raised Sefi and her four siblings from then on, and watching her mother take charge as the head of the household shaped her feminist sensibilities.

Atta discovered storytelling as a student in Queen's College, Lagos, where she was active in the drama society and was the class playwright, and at the age of fourteen she was sent to Millfield, a boarding school in England. At Millfield, she studied English and French for A levels, and her fiction readings sparked her interest in literary fiction, but not strongly enough for her to begin writing fiction. She went on to Birmingham University from where she graduated with a business degree, and then moved to London to train as a chartered accountant. In 1994 she moved to New Jersey with her husband, Gboyega Ransome-Kuti, a medical doctor, and practiced as a CPA. After giving birth to a daughter, she enrolled in a creative-writing course at New York University, and when her family's relocation to Mississippi in 1997 left her without a job she began to write full-time. She also completed an online masters degree in creative writing from Antioch University, Los Angeles, graduating in 2001. She teaches at Missis-sippi State University and Meridian Community College.

Atta's short stories have won prizes from *Zoetrope*, Red Hen Press, the BBC, and Commonwealth Broadcasting Association, and have appeared in *Glendora Review*, *Farafina*, *In Posse Review*, *Carve*, *Eclectica*, *Los Angeles Review*, *Mississippi Review*, *storySouth*, and *Crab Orchard Review*. Her memoirs have been anthologized in *The Penguin Book of New Black Writing in Britain* and *Roar Softly and Carry a Great Lipstick*. She is a two-time winner of the BBC African Performance Competition for plays, and in 2002 the opening section of her debut novel was short-listed for the Macmillan Writers Prize for Africa. The novel entitled *Everything Good Will Come* was published in the United States and the United Kingdom in 2005, and later in Nigeria also. It is the story of Enitan Taiwo's experiences as she grew up in Lagos in the years spanning the eruption of the Nigerian civil war and the increasingly tumultuous military rule of the 1990s. It is also the story of Enitan's relationship with her unconventional friend Sherri Bakare, and with both her activist father, a lawyer who cannot stomach soldiers' rule, and her fanatically religious mother. Educated in England as a lawyer herself, Enitan works for her father in Lagos and lives with him until she becomes convinced that he is a hypocrite who had hurt her mother and was to blame for their divorce. The story is for the most part an interrogation of gender relations, much of it unedifying, until the end when the "good thing" in the title—the promise of a rapprochement with her father—does come.

Her second novel, *Swallow*, which she has completed but has not yet placed, is set in the 1980s, also in Lagos. It involves two young women, Tolani and Rose (who are forced by circumstances to become involved in drug trafficking), and also of

Arike, Tolani's mother, who is herself a survival of a troubled youth.

FURTHER READING

Newland, Courttia, and Kadija Sesay, eds. *The Penguin Book of New Black Writing in Britain*. London: Penguin, 2000.

Stephens, Autumn, ed. *Roar Softly and Carry a Great Lipstick: 28 Women Writers on Life, Sex, and Survival*. Maui and San Francisco: Inner Ocean Publishing, 2004.

Autobiography One can confidently assert that the autobiography as a genre in African writing emerged from the African encounter with Europe, and that it has no antecedent in traditional cultural production. The suggestion that some version of the genre existed before the advent of the Europeans, albeit quite different from the new version, is quite untenable. Proponents of a pre-European autobiographical tradition point to such performances as the Yoruba praise form *oriki* and similar ones in other cultures as examples, but these can hardly qualify as autobiographies, narratives of individual lives by the individuals who lived them. Such a performance occurs in Chinua Achebe's *Arrow of God*, where the hero Ezeulu, chief priest of the god Ulu, sings his own praises in a sort of "autobiography" during the festival of the Pumpkin Leaves. Inasmuch as he was in that role an impersonation of his god testifying to the awesomeness of the god, one should properly say that he was singing the praises of Ulu. Another example occurs in Karin Barber's work on Yoruba women's praise singing, *I Could Sing Until Tomorrow*, wherein she describes how Yoruba brides go in a bridal procession to their grooms' homes, tearfully singing praises (*ekun iyawo*). An autobiographical dimension is detectable in such praises, inasmuch as their content refers to the bride's loving upbringing at the hands of her parents, but the praises concentrate on the excellence of the bride's lineage, and therefore of herself.

Apart from such ceremonial and ritual occasions it is difficult to imagine any circumstance in traditional African life when a person would deem it necessary or proper to regale listeners with the story of his or her life. Since people lived their lives fully in the sight and knowledge of the community, any person who insisted on subjecting others to tales about his or her exploits would be a boor. That is not to deny that there were occasions when a hunter, say, might recount or dramatize a memorable hunting triumph he once achieved, as in Yoruba *ijala* (hunter's chant) for example, but such performances would fall under the classification of boasts, would occur in formal or semiformal contexts (such as when groups drink and swap experiences), and would not account for whole lives or substantial parts thereof.

Significantly, scholars who have studied African (and African American autobiography) trace its origin to the effort by freed slaves in North America to prove their humanity by, in Henry Louis Gates's words, "writing themselves into being." Since the rhetoric that rationalized and justified the Atlantic slave trade, and later colonialism, asserted that Africans were subhuman and buttressed the assertion by pointing to the absence of literacy in African cultures, the freed slaves—for example Olaudah Equiano and Frederick Douglass—by writing, and especially by writing autobiographies, in effect proved their humanity. James Olney has advanced three reasons for African autobiographical writing (in addition to the four Benjamin Franklin cited for himself), which, he says, pertain more to the African genre than to comparable ones in other cultures: "to preserve a disappearing world; to describe the African milieu for outside readers; and ... to describe a representative case of a peculiarly African experience"

(Olney 1973, 27). It should be obvious, at a glance, why none of these would appeal to the African of the pre-European era, and why they would be preoccupations peculiar to Africans who feel the urge to address themselves to the external world.

Moreover, the early autobiographies—among them *Akiga's Story: The Tiv Tribe as Seen by One of Its Members* (1939, 1965) and the Sierra Leonean Robert Wellesley Cole's *Kossoh Town Boy* (1960)—were "ethnographic" (after Olney) in that they were exposés of the narrators' cultures through the experiences of the narrators; they were, in effect, group (auto)biographies, or, to use Olney's term, autophylography (218). These soon gave way as far as popularity was concerned to the memoirs of the principal players in the anticolonial struggle. Among these anticolonial autobiographies are Kwame Nkrumah's *Autobiography of Kwame Nkrumah* (1957); Ahmadu Bello's *My Life* (1960); Chief Obafemi Awolowo's *Awo: The Autobiography of Chief Obafemi Awolowo* (1960), *My March Through Prison* (1985), and *The Travails of Democracy and the Rule of Law* (1987); Chief Anthony Enahoro's *Fugitive Offender* (1965); and Nnamdi Azikiwe's *My Odyssey: An Autobiography* (1970). The authors of these works were mindful of having played important roles in momentous historical developments, and they wished to avail posterity of their insider's knowledge of what really happened, sometimes to congratulate and sometimes to vindicate themselves (if they had any reason to do so), and also to inspire younger readers to emulate their accomplishments.

The more recent African experience of coups, civil wars, and military rule in the postcolonial period has yielded a crop of autobiographies in which the protagonists have recounted their roles, just as the earlier politicians did; these have tended to focus on climactic events rather than the entire lives of the authors. Thus Colonel Akwasi Amankwa Africa, who led the coup that deposed Nkrumah of Ghana in 1966, wrote *The Ghana Coup, 24 February 1966* (1966); Olusegun Obasanjo, who was a Nigerian officer during the war to prevent Biafra's secession and served first as a military dictator and then on two occasions as an elected president, wrote *My Command: An Account of the Nigerian Civil War, 1967–70* (1981).

Some creative writers have also written autobiographies. First among them is Nigeria's Nobel laureate Wole Soyinka, who has already written three installments, *Aké: the Years of Childhood* (1981), *Ibadan: the Penkelemes Years* (1994), and *You Must Set Forth at Dawn* (2006). He has been joined by fellow Nigerians Buchi Emecheta, who published *Head Above Water* in 1986, and Tanure Ojaide, whose *Great Boys: An African Childhood* came out in 1998.

FURTHER READING

Olney, James. *Tell Me Africa: An Approach to African Literature.* Princeton: Princeton University Press, 1973.
Owomoyela, Oyekan. "The Self as Exemplum: African Autobiography as Celebratory Performance of the Self." In *African Writers and Their Readers: Essays in Honor of Bernth Lindfors*, ed. Toyin Falola and Barbara Harlow, 2:1–25. Trenton, NJ: Africa World Press, 2002.
Research in African Literatures 28, no. 2 (1997). Special issue on autobiography.

Awoonor, Kofi (1935–) Kofi Nyidevu Awoonor (formerly George Awoonor-Williams) was born in Wheta in 1935, in the Ewe-speaking Asiyo division of the Volta region of Ghana, and grew up listening to the singing of Ewe dirges, which was his grandmother's specialty. After primary schooling at the Catholic and Presbyterian primary schools in Dzodze and Keta, and secondary education, first at Zion College, Anloga, and later at Achimota Secondary School, he went to the University of Ghana at Legon. There, he honed his interest in traditional poetry at the Institute of African Studies, and received his degree in English in 1959. He served as editor of the literary journal *Okyeame* in the early 1960s, and also as an associate editor of *Transition*. He was also the director of the Ghana Film Corporation. On the overthrow of Kwame Nkrumah with whom he was closely associated in 1966, he left Ghana and pursued graduate study in exile, earning his MA from London University in 1968, and his PhD from the State University of New York at Stony Brook in 1972.

Awoonor began writing his own poetry at the age of fourteen—translations of dirges he heard from his grandmother—and his exposure to varied poetic traditions and styles is reflected in the infusion of his poetry with various flavors, the traditional, the Western, and the Christian.

In 1964 the Mbari Press published his first volume of poems, *Rediscovery and Other Poems*, which includes his Ewe dirge translations. In 1971, five years after he went into exile, his second collection, *Night of My Blood*, was published. Because of its theme of exile, its laments of a prodigal alienated from his cultural roots and yearnings for a spiritual return, it has been compared to the poetry of the Nigerian Christopher Okigbo. Ezekiel Mphahlele remarks in his introduction to the volume that the poetry is "characterized by the aura of a sage's words: now pleading, now cautioning, now ruminating over Africa's position in relation to the ancestors" (9). *Ride Me, Memory* (1973), which he wrote in the United States, also deals with the sense of exile and an anticipation of return, while *Guardians of the Sacred Word* (1974) comprises English renditions of the Ewe-language poetry of the innovative Ewe dirge composer Henoga Vinoko Akpalu. It also bespeaks Awoonor's belief

that the function of the traditional Ewe bard (the *heno*) is to help the community to position itself meaningfully in changing times, a function Awoonor believes the modern artist must also assume.

Awoonor returned home from exile in 1975 and took a teaching post at Cape Coast University. He soon got into trouble with the Acheampong government, however; he was accused of complicity in a coup plot and imprisoned for a year. The experiences yielded two works, *The House by the Sea* (1978) and *Until the Morning After: Collected Poems* (1987). They encompass the exile's return from his American sojourn to imprisonment at home and affirm his dedication to a future for the continent that will be better than its troubled present. His fortunes changed for the better with the accession of Jerry Rawlings to power: he was appointed his country's ambassador to Brazil in 1985 and to Cuba in 1989; and from 1990 to 1994 he served as Ghana's permanent representative to the United Nations.

Awoonor's first novel, *This Earth My Brother ... An Allegorical Tale of Africa*, which deals with corruption, disorientation, and alienation in independent Ghana, was published in 1971. Awoonor conceived it as a poem, and it fully justifies critics' reference to it as a prose poem. The hero Amamu, a foreign-educated ("been-to") lawyer, is neither capable of coping with the corruption around him nor able to retreat into the safety of a traditional order; he eventually suffers a breakdown and dies. His second novel, *Comes the Voyager at Last: A Tale of Return to Africa* (1992), reenacts the reconnection with roots that features prominently in Awoonor's consciousness. The "voyager," Marcus Garvey MacAndrews, is uneasy in his spiritual exile in the United States and returns home to Africa. The work also serves as a vehicle for the author to bemoan Africans' participation in, and culpability for, the transatlantic slave trade.

Awoonor is coeditor, with A. Adali-Mortti, of *Messages: Poems from Ghana* (1971), and he published his PhD dissertation on the development of African literatures as *The Breath of the Earth: A Critical Survey of Africa's Literature, Culture and History* in 1976. His other publications include the political commentaries *The Ghana Revolution: A Background Account from a Personal Perspective* (1984) and *Ghana: A Political History from Pre-European to Modern Times* (1990). He was honored with his country's National Book Council Award for poetry in 1979.

FURTHER READING

Elimimian, Isaac. "Kofi Awoonor." *Theme and Style in African Poetry.* Lewiston, NY: Edwin Mellen Press, 1991.

Kolawole, Mary Ebun Modupe. "Kofi Awoonor as a Prophet of Conscience." *African Languages and Cultures* 5, no. 2 (1992): 125–32.

McKoy, Sheila Smith. "'This Unity of Spilt Blood': Tracing Remnant Consciousness in Kofi Awoonor's *Comes the Voyager at Last.*" *Research in African Literatures* 33, no. 2 (2002): 194–209.

B

Bandele-Thomas, Biyi (1967–) Biyi Bandele-Thomas was born in Kafanchan, in northern Nigeria, in 1967. He became captivated by the theater when as a young boy he saw John Osborne's *Look Back in Anger* on his father's brand-new television set. In 1987 he gained admission to Obafemi Awolowo University, Ile-Ife, to study drama, receiving his degree in 1990. Upon graduation he emigrated to London, where he has established his residence and his reputation as a poet, a playwright, and a novelist. In 1989, while he was still in Nigeria, his poetry collection *Waiting for Others* won the British Council Award, and his play *Rain* won the International Student Playscript Competition. In 1991 the BBC broadcast his play *The Female God and Other Forbidden Fruits* in its World Service, and two years later Radio 5 broadcast *Marching for Fausa*, which was also performed at the Royal Court Theatre. His other theatrical successes include *Resurrections* (1994), *Two Horsemen* (1994), which was voted the best new play at the 1994 London New Play Festival, *Death Catches the Hunter* (1995), and *Me and the Boys* (1995). In addition to writing several other plays for radio and television—for example, the 1995 crime thriller *Bad Boy Blues*. He also adapted Chinua Achebe's *Things Fall Apart* for stage at Leeds and London in 1997.

Bandele-Thomas wrote the novels *The Man Who Came in from the Back of Beyond* (1991) and *The Sympathetic Undertaker and Other Dreams* (1991). Both are indictments of the rampant corruption in public life. *The Man Who Came in from the Back of Beyond* incorporates a story reminiscent of Ken Saro-Wiwa's short story, "Africa Kills Her Sun": a young man engages in illicit trade in order to earn the means to fight official corruption. Another novel, *The Street*, appeared in 2000, with the author's name rendered as Biyi Bandele. It is set in the Brixton neighborhood of London and examines life in the multiracial community.

FURTHER READING

Agho, Jude. "Scatology, Form and Meaning in the Novels of Alex La Guma and Biyi Bandele-Thomas." *Neohelicon* 30, no. 2 (December 2003): 195–208.

Negash, Girma. "Migrant Literature and Political Commitment: Puzzles and Parables in the Novels of Biyi Bandele-Thomas." *Journal of African Cultural Studies* 12, no. 1 (June 1999): 77–92.

***Beasts of No Nation* (2005)** Although the setting of Uzodinma Iweala's debut novel, *Beasts of No Nation*, is not specified, certain details suggest Nigeria during the Biafran War. The backdrop for the story is a civil war in which rebel soldiers short on ammunition, food, clothing, and other supplies are fighting a government that pursues them with helicopters and airplanes. Moreover the government forces are referred to as being from the north, and the youthful hero Agu has a childhood best friend named Dike.

Agu, whose father was a teacher, learned to love books thanks to his father's sizeable library and had earned the nickname "the professor" from his Bible-reading mother because of his bookishness. His teacher, Mistress Gloria, who taught every class up to sixth grade, also encouraged his learning with the promise that he would in time become a doctor or an engineer. But then the civil war intrudes into his life, his father is killed and he is forced to join the rebel ranks as a child-soldier. He is quickly initiated into killing, cheered on by the laughter of the other soldiers and the Commandant's encouraging smile, and growing hard between his legs.

His career as a killer begins when he is still too young to carry a gun, so he makes do with a knife—there are not enough guns to go round anyway—but that serves well enough for him, fortified with gun juice, to be able to sever a girl's hand to get her away from her mother, and to finish her off with his weapon. But he is also often at the receiving end of awful experiences, especially because the Commandant takes a liking to him and repeatedly uses him to satisfy his sexual cravings.

The author includes some folkloric touches in the narration, one concerning the legend about the creation of Agu's village, and another about the mysterious Town of Abundant Resources. And although a gruesome account, the ending is optimistic: Agu winds up in an idyllic refugee camp by the ocean, where he can read as much as he likes and walk the beach, dreaming realistic dreams of becoming a doctor or an engineer eventually.

Although the story has a war as its backdrop, a war whose details recall the Nigerian civil war, this young Igbo writer, unlike others in his generation, does not devote his attention to the interethnic issues of the conflict, but to the evil of forcing underage children to become killers.

Beautyful Ones Are Not Yet Born, The (1968) Ayi Kwei Armah's subject in his first novel, *The Beautyful Ones Are Not Yet Born,* is the corruption that pervades the society during the rule of Ghana's founding president, Kwame Nkrumah. His leadership during Ghana's campaign for independence had inspired idealistic Ghanaians, and with them many Africans; expectations were high that under his dynamic leadership the country and the continent would embark on an era of freedom and prosperity that would reverse the debilitating legacies of the slave trade and colonialism. As Armah dramatizes in his novel, by presiding over a corrupt administration and squandering the resources of the nation on megalomaniacal projects, the new leader quickly betrayed the hopes the people had reposed in him. The novel also demonstrates Armah's conviction that the political leadership was not alone in wallowing in corruption, but that the disease had worked its way into practically every nook and cranny in the life of the nation.

The hero of the novel is "the man," an anonymous designation that makes him somewhat representative of the general population. He works as a clerk for the national railway company, an employment that is not only boring—he spends much of his time exchanging pointless and sometimes meaningless messages on the Morse machine with other clerks like himself at different stations on the railway line—but also exposes him to the filth and blight everywhere. On his way to work he rides buses crowded with disgusting, drooling fellow passengers; at work he has to put up with banisters encrusted with assorted grime, fecal matter, mucus, and other such nasty things, and he is forced to fend off invitations to engage in official corruption.

He cannot count on his home as a refuge from the plague, because it has infested his wife Oyo, who, urged on by her mother, berates the man for not pursuing "the gleam" like his old friend Koomson. Koomson had astutely joined Nkrumah's party and had made the social and economic leap from dockworker to minister of state, in which capacity he is able to live "the gleam"—to ride luxury cars, live lavishly, and generally be a "white man." Oyo envies Koomson's wife Estella, for whom "the gleam" means, among other things, the ability to indulge her taste for imported foods and drinks. Together "the loved ones" have turned even his children against him, and have made home such an inhospitable place that he silently agrees with his co-worker's statement regarding their bleak working environment, "I can almost like it here when I think of home."

The prevailing attitude of the average Ghanaian, variously described as "walking corpse," "living dead," "walking dead," and the like, is of impotence, the prevailing belief that "honesty could only be a social vice." In their perversion they even assault and undermine the authorities' weak attempts at decorum. They had placed "receptacle[s] for the disposal of waste" at strategic points in the city in a campaign to "Keep [the] Country Clean by Keeping [the] City Clean," but the people had asserted themselves and their nature by depositing their offal everywhere around the receptacles, but not inside.

The exceptions to the rottenness seem to be the man and his friend, Teacher, whom despair had forced to write society off as hopeless, and therefore to withdraw from it. But even he admits that his flight from society, from the deadly embrace of loved ones has condemned him to living a half-life. Escape is thus not the answer. The man himself, for all his righteousness, finds that he cannot escape from being smeared with others' filth. Toward the end of the novel a coup takes place in which the government is overthrown, and a hunt is on for the top officials in the overthrown regime. Koomson has taken refuge at the man's home, and when the searchers approach, both men are forced to slip out through the human feces in and around the latrine hole. The man can at least take some solace from his wife's final admission that the way of the gleam was not the best after all: "I am glad you never became like him," she tells him at last. But Armah's verdict on the change of government is that it only means that "new men would take into their hands the power to steal the nation's riches and to use it for their own satisfaction," and the "beautyful ones" who would redeem the nation and people were yet to be born.

Critics have compared *The Beautyful Ones* to works by the existentialist writers Jean-Paul Sartre and Albert Camus in which characters are alienated from themselves and their milieu and are beset by questions about the meaning and purpose of living. One inescapable feature of the novel is its strong scatological quality, its obsession with excrement, vomit, and assorted forms of putrefaction. The filth envelops the society and its people and even finds its way inside the characters, where it makes its presence known through "half-audible rumblings from [the] belly and full, loud farts from below."

Besong, Bate (1954–2007) Bate Besong was born to Cameroonian parents at Ikot Ansa, Calabar, in eastern Nigeria on May 8, 1954, when Cameroon was still part of Nigeria. He attended St. Bedes Secondary School, Ashing Kom, and after receiving his General Certificate of Education (GCE), Ordinary Level there he went on to the Hope Waddell Institute, Calabar for his GCE Advanced Level certificate. From there he proceeded to the University of Calabar for his BA Honors degree in English and literary studies, and later to the University of Ibadan for his MA in English, with an emphasis on African poetry and drama. He returned to the University of Calabar and there took his PhD in English and literary studies.

His artistic inclinations became evident while he was in high school; he played in the school orchestra and earned himself the nickname James Brown (JB). As a university student in Nigeria he was prompted by the political crises in the country, especially the succession of military coups, to redirect his attention to politics, about which be began to express himself in poetry published in such places as *Opon Ifa, Okike, Anthology of Oracle Poets, West Africa Magazine, Quest Magazine, Drumbeats*, and *African Concord*. In addition, he was a ghostwriter for several prominent figures, among them General Mamman Vatsa. He has also published a number of plays. He taught literature at the Bilingual High School, Molyko, in Buea, and in 1999 was appointed a senior lecturer in drama and critical theory at the University of Buea. A versatile scholar and teacher, his activities include teaching drama, critical theory, cultural studies, creative writing, and play production.

Besong is one of the best-known Anglophone writers of Cameroon, having scored some successes with his poems and plays. His topical works critically engage the so-cial and political problems that plague his country and others in Africa, and call for radical change, although he is sometimes criticized for writing above the heads of most Cameroonian readers. The political stance places him in the same tradition and grouping as such Nigerian writers as Niyi Osundare, Tanure Ojaide, and Odia Ofeimun. His publications include the poetry collections *Obasinjom Warrior with Poems After Detention* (1991) and *Just Above Cameroon (Selected Poems 1980–1994)* (1998), and the dramas *The Grain of Bobe Ngom Jua* (1997), *Change Waka & His Man Saw-aBoy* (2003), and *The Achwiimgbe Trilogy* (2003).

The year 1992 was a banner one for Besong; he was named the *Cameroon Post* Literary Man of the Year, and he also won the drama award of the Association of Nigerian Authors (ANA). His life ended in an auto accident on March 8, 2007.

FURTHER READING

Ngwane, George. *Bate Besong (Or the Symbol of Anglophone Hope)*. Limbe: Noomerac Press, 1993.

Biafran War/Nigerian Civil War (1967–70) The constitutional gerrymandering through which the departing British colonizers hoped to determine the future of Nigeria even as they handed the country its independence in October 1960 perhaps inevitably precipitated the ethnic crisis that resulted in the military coup of January 1966. Igbo officers led it, and it saw the elimination of the political leaders of both the Yoruba-identified party, the Action Group (AG), and the Hausa-identified party, the Northern People's Congress (NPC). The suspicion that the coup was an Igbo plot to impose their dominance on the country was not eased by the nature of the government that Major General Aguiyi-Ironsi, an

Igbo, formed or the policies he initiated. Lieutenant Colonel Yakubu Gowon from the Middle Belt area of the country led a countercoup in July in which Aguiyi-Ironsi was killed. In a subsequent bloodbath in the northern parts of the country a large number of Igbo residents were killed, with the result that the Igbo fled not only the north but also all non-Igbo-speaking parts of the country to seek refuge in the Igbo heartland east of the Niger and south of the Benue.

In May 1967, the Igbo leader, Lieutenant Colonel Odumegwu Ojukwu, declared the secessionist Republic of Biafra, made up of the whole of the Eastern Region including the non-Igbo areas. Several attempts to heal the rift by peaceful means failed, and the civil war between the armed forces of the federal government of Nigeria and the secessionist Republic of Biafra, also known as the Biafran War, broke out on July 6, 1967. It was fought mainly on Biafran territory, and therefore the people who felt the attendant hardship most severely were those who lived in the contested republic. As the fighting dragged on, people closely involved in the events as well as observers saw instances in which the actions of the leaders on both sides failed to match their high-minded proclamations or to justify the sacrifices they urged on their followers. The war ended in January 1970, after Ojukwu fled the fighting for Ivory Coast, leaving a lieutenant behind to sue for peace.

The principals on both sides, especially the southerners, were often close associates: friends who were students together in high school and university, who were either employed in the same organizations, or at least frequenters of the same social occasions before the war. The necessity to choose sides meant that associations and friendships were disrupted or destroyed by the outbreak of hostilities. Among the writers for whom the trauma of the war and its aftermath has proved to be an attractive subject is John Pepper Clark-Bekederemo, who had remained loyal to the federal side while close friends and colleagues Chinua Achebe, Christopher Okigbo, and Gabriel Okara cast their lot with the rebels. Of the many works that the war has generated the following are among the most noteworthy: Clark-Bekederemo's *Casualties* (1970), Achebe's *Girls at War and Other Stories* (1972), Kole Omotoso's *The Combat* (1972), Eddie Iroh's *Forty-Eight Guns for the General* (1976) and *Toads of War* (1979), Cyprian Ekwensi's *Survive the Peace* (1976; 1979) and *Divided We Stand* (1980), Flora Nwapa's *Wives at War and Other Stories* (1980), Buchi Emecheta's *Destination Biafra* (1981), Odia Ofeimun's *The Poet Lied* (1983), and Festus Iyayi's *Heroes* (1986).

The role people played during the conflict has also tended to affect how people have perceived and reacted to their postwar fortunes. For example, Ken Saro-Wiwa, who was a commissioner on the federal side during the war, lost much sympathy later on when he took on the federal military government on behalf of his Ogoni people. The prevalent feeling in the country was that his predicament resulted from his too-close chumminess with the soldiers during the war, a chumminess that was moreover the foundation for his later prosperity and influence.

FURTHER READING

Cronje, Suzanne. *The World and Nigeria: The Diplomatic History of the Biafran War.* London: Sidgwick and Jackson, 1972.

McLuckie, Craig W. *Nigerian Civil War Literature: Seeking an Imagined Community.* Studies in Lewiston, NY: Edwin Mellen Press, 1990.

Nafziger, E. Wayne. *The Economics of Political Instability: the Nigerian-Biafran War.* Boulder, CO: Westview Press, 1983.

Cheney-Coker, Syl (1945–) Syl Cheney-Coker was born on June 28, 1945, in Freetown, Sierra Leone, to Christian Creole parents and received his early education there. At twenty-one he left for the United States and did his university studies at Oregon and Wisconsin. Soon after returning home upon graduation he took a teaching job at the University of the Philippines in 1975, and after two years he accepted another teaching position at the University of Maiduguri in Nigeria. In 1988 he went to the University of Iowa as writer in residence, and in the late 1980s through the early 1990s he worked as editor and publisher of the Freetown newspaper, the *Vanguard*.

Cheney-Coker made his mark as a poet with the publication of his two volumes *Concerto for an Exile* (1973) and *The Graveyard Also Has Teeth with Concerto for an Exile* (1980), the second of which combines the contents of the earlier volume with several new poems. A third collection of poems, *The Blood in the Desert's Eyes*, came out in 1990, the same year as the publication of his ambitious novel, *The Last Harmattan of Alusine Dunbar*. His early poems indicate that he was an admirer of the negritude poets, especially with regard to their celebration of the beauty of things African, but they avoid excesses of romanticism. He soon moved on, though, to wrestle in his collected works with his Creole identity, attempting to reconcile his privileged background with his sense of commitment to the struggling masses. They also reflect the anguish of exile, understandably inasmuch as he has lived abroad longer than he has in Sierra Leone.

The long epic novel *The Last Harmattan of Alusine Dunbar* marks a new direction in Cheney-Coker's writing, for it incorporates many of the features that are associated with Latin American magical realism, and that place him in the same grouping with the Ghanaian Kojo Laing and the Nigerian Ben Okri. The novel covers many eras in the development of the fictional country of Malagueta, which one presumes to be a stand-in for Sierra Leone, from its founding by immigrants from the New World to its later violence-riddled years. The figure of the eternal mystic Alusine Dunbar (or Sulaiman the Nubian) moves in and out of the story, making his appearances at strategic points and then departing. The work won the 1991 Commonwealth Writers Prize for the Africa Region.

Cheney-Coker fled his home in 1997 because of threats to his life during the civil strife that ravaged the country, and toward the end of 2000 he arrived in Las Vegas as the first writer and member of the International Parliament of Writers to take advantage of that city's designation as one of the cities of asylum, refuges sponsored by the parliament for the benefit of endangered writers. There, at the International Institute of Modern Letters, he continued work on two new projects, a book of poetry with the working title *Stone Child* and a novel with the title *The Sacred River*. Both are attempts to come to terms with the horrors of the war that had lately devastated his country, an event that he says affected him "to the point of making literature the only alternative to grief, silence, and outrage." He returned to a more peaceful Sierra Leone in 2003, confessing to the weariness of exile.

FURTHER READING

Bertinetti, Paolo. "Reality in Magic in Syl Cheney-Coker's *The Last Harmattan of Alusine Dunbar*." In *Coterminous Worlds: Magical Realism and Contemporary Post-colonial Literature in English*, ed. Elsa Linguanti et al., 197–207. Amsterdam: Rodopi, 1999.

Cooper, Brenda. *Magical Realism in West African Fiction: Seeing With a Third Eye.* London: New York: Routledge, 1998.

Knipp, Thomas. Review of *The Blood in the Desert's Eyes: Poems. African Studies Review* 35, no. 1 (April 1992): 136–37.

Nwankwo, Chimalum. Review of *The Last Harmattan of Alusine Dunbar. African Studies Review* 35, no. 1 (April 1992): 134–35.

Whyte, Philip. "Gender and Epic in Syl Cheney-Coker's *The Last Harmattan of Alusine Dunbar.*" *Commonwealth: Essays and Studies* 26, no. 1 (2003): 53–60.

Chinweizu (1943–) Chinweizu was born in Eluama-Isuikwato in eastern Nigeria. His university education was at the Massachusetts Institute of Technology and at the State University of New York, Buffalo. At the first institution he studied mathematics and philosophy as an undergraduate, and later returned there for graduate studies in economics. In between he pursued American studies and history.

In his first book *The West and the Rest of Us* (1975) he detailed the Western world's exploitation of non-Western peoples and argued for pan-African solidarity. He also decried the cultural alienation of the African elite and its slavish adoption of Western values. Working as a journalist for the Lagos publications *Guardian* and *Vanguard* in the 1980s, he established himself as a strident propagator of those and similar ideas. His work that has attracted the greatest attention is the book on African writing, *Toward the Decolonization of African Literature* (1980), which was a collection of essays he and his collaborators Onwuchekwa Jemie and Ihechukwu Madubuike had earlier published in *Okike.* In it the authors roundly condemn both Eurocentric approaches to the criticism of African literature, and what they saw as the obscurantist tendencies of writers like Wole Soyinka, Christopher Okigbo, Michael

Echeruo, and others they characterized as "the Ibadan-Nsukka poets" and whom they dismissed as suffering from "the [Gerard Manley] Hopkins disease." Chinweizu was unsurprisingly dismissive of Wole Soyinka's Nobel Prize, saying that the poet and the prize deserve each other.

Chinweizu has published both poetry—*Energy Crisis* (1978) and *Invocations and Admonitions* (1986)—and short fiction—*The Footnote* (1981). In these he maintains his critique of the West and African derivativeness, as he continues to do in the collection of essays, *Decolonising the African Mind* (1987). True to his established polemical form, he turned his caustic attention to women in *Anatomy of Female Power* (1990), which replaces matriarchy with patriarchy as the offender in gender relations. *Voices from Twentieth Century Africa: Griots and Towncriers* (1988), an anthology he edited, is eclectic, covering both popular and highbrow literature, and works from both the oral and the written traditions in their variety of genres. It comprises works that meet Chinweizu's criteria that their production and consumption must be acts within the social history of their originating communities; be integral parts of the public conversation; be moving or memorable and affect the reader or hearer emotionally, intellectually, morally, or aesthetically; and be for Africans by Africans and in African languages but translate well into English.

Early in 2006 Nigerian writers and artists gathered at the Muson Center in Lagos to honor Chinweizu, who was recovering from a stroke. At the event he reiterated his familiar arguments, dwelling especially on the feat Nigeria has accomplished of running a country endowed with immense wealth into the ground in record time. One of the highlights was the performance of Okot p'Bitek's two poem, *Song of Lawino* and Song of *Ocol*, which Chinweizu had adapted for the stage.

FURTHER READING

Chinweizu. *The West and the Rest of Us: White Predators, Black Slavers and the African Elite*. New York: Random House, 1975.

———. *Voices from Twentieth Century Africa: Griots and Towncriers*. London, Faber & Faber, 1988.

———. *Anatomy of Female Power: A Masculinist Dissection of Patriarchy*. Lagos: Pero Press, 1990.

Chinweizu, Onwuchekwa Jemie, and Ihechukwu Madubuike. *Toward the Decolonization of African Literature,* vol. 1, *African Fiction and Poetry and Their Critics*. Enugu: Fourth Dimensions, 1980.

Clark-Bekederemo, J. P. (1935–) John Pepper Clark-Bekederemo (perhaps better known as John Pepper Clark or J. P. Clark) was born in Kiagbodo in the Delta area of southern Nigeria on April 6, 1935. His father was Chief Clark Fuludu Bekederemo, his mother Poro Amakashe Adomi, an Urhobo princess. He grew up in a polygamous household and experienced the relational tensions that often characterized such households. After his primary education at the local Native Administration school, he went on to Government College, Ughelli, for his secondary education, which he completed in 1954. After working for a year in the civil service in Lagos he was admitted to the University College, Ibadan, to study English. He received his BA Honors in 1960. While a student at the university in 1957 he founded *The Horn*, a journal for student poetry in which his own first poems were published. He also served as editor of the student journal *The Beacon*.

On graduating, Bekederemo went to work for the Western Nigeria Ministry of Information in Ibadan, and after a year (in 1961) he took a job with *The Daily Express*, a newspaper based in Lagos, as editorial writer and head of features. It was at this time that he published his poetry collection *Po-ems*, made up of some forty poems on various subjects, and the play *Song of a Goat*, an exercise in writing Greek-style tragedy. In 1962 he went to Princeton for a year of study on a Parvin fellowship, but the experience proved most unsatisfying for host and guest alike, and it culminated in his being unceremoniously asked to leave the country. He later documented that unhappy American experience in *America, Their America* (1964), a scathing condemnation of the country and its people, both black and white.

Back in Nigeria, Bekederemo worked as a research fellow at the Institute of African Studies, University of Ibadan, an appointment that gave him the opportunity to research and record the Ijo *Ozidi Saga*. He also published *Three Plays* (1964) before again leaving Ibadan for Lagos to embark on a career as a lecturer at the University of Lagos. He kept up the pace of his productivity with the publication of the collection of poems *A Reed in the Tide* (1965), poems on the poet's African experiences and his travels in America and elsewhere, and the play *Ozidi* (1966), which is based on an Ijo legend that is performed over a period of several days. In the same year of the play's publication, he became coeditor of the literary journal *Black Orpheus*.

The outbreak of the Biafran War that same year confronted him with a painful dilemma. Close friends and contemporaries such as Christopher Okigbo and Chinua Achebe, among others, espoused the cause of the rebel Biafrans, while Bekederemo's allegiance remained with the federal side. His loyalty to the ideal of a united Nigeria resulted in the loss of valued friendships, some irretrievably as in the case of Okigbo, who died very early in the conflict. Bekederemo gave expression to his sense of loss in the postwar poetry collection *Casualties: Poems 1966–68* (1970), and during the same year he also published *The Example of Shakespeare* (1970), five previously published essays.

In the years before his retirement from his professorship at the University of Lagos in 1980, Bekederemo worked with the filmmaker Francis Speed to produce a film of the Ozidi saga, *The Ozidi of Atazi* (1972), and later published the literary version *The Ozidi Saga* in 1977. After his retirement he turned his attention to running the PEC Theater, which he founded with his wife Ebun in 1982, but he still kept up his writing as well as the repackaging of his earlier works for publication: *A Decade of Tongues* (1981); *State of the Union*, new poems on the Nigerian situation (1985); *The Bikoroa Plays*: *The Boat*, *The Return Home*, and *Full Circle* (1985); and *Mandela and Other Poems* (1988). *Once Again a Child*, a collection of new poems, came out in 2004. In these poems Bekederemo confronts and comes to terms with the realities of the human passage through time, a process in which as one moves farther from the womb and childhood and approaches the tomb one paradoxically becomes more and more a child. The poems have a marked autobiographical feel, with allusions to the poet's physical and spiritual journeys through life. The volume ends with "The Second Coming," an allusion to the belief in reincarnation, and perhaps the poet's anticipation of a second chance to do some things over. In September 2000 he marked forty years of Nigeria's independence with a new play *All for Oil*, which was performed at the Tennis Club in Lagos. It laments the rape of the Niger Delta area, which, in return for bringing seemingly boundless wealth, has mired the country in pollution and poverty.

Bekederemo enjoys a respectable reputation as a dramatist whose sense of theater was as evident in the early *Three Plays*, in which he emulated classical Greek drama, as in his later plays, which privilege indigenous expressive devices. Most critics are however of the opinion that his reputation derives mostly from his poetry, although he also excels in drama. His early poetry, like the early works of his novelist colleagues, can be described as "tutelage" or derivative, the derivative ones earning him inclusion among the writers whom Chinweizu and company diagnosed as suffering from "Hopkins disease"—the tendency to emulate the opacity of the British poet Gerard Manley Hopkins, that is. By the time of *Casualties*, though, he had developed a distinctive individual voice that continued to be sometimes obscure—the late volume, *Once Again a Child*, being perhaps the most accessible of his works. The subjects he dealt with run the gamut from his celebration of natural phenomena, childhood experiences (including his exile from the ancestral hearth in search of education and employment), the traumas of interpersonal relationships, colonialism, and political corruption.

Bekederemo was honored with the Nigerian National Merit Award in 1991 for his literary works, and with an honorary doctorate from the University of Benin.

FURTHER READING

Adepitan, Titi. "Between Drama and Epic: Toward a Medium for Ozidi." *Research in African Literatures* 33, no. 1 (Spring 2002): 120–32.

Eyoh, Luke. "African Musical Rhythm and Poetic Imagination: A Phono Stylistic Interpretation of Clark-Bekederemo's 'Return of the Fishermen.'" *Research in African Literatures* 32, no. 2 (Summer 2001): 105–18.

Izevbaye, D. S. "J. P. Clark-Bekederemo and the Ijo Literary Tradition." *Research in African Literatures* 25, no. 1 (1994): 1–21.

Conteh, J. Sorie Sorie Conteh, a Sierra Leonean scholar, received his BA from the University of Rochester and his PhD in anthropology and African studies from Indiana University, with the 1999 dissertation "Diamond Mining and Kono Religious Institutions: A Study in Social Change." He was a research fellow at the Department of African Studies of Fourah Bay College, the University of Sierra Leone, and of the Afrika-Studiecentrum in Leiden, the Netherlands; he was also a political affairs officer at the Permanent Observer Mission of the Organization of African Unity at the United Nations, as well as a member of the United Nations Iraq-Kuwait Observer Mission (UNIKOM) in Kuwait.

Conteh has written several short stories and essays in which he explores such issues as diamond smuggling, female circumcision, democracy in Africa, and such like. *The Diamonds* (2001), his first novel, is the story of Gibao and his love for diamonds and women, and of the horrors such a combination can engender. Moreover, it deals with the collapse of the communal spirit in the face of desire and materialism. It is a story of greed, lust, murder, and redemption, a story that is especially topical and significant, given the role diamonds played in fueling the bloody civil war that Sierra Leone had only recently come through.

Conton, William (Farquhar) (1925–) William Conton, one of the pioneers of modern Anglophone literature, was born in 1925 in Bathurst, now Banjul, the capital of The Gambia. He received his primary and secondary education in Gambia, Guinea, and Sierra Leone, and his university education first locally at Fourah Bay College and later abroad at the University of Durham. His has spent his professional life in Sierra Leone, where he was for some time the principal of the government secondary school at Bo, and later an education officer in the civil service.

His novel *The African* (1960) was among the earliest in the Heinemann African Writers Series. Reflecting the political ferment of the period, it depicts the career of Kisimi Kamara, a heroic politician who leads his fictional country of Songhai to independence, and is then persuaded by other African leaders to spearhead the formation of a United States of Africa, and the eventual liberation of South Africa from the grips of its apartheid regime. The novel is written in the first person, in the voice of its hero. It has suffered, though, because of the naiveté of its plot and its pedestrian language, which have combined to confine the work's significance to the realm of history (incidentally the author's specialty) rather than art.

Conton is also the author of the novel *The Flights* (1987), published by Heinemann (Nigeria), in some respects a sequel to *The African*. It features Saidu, a political exile in England from his fictional West African country of Songhai. Under the sociological and psychological stress his exile imposed on him, he commandeers a commercial airplane and threatens to kill a Songhai diplomat on board unless his government accedes to his demands. Badly written and badly printed, the work has understandably attracted little, and quite ephemeral, attention.

FURTHER READING

Soyinka, Wole. *Myth, Literature, and the African World*. London: Cambridge University Press, 1976.

Contract, The (1982) Festus Iyayi's second published novel, *The Contract*, depicts the culture of brazen embezzlement that pervaded Nigeria during the 1970s and 1980s, highlighting the accepted practice of grossly inflating the costs in awarding government contracts in order to ensure that all involved could reap illegal windfalls, and with the understanding that the projects in question would not necessarily be carried out. The hero is Ogie Obala, who has just returned from studying abroad.

His initial idealism enables him to resist the efforts of his father, Chief Eweh Obala, to lure him into corrupt practices. Chief Obala is the chairman of the city council and controller of contracts. His good friend Mallam Mallam has accumulated immense wealth through signing contracts with government officials for nonexistent projects and splitting the proceeds with them. The pressure on Ogie to become a practical, "liberal realist" eventually wears him down; he succumbs to the culture of corruption, but assuages his conscience by vowing to keep his loot within the country, where it would help the economy, instead of stashing it (as others did) in banks abroad. By thus engaging in "corruption with a human face" he would be demonstrating that he had a conscience.

The contract in the story is for low-cost housing; its original cost is estimated at 100,000 naira, but after highly placed officials have padded it to allow for their cuts the cost balloons to 500,000,000 naira. The novel exposes the lack of accountability that is at the root of official corruption in the country, as well as the utter contempt on the part of high public officials for the people, whom they consider ignorant anyway. In the end, Ogie's attempt at putting a human face on his corruption costs him his life at the hand of his father, whose overriding concern to protect his loot trumps his paternal obligations.

Iyayi wrote the novel before *Violence* (1979), but its publication was apparently held hostage by the publisher's reluctance to offend those in power in Nigeria at the time.

Dance of the Forests, A (1960) Wole Soyinka wrote *A Dance of the Forests* to commemorate Nigeria's attainment of independence in

October 1960, and its premiere performance took place during the festivities, although it was not part of the official celebrations. The refusal of the official planners to include the play in their program is easily understandable, given its import with regard to the legitimacy of any celebration and its outlook for the nation coming to birth.

The play centers on a mythical festive occasion, similar to the independence celebrations, when humans had hoped to celebrate their glorious achievements and asked the gods to send them illustrious past heroes to grace the occasion. Instead, the gods send accusers with grievous stories of having been ill used by the forebear of the celebrants. The gods also contrive to transform the celebrations into a trial of humankind, in which the celebrants would be confronted by tableaux of their past crimes, in which their victims would state their cases and sue for relief. The gods themselves serve as judges and prosecutors: Forest Head is at their head, with Aroni as his chief aid and master of ceremonies. The chief accusers, or plaintiffs, are the Dead Warrior and his wife. Their complaint is that when the Dead Warrior had refused Mata Kharibu's order to mount a military expedition for the recovery of the trousseau that had been stolen from Kharibu's consort, the whorish Madame Tortoise, Kharibu had had him castrated and sold into slavery, and his pregnant wife had also died with her pregnancy. The Dead Warrior now seeks vindication, and his wife relief from the pregnancy she has endured these one hundred generations.

Some of the gods are also involved in their own rivalry: Eshuoro is in conflict with Ogun over the fates of their human charges. Demoke, a master carver and Ogun's protégé, had killed his apprentice Oremole, Eshuoro's protégé, because the latter was about to surpass him in glory. Their antics and those of other agencies combine with the trials of the ancestors and their modern replicas to make for a most complicated and tedious drama.

In the final tableau all the contending characters are assembled before the presiding Forest Head in a contest for the ultimate prize, the Half-Child of which the Dead Woman has finally been delivered. Wagering for its possession are such claimants as the sinister Figures in Red, the Triplets (End that Justifies the Means, The Greater Cause that Justifies the Crimes, and Posterity), and the diabolical Eshuoro. In the original version Eshuoro claims the child whom he carries off with an evil grin. In a later concession to the spirit of independence, though, Soyinka rewrote the ending to suggest some optimism, awarding the Half-Child to Demoke, who later hands it to its mother. Forest Head withdraws in what seems to be utter disgust at the futility of making humans better.

The Half-Child represents the new nation, and Soyinka has proved prescient in his prognostications for it, even if his symbolic reconstruction of its history is unjustifiably vilified. The Warrior's declaration that "Unborn generations will be cannibals … Unborn generations will, as we have done, eat up one another," might be applicable to the future (as we now know), but hardly to the past that we do know. There seems to be little question, though, about the veracity of his point that human wickedness is perennial and self-repeating; to drive home the point, he provides for each major past miscreant a modern replica who repeats the forebear's misdeeds.

***Danda* (1964)** *Danda* (1964) is Nkem Nwankwo's rollicking story of the irrepressible thirty-year-old Danda. His father Araba is an *ozo* titleholder and therefore one of the most important men in Aniocha. He boasts a long barn full of yams, presides over a family of respectable size, and, as they say in the village, his name makes noise. Danda, by contrast, is an *akalogholi*, a ne'er-do-well. He has no gainful employment and no sense of responsibility, but he is nevertheless very popular with the women and youth of the village because he is irrepressibly cheerful, carefree and witty. Nicknamed "Rain," his characteristic garb is a cloak bedecked with little bells that announce his approach, often as accompaniment to the tunes he plays on his flute. He is also a favorite at any festival, where he entertains the participants with his colorful wisecracking, flute playing and singing, and where he indulges his insatiable appetite for palm wine.

Danda is the scourge of all sticklers for conventions and rules, especially rules about entitlement, proprietorship, or ownership. He is introduced brazenly taking possession of his kinsman Ndulue Oji's brand-new car in the owner's absence; Ndulue has no choice but to accommodate Danda because, as an onlooker comments, the law does not say that when a man acquires a land-boat he should forget his kindred. He next shows up at a festival carrying an *ozo* staff, an insignia only the *ozo* may carry, and even flaunts it before the gathered *ozo*. To the warning that the offended chiefs might punish him he responds, "They are not fit," and he later proves his invulnerability by nonchalantly seducing the young wife of a village dignitary. Invited to join the church, he casually accepts, and even accepts instruction preparatory to baptism. But when he is tested on the instruction, he relies on the examiner to supply all the answers, and when a date for his baptism is set nonetheless, he fails to show, later explaining casually that he had been invited to a drinking party. The church episode is an opportunity for Nwankwo to highlight the high-handedness of the Christians in those early days of conversion.

It is quite obvious that Danda's father Araba has no control over him. Indeed, he seems disinclined to control his son, limiting himself to occasional feeble reprimands. In fact, he indulges Danda, taking it upon himself to tell his son it is time for him to take a wife, taking the trouble to find a wife for him, and paying all the expenses. He goes so far on the wedding night as to drag Danda away from his drinking, shove him into the room where his wife awaits him, and shut the door on them. Araba also would have bought the *ozo* title for Danda if someone's remembering that Danda had in his youth run away when the ici was to be cut on his face had not foiled him, and no fugitive from the *ici* knife is allowed to become an *ozo*. No matter; another *ici* cutting date is arranged for Danda, but he again flees at the sight of the knife, thus bringing disgrace on his extended family.

Although the novel bears the title *Danda*, Nwankwo's interest seems to include more than his eponymous hero. He lets the reader in on the details of village life—festivals, chiefly deliberations, nuptial negotiations, and the like—and digresses often from Danda's story to concentrate on other matters, like the rivalry between Araba and Nwokeke and their dispute over the right to keep the clan *ozala* staff, and the return of Araba's other son Onuma to the village to take a wife.

Nwankwo's novel is highly humorous and its language, especially Danda's dialogue, is lively, featuring proverbial anecdotes and witty idioms. On a few occasions the author sets the reader wondering who the narrator is, when he makes a first-person voice intrude into the prevailing omniscient: "It was old Imedu that told me the story," "We were all anxious to know how the new couple got on," "For some time after this we heard nothing more."

Darko, Amma (1956–) Amma Darko was born in Tamale, Ghana, in 1956. She grew up in Accra and studied at the University of Science and Technology at Kumasi, graduating in 1980. She worked briefly for the Technology Consultancy Centre in Kumasi before leaving for Germany, where she spent seven years living off menial jobs. She returned to Ghana in 1987 and studied taxation, subsequently taking a job as a tax inspector in the Ghanaian public service. She was a fellow of the International Writing program at the University of Iowa in 2002.

Darko published her first novel, *Der Verkaufte Traum* (1991; *Beyond the Horizon*, 1995), while she was still in Germany. It chronicles the experiences of the young and naive Ghanaian woman Mara, whose family forces her to marry the duplicitous Akobi just for the bride price. Akobi takes her from her rural home to the city where he freely misuses her and then abandons her to travel to Germany. Years later, already married to a German woman, he brings Mara to Germany, makes her pass herself off as his sister, and forces her into prostitution. With the money he makes from selling her sexual services he imports another hapless Ghanaian woman to augment his German holdings. Mara is eventually able to expose him and escape his clutches.

Her second novel, *The Housemaid* (1998), which follows the pattern of decrying Ghanaian men's unconscionable abuse of women, features a plot that turns around the discovery of a dead baby, the subsequent disclosure of the identity of the mother, Efia, and horrific circumstances that forced her to infanticide. Her third novel *Faceless* (2003) is also a naturalistic study of the squalid life of Accra slums and the conditions that pull their habitués into drugs, sex, and violence. The focus in this ultimately regenerative story is on fourteen-year-old Fofo and her friends; they have the good fortune of attracting the attention of four activist women intent on defeating the oppressive forces of patriarchy, and who are successful in drawing needed attention to the social problems

FURTHER READING

Higgins, Ellie. "Creating an Alternative Library." *Journal of Commonwealth Literature* 39 (2004): 111–20.

Kohrs-Amissah, Edith. *Aspects of Feminism and Gender in the Novels of Three West African Women Writers (Aidoo, Emecheta, Darko).* Heidelberg: Books on African Studies, 2002.

Odamtten, Vincent O., ed. *Broadening the Horizon: Critical Introductions to Amma Darko.* Accra, Ghana: Ayebia Clarke, 2006.

Zak, Louise Allen. "Writing Her Way: A Study of Ghanaian Novelist Amma Darko." PhD dissertation, University of Massachusetts, Amherst, 2001.

De Graft, Joe (Joseph Coleman) (1924–78) Joseph Coleman de Graft, more popularly known as Joe de Graft, was born in Cape Coast in the (then) Gold Coast on April 2, 1924. He received his primary education at Mfantsipim School from 1939 to 1943, and his secondary education at Achimota College from 1944 to 1946. He entered the University College of the Gold Coast (now the University of Ghana, Legon) in 1950 and became one of its first graduates in 1953. In 1955 he went back to Mfantsipim, his old school, to teach, also directing the Mfantsipim Drama Laboratory. In 1960 he took advantage of a UNESCO fellowship to study drama for a year in the United Kingdom. When Kwame Nkrumah opened the Ghana Drama Studio in Accra in 1961, de Graft was named its first director, and he had his play *Village Investment* produced there in the same year. He also collaborated with Efua Sutherland to establish the School of Music and Drama at the University of Ghana. In 1969 he left Ghana to work for UNESCO in Nairobi, Kenya, where he also taught drama

at the university before returning to Ghana in 1977.

De Graft's literary production included popular fiction, poetry, and drama. *The Secret of Opokuwa: The Success Story of the Girl with a Big State Secret* (1967) and *Visitor from the Past* (1968) are early works of fiction of his that enjoyed wide popularity, and several of his poems were anthologized in *Messages: Poems from Ghana* (1971), edited by Kofi Awoonor and G. Adali-Mortty. In 1975 a collection of his poems was published in *Beneath the Jazz and Brass*. His plays were among the early fare that nurtured the nascent Anglophone West African drama, among the most important of them *Sons and Daughters* (1963), a play about the relative merits of careers in the sciences and the arts, and *Through a Film Darkly* (1970), a drama about culture conflict and racial suspicions. The latter was originally performed in the Ghana Drama Studio, Accra, as *Visitors from the Past* in September 1962.

De Graft is also the author of *Muntu*, an ambitious epic on African history from creation to the present, and *Mambo*, an adaptation of Shakespeare's *Macbeth*, which was produced in 1978 shortly before the playwright's death on November 1, 1978.

Dei-Anang, Michael Francis (1909–77) Born in Mampong-Akwapim in what is modern-day Ghana, Dei-Anang was educated at the Achimota College near Accra, then at London University. A career civil servant, he joined the colonial government of the Gold Coast in 1938 and remained a civil servant after his country became independent as Ghana in 1957.

Dei-Anang was among the first Anglophone West African poets to be published, his early, patriotic works including *Wayward Lines from Africa* (1946), and *Africa Speaks* (1962). His other poetic works are *Ghana Semi-Tones* (1962) and, with Yaw Warren,

Ghana Glory: Poems on Ghana and Ghana-ian Life (1965), for which Kwame Nkrumah wrote the introduction. His poems also appeared in the literary magazine *Okyeame* and in anthologies such as Langston Hughes's *An African Treasury* (1961). He is the author of the historical drama *Okomfo Anokye's Golden Stool* (1960), whose subject is an indication of the author's interest in Ghanaian folklore and folk history, and the historical sketches *Cocoa Comes to Mampong: Brief Dramatic Sketches Based on the Story of Cocoa in the Gold Coast* (1949, 1971).

Dei-Anang emigrated to the United States in 1966 and died there in 1977.

Diaspora More and more, studies pertaining to Africa take on diasporic dimensions, whereby developments on the continent are linked to the fates and experiences of Africans who over the centuries have been displaced to other continents, most notably the America, the Caribbean, and Europe. The trend has been catalyzed by the new exodus of Africans from the continent to other parts of the world, partly in response to diminishing opportunities at home and partly as a result of sometimes deadly hostility toward intellectuals on the part of intolerant rulers.

Although the dispersal of Africans to other parts of the world began long before the transatlantic slave trade, Africans having been transported to Europe and Asia since antiquity, the forceful relocation of large numbers of Africans to the Americas (and the Indies) beginning in the fifteenth century is what scholars identify as the origin of the African diaspora. And because the largest concentration of peoples of African descent outside the continent is in the United States, the focus of interest for students of the diaspora has been the ramifications of the connections between Africa and the United States. It is not surprising, therefore, that the United States is the home

of arguably two of the most influential scholarly associations whose main focus is Africa—the African Studies Association and the African Literature Association.

The activities of freed slaves in North America, the civil rights movement, the emergence of independent African states after colonialism, and the struggle against apartheid in South Africa all played a role in kindling interest in the conceptualization of the totality of Africans, in Africa and elsewhere in the world, as constituting a family, a diaspora. The first clear articulations of the notion occurred during the colonial period, when educated Africans and descendants of African in the new world began promoting the doctrine of pan-Africanism, of which W. E. B. Du Bois was the primary proponent. The desire among freed slaves in America was to rescue Africa from what they saw as its primitive and (to some) godless state, to "civilize" the people and ameliorate their shameful condition, and to replace the European colonizers. During the Harlem Renaissance African American interest found expression in the form of primitivism in various art works, African American artists incorporating African elements into their productions, thus attesting to the belief that there was some basic quality that characterizes blackness, some common element that all black people shared. The idea received an intellectual boost when in 1922 Howard University established an African studies program. A little over half a century later, in 1979, it hosted the First African Diaspora Studies Institute (FADSI).

The development has not met with universal approbation among African intellectuals. Consistent with the prevailing trends in postmodernism regarding identity, essentialism, and related notions, African scholars have cast doubt on the validity of race as a basis for identity, and questioned the notion of any sort of imperative for transterritorial or transtemporal black solidarity. Such doubts form the burden of Anthony Kwame Appiah's "African Identities," published in *In My Father's House* (1992), and Paul Gilroy's *The Black Atlantic* (1993), the latter arguing that *route* is more important than *root*, that the experience of the Atlantic crossings and their legacies should take precedence in people's imagination over a race-based diaspora.

As far as disciplinary homes are concerned, the realities of the place of Africa and Africans in the modern world have inevitably located African diaspora studies, at least initially, in such disciplines as history and political science; lately, though, it has assumed considerable importance in cultural studies and literature. For their part, several African writers have in their works demonstrated their awareness of the black presence outside Africa. It is evident, for example, in Ama Ata Aidoo's *The Dilemma of a Ghost*, in which she shows that Africans and African Americans have widely different conceptions of social relationships despite their shared blackness; in Ayi Kwei Armah's *Osiris Rising*, Kofi Awoonor's *Comes the Voyager Home at Last*, and Isidore Okpewho's *Call Me by My Rightful Name*, all of which focus on the legacy of the slave trade and to some extent Africans' share in the culpability for the traffic, and in one form or another suggest a reconciliation. Buchi Emecheta, on the other hand, in *The Family* depicts the separation of diasporic Africans from the continent and their consequent severance from its regulatory ethos as a cause for the attenuation of their ethical and moral moorings, and in *The Last Harmattan of Alusine Dunbar*, Syl Cheney-Coker traces the career of the returning ex-slaves in their new home in West Africa and their troubled efforts at creating a new nation there. Armah, again in *Osiris Rising*, holds out the promise that from out(side) of Africa, from out of the

diaspora, will come redemption from the moral degeneration rife on the continent, the new world coming to the rescue of the old, and Wole Soyinka in *Isara: A Voyage Around Essay* looks to America for validation for (or vindication of) ethical choices made by Africans in Africa.

FURTHER READING

Appiah, Kwame Anthony. *In My Father's House: Africa in the Philosophy of Culture*. New York: Oxford University Press, 1992.

Gilroy, Paul. *The Black Atlantic: Modernity and Double Consciousness*. Cambridge, MA: Harvard University Press, 1993.

Harris, Joseph E., ed. *Global Dimensions of the African Diaspora*. 2nd ed. Washington, DC: Howard University Press, 1993.

Jalloh, A. and S. E. Maizlish, eds. *The African Diaspora*. College Station: Texas A&M University Press, 1996.

Okpewho, Isidore, Carole Boyce Davies, and Ali A. Mazrui. *The African Diaspora: African Origins and New World Identities*. Bloomington: Indiana University Press, 1999.

Dipoko, Mbella Sonne (1936–) Mbella Sonne Dipoko was born in Missaka near Douala in 1936, in what was then (Anglophone) Western Cameroon, and spent his early years in both Cameroon and Nigeria. On completing his education he worked for a while for the Development Corporation at Tiko before joining the Nigerian Broadcasting Corporation in 1958 as a news reporter. In 1960 he moved to Paris, where he worked for *Présence Africaine* and began to study law at Paris University. He soon abandoned his studies, though, because he was dismayed at the totalitarian policies of the Ahidjo government in his country, and believed that it made no sense for him to become a lawyer; he would write full time instead. He returned to Cameroon in 1968, but later went to the university in the United States, enrolling in Anglo-American studies and majoring in English. Back in Cameroon he entered politics and was for a while mayor of Tiko during the regime of Paul Biya.

Dipoko wrote two novels, *A Few Nights and Days* (1966) and *Because of Women* (1969), and a volume of poetry, *Black and White in Love* (1972). He also wrote the play *Overseas*, which the BBC broadcast in 1968. *A Few Night and Days* is about the romantic involvement of a young African man with a French woman and his sexual escapade with her Swedish friend, while *Because of Women* deals with the love life of a young African and his two women. Although the two works were supposed to be part of a trilogy, Dipoko has yet to write the third part.

He enjoys a good reputation as a writer, because of his early writings, but his political involvement, which many see as collaboration with totalitarian rulers, and his leftover beatnik beard have earned him some disdain. He continues to write essays and poems that are published in the local media.

Djoleto, Amu (1929–) (Solomon Alexander) Amu Djoleto was born in a small Ghanaian village in 1929. He did his early schooling at the Accra Academy and St Augustine's College, Cape Coast, and later studied English at the University of Ghana, Legon. After graduation he worked in the 1960s as a schoolteacher and an education officer before going to the Institute of Education at the University of London to study textbook production. On completing the course he returned to Ghana and took up the editorship of the *Ghana Teacher's Journal*. He was also for some time charged with directing the nascent publishing program for the country's ministry of education. He has remained a career officer of that ministry in Accra.

In 1967 Djoleto published his first novel, *The Strange Man*, the story of young Mensa's early struggles with school, village hostilities, and family problems, and his later difficult experiences as a civil servant and a father. Djoleto followed with *Money Galore* (1975), a satire that earned him comparison

to Nigeria's T. M. Aluko. It enacts the experiences of Abraham Kofi Kafu, who despairs of the meager rewards of teaching and takes on politics instead. He achieves success by the usual means, graft and corruption, and enjoys the desultory living the success permits, until life catches up with him in the end. Another of his novels is *Hurricane of Dust* (1987), which, set in the period of military rule in Ghana, is about an unscrupulous man whose support of the revolution led eventually to disaster for him.

More recently Djoleto has been a productive writer of books for adolescents. His works in this genre include *Kofi Loses His Way* (1996), the adventures of Kofi, who has to find his own way home because his father is late in picking him up from school; *Akos and the Fire Ghost* (1998), about young Akos's nightmares after her father dies by drowning; *The Frightened Thief* (1992), which recounts Amanor's victimization by school bullies; *The Girl Who Knows About Cars* (1996), a girl-who-can story about Esi, who learns about cars from the family driver and later helps her father repair a punctured tire; and *Twins in Trouble* (1991), the hair-raising experiences of young Lawo.

Djoleto's poems were anthologized as early as the 1950s in *Voices of Ghana* (1958), and later in *Messages: Poems from Ghana* (1970). His poems are also published in the collection *Amid the Swelling Act Haps* (1992). He also collaborated with T. H. S. Kwami in collecting and editing the anthology, *West African Prose*, in 1972.

Easmon, Sarif (1913–) Raymond Sarif Easmon, a Sierra Leonean of Creole and Susu ancestry, was born in Freetown in 1925. After his early education in Guinea and Sierra

Leone he went to the United Kingdom and studied medicine at Newcastle University. On completing his studies he returned to Sierra Leone and embarked on a medical career in the public service. The corruption everywhere evident in government proved too much for him, however, and he consequently resigned from the government medical service to set up his own private practice.

He had his literary and dramatic debut in 1961 when The 1960 Masks, Wole Soyinka's acting company, staged his play *Dear Parent and Ogre* at the Arts Theatre of the University of Ibadan. In it Easmon dramatizes the corruption that bedeviled his society to the extent of marring even marriage negotiations, and he also castigates pervasive incompetence, tribalism, and class stratification. The play won the first *Encounter Magazine* play writing prize, but it also drew negative criticism because of the pretentious Western affectations of its dialogue and atmosphere. His second play, *The New Patriots*, was published in 1966. It premiered in Ghana after the demise of the Nkrumah regime in 1966, and it played at other locales in West Africa before it was staged for the first time in Sierra Leone in 1968. In this, as in the earlier play, Easmon again vents his anger at the corruption and crass materialism of the new ruling class.

Easmon has been criticized for showing little interest in African cultures in his early works, including his one novel, *The Burnt-Out Marriage* (1967), and some critics have suggested that he was in fact at best impatient with them. He moderated his lack of interest, though, in his collection of twelve short stories, *The Feud and Other Stories* (1981), which deals with various subjects, such as traditional marriage practices and social expectations of women, interracial relationships, and class divisions. A novel with the title *Genevieve*, which he submitted

to *African Arts / Arts d'Afrique* in 1969, was a close runner-up to Ezekiel Mphahlele's winning entry, *The Wanderers*.

FURTHER READING

Hunt, Caroline C., and Joko M. Sengova. "Coming of Age in West Africa: Contemporary Fiction from Sierra Leone." *English Journal* 84, no. 3 (March 1995): 62–66.

Echeruo, Michael Joseph Chukwudalu (1937–) Michael Echeruo was born on March 14, 1937, in Okigwi, eastern Nigeria. He began his undergraduate education at the University College, Ibadan (now University of Ibadan), in 1955 and was awarded a prestigious college scholarship in 1957 and a Shell English scholarship the following year. He graduated with a honors degree in English in 1960. In 1961 he took a lecturing position at the Nigerian College of Arts, Science and Technology in Enugu, transferring to a similar position at the University of Nigeria, Nsukka, a year later. While still thus employed he went to Cornell University for his graduate studies. He took his MA in 1963 and his PhD in 1965, both in English and American Literature, and returned to teach at Nsukka. Having risen to the rank of professor, he moved to the University of Ibadan as professor of English in 1974. He remained in that position until he left to take a visiting professorship and the University of Indiana, Bloomington, in 1989. He was appointed the William Safire Professor of Modern Letters at Syracuse University in 1990.

Echeruo is primarily a respected and well-regarded academic, but he qualifies for inclusion among creative writers on the strength of the poetry he published early in his career. The collection *Mortality* was published in 1968 and reissued with additional poems as *Mortality and Other Poems* in 1995. In the interim he published the anthology *Distanced: New Poems* in 1975. *Mortality* and *Distanced*, both published in Nigeria, earned Echeruo the Distinguished Author award in 1986, but they also earned him the disapproval of Chinweizu and his collaborators, who lumped him with the "Euro-modernists" (such as Soyinka and Okigbo) whose deliberate obscurantism they dislike. In particular they object to the Latinisms in the poems in *Mortality* and his advice to poets in an article urging them to avoid being explicit, "to cultivate deliberate obscurity."

Echeruo is the compiler of the online Okigbo Concordant, as well as the author of *Chinua Achebe Revisited* (1999).

Echewa, T. Obinkaram (1938–) Born in Aba in the eastern part of Nigeria in 1938, T. Obinkaram Echewa received his higher education in the United States—at the University of Notre Dame, Columbia University, and the University of Pennsylvania. He has taught English at Cheyney College, Pennsylvania, and is a professor of English at West Chester University, Pennsylvania. He has written stories, poems, and articles for several newspapers and magazines, including *America*, *Essence*, *New York Times*, *The New Yorker*, *Newsweek*, *Time*, and *West Africa*. His interest as an author has been more focused on the impact of colonization on Africa than on the postcolonial traumas that have plagued the continent.

His first novel, *The Land's Lord* (1976), pits European colonizers and their Christian allies against Africans desirous of holding on to their traditional ways. He followed it with *The Crippled Dancer* (1986), which deals with village feuds and the problems of negotiating the passage from the past to the present. In *I Saw the Sky Catch Fire* (1992), which the *New York Times* described as "exquisite," Echewa returns to the colonial period to take up the 1929 revolt by Aba women against colonial attempts

to tax them. *The Land's Lord* won the 1976 English-Speaking Union Prize, while *The Crippled Dancer* was regional finalist for the 1986 Commonwealth Book Prize.

Apart from books for adults, Echewa has also written several works for children. These include *The Magic Tree: A Folktale from Nigeria* (1999), which is based on *The Crippled Dancer* and features an aged storyteller who inculcates morals into children using folktales and is honored after his death, thanks to the children's efforts, and *Mbi, Do This; Mbi, Do That: A Folktale from Nigeria* (1998). He also collaborated with Elanim Ekeh, and Efanim Ekeh on *How Tables Came to Umu Madu: The Fabulous History of an Unknown Continent* (1993), a political satire.

Echewa's writing has enjoyed quite favorable reviews, with particular praise for his ability to capture women's sensibilities, for instance in *I Saw the Earth Catch Fire*. He is also a captivating performer of his folktales before schoolchildren.

FURTHER READING

Brodzki, Bella. "History, Cultural Memory, and the Tasks of Translation in T. Obinkaram Echewa's *I Saw the Sky Catch Fire*." *PMLA* 114, no. 2 (March 1999): 207–20.

Efuru (1966) Flora Nwapa was the first published Nigerian female novelist. *Efuru* (1966) is her first work, and one of the earliest volumes in Heinemann's African Writers Series. Appropriately, its subject is the unfair burden tradition places on the woman, as a mandatory mother, and the suffering she experiences if she fails in that role.

The eponymous Efuru is the independent-minded daughter of the prosperous Nwashike Ogene, "the mighty man of valour … who single handed, fought against the Aros." Five years after her mother died, Efuru decides to marry Adizua, a poor farmer, without so much as telling her father, let alone seeking his consent. She also defies his repeated demands that she return home and stop disgracing the family with her behavior. She further demonstrates her independence by refusing to join her husband in farming, deciding to trade instead. It is a fortunate choice, for she prospers as a trader. Her marriage, however, does not produce a child for a while, and there is concern that Efuru might be infertile. Eventually she does conceive and gives birth to a daughter whom she names Ogonim. The child soon dies, though, and no other follows. Adizua's attitude toward Efuru changes: he abuses her and takes up with another woman, prompting Adizua to return to her father's compound and dissolve the marriage. Another marriage fails to produce a child, and she finds out that her plight results from her adoption by the goddess Uhamiri, "the lady of the lake," who prefers to favor her followers with wealth and prosperity but not children. But the goddess' predilections also earn her favorites mistreatment from their frustrated husbands, and Efuru in the end must return to her natal home. The last sentence of the work (which express Efuru's thoughts regarding the lady of the lake): "She had not experienced the joy of motherhood," suggested the title for Emecheta's novel *The Joys of Motherhood*.

Efuru appeared at a time when critics, especially African women, were complaining about the failure of African writers, all male up to that point, to portray women in meaningful and positive roles. It is certainly an early example of feminism in African literature, albeit according to the standard Western conception of feminism, inasmuch as it asserts the availability to women of fulfillment outside the context of marriage and motherhood. It is also significant for inaugurating some of the literary devices that critics have identified as typifying African women's writing, especially a reliance on conversations among women, which suggest the establishment of a sharing and supportive community. The device, however, has not impressed some critics of the novel, who regard it as too "gossipy." Others have objected to the novel's superstitiousness, especially given the credence it gives to the determining role of Ohamiri on Efuru's fortunes.

Coming as early as it did in the history of modern African literature and out of the Igbo culture, it inevitably invited some comparison with Achebe's works. No critic suggested that it came close to the literary quality of the latter, but it is clear that it benefited from the comparison. For example, *Efuru* is free of the direct translations that are a prominent feature of *Things Fall Apart*; unlike the early Achebe, Nwapa allows the context to indicate the import of her Igbo expressions. Such expressions, along with the device of translating greetings directly from Igbo into English, "Let day break," for example, for "Goodnight," serve to give the work the Igbo flavor she desired.

Some critics have observed that the world of *Efuru* is one in which Western influence is absent, for example as an explanation for Efuru's independence, but there is in fact some reference to the operation of Western influence in the affairs of the community. For example, some of its members attribute her father's failure to enforce his will (regarding Efuru's marriage to Adizua) to the new dispensation the white people had inaugurated: "Things are changing fast these days," they observe. "These white people have imposed so much strain on our people. The least thing you do nowadays you are put into prison."

FURTHER READING

Banyiwa-Horne, Naana. "African Womanhood: The Contrasting Perspectives of Flora Nwapa's *Efuru* and Elechi Amadi's *The*

Concubine." In *Ngambika: Studies of Women in African Literature,* ed. Carole Boyce Davies and Anne Adams Graves, 119–29. Trenton, NJ: Africa World Press, 1986.

Duruoha, S. I. "The Language of Flora Nwapa's *Efuru* and *Idu*: A Study in Ambiguity." In *Feminism and Black Women's Creative Writing: Theory, Practice, and Criticism,* ed. Adebayo Aduke, 245. Ibadan, Nigeria: AMD, 1996.

Githaiga, A. *Notes on Flora Nwapa's Efuru.* Nairobi: Heinemann, 1978.

Maja-Pearce, Adewale. "Flora Nwapa's *Efuru*: A Study in Misplaced Hostility." *World Literature Written in English* 25 (Spring 1985): 10–15.

Ogunyemi, Chikwenye Okonjo. *Africa Wo/Man Palava: The Nigerian Novel by Women.* Chicago: University of Chicago Press, 1996.

Egbuna, Obi (1938–) Obi Benedict Egbuna was born on July 18, 1938, at Ozobulu, near Onitsha, Nigeria. He got his education up to the secondary level in Nigeria before he left the country for England in 1961 to study law. Soon after, he became a radical pan-Africanist and was elected president of the British Black Power movement, the Universal Coloured People's Association, and publisher of its journal *The Voice of Africa.* He embraced the ideology of negritude, while also predictably expressing strong support for Kwame Nkrumah and his pan-Africanist ideas. In 1968, while the war of Biafran secession was raging in Nigeria, he published the essay, *The Murder of Nigeria: An Indictment,* an attack on imperialism and its devastation of Africa.

Egbuna was instrumental in the founding of a Black Panther chapter in Britain, and his political activism, specifically a charge that he was involved in plotting to murder a policeman, led to his arrest and conviction; his sentence to prison was, however, suspended. He returned to Nigeria to work in television, also writing politi-

cal commentaries that were later published in *Diary of a Homeless Prodigal* (1976). He attended the International Writing Program at the University of Iowa in 1976. He earned a master's degree the following year, and went on to earn a PhD from Howard University in 1980. As late as 2003, he reconfirmed his radical anti-imperialism at the Martin Luther King memorial rally held in August on the Capitol grounds in Washington, when he took the stage and made an impassioned attack on President George W. Bush and Attorney General John Ashcroft while lavishing praise on Robert Mugabe, the controversial president of Zimbabwe, for "reclaiming African lands from the colonialists."

Egbuna's early writings include the novel *Wind Versus Polygamy* (1964), about the polygamous Chief Ozuomba, who was so attracted by a woman brought before him by two rival suitors that he decided to marry her himself in defiance of a new antipolygamy law. The ensuing trial offers him an opportunity to assert the virtues of polygamy and its superiority over monogamy. In something of an irony, it served as Britain's official entry at the First World Black Festival of Arts in Dakar, Senegal in 1974. He later retitled and published it as *Elina* (1978). *The Minister's Daughter* (1975), another novel, is a satire aimed at the country's government and its feckless youths; it features an attempted coup in which an idealistic major attempts to change things for the better. In *The Madness of Didi* (1980), Egbuna writes himself, sometimes with his real name, into the story of an activist who returns to his society from abroad in search of a role to play therein. Didi, a been-to and a Black Power activist, antagonizes people with his activities and is killed in a fire set by his enemies, but his ideals live on in Obi whom he had befriended. In another novel into which Egbuna again writes himself, *The*

Rape of Lysistrata (1980), a white woman accuses a black Brazilian studying in Iowa of raping her.

Egbuna has also published plays, including *The Ant Hill* (1965), which deals with the experiences of African students in London, as well as collections of short stories, among them *Daughters of the Sun and Other Stories* (1970) and *Emperor of the Sea and Other Stories* (1974).

FURTHER READING

Lindfors, Bernth, ed. *Dem-say: Interviews with Eight Nigerian Writers.* Austin: University of Texas Press, 1974.

Taiwo, Oladele. *Culture and the Nigerian Novel.* New York: St. Martin's Press, 1976.

Ekwensi, Cyprian (1921–) Cyprian Odiatu Duaka Ekwensi, whose Igbo parents were resident in northern Nigeria, was born on September 26, 1921 in Minna in what is now the Niger State. His early schooling was in predominantly Hausa northern Nigeria, and his secondary schooling at Government College, Ibadan, in the Yoruba area of western Nigeria. He spent practically all of his early professional career in Lagos, also in the Yoruba area of Nigeria. His formative years spent in different parts of the country endowed him with a thorough familiarization with the cultures of the dominant ethnic groups, and he also became fluent in the country's three major languages.

He trained as forestry officer in Nigeria before departing for London in 1951 to study at the Chelsea School of Pharmacy. His study complete, he returned to Nigeria in 1956. He worked only briefly in the pharmacy profession, though, soon abandoning it to pursue other interests. Even before leaving for the United Kingdom he had demonstrated his talent as a writer, and had had his stories broadcast by the Nigerian Broadcasting Corporation (NBC). On his return home to Nigeria he worked as the head of features for the Corporation, and in 1961 he became director of information for the Federal Ministry of Information in Lagos. When the Biafran War broke out, he affirmed his loyalty to his Igbo roots and threw in his lot with the Biafrans. He relocated to Enugu, the Biafran capital, and served during the war as the director general of the Broadcasting Corporation of Biafra. In that capacity he visited the United States to raise money for Biafran broadcasting. On the conclusion of the war he remained in eastern Nigeria, occupying such positions as chairman of the East Central State Library Board and commissioner for information in Anambra State.

As an author, Ekwensi has been described as the one Nigerian writer whose writing best exemplifies the pulsating diversity of the country's cultures as well as the heady restlessness of Nigerian cities—the spectacle and excitement as well as the squalor, the violence, and the corruption. His early works, which include the novellas *When Love Whispers* (1947) and *The Leopard's Claw* (1950), are exemplary in depicting both the appeal and repulsion of urban life. The aptly named *People of the City* (1954; rev. 1969) is also a study of life in urban Nigeria, which the author portrays through the experiences of a Lagos crime reporter and dance-band leader as rife with criminality and corruption alongside the good life.

His most successful, and most popular, work has been *Jagua Nana* (1961), the rollicking story of the thoroughly engaging prostitute Jagua Nana and her young paramour Freddie. Their story enables Ekwensi to showcase the lifestyles of different opportunistic characters who had escaped from the drab life of the villages to experience the pulsating excitement of the city. In this and other works Ekwensi, who considers himself a writer for the masses, and who was early identified with the popular Onitsha market literature tradition, demonstrates his understanding of what Nigerians wish to read—namely, spectacular and scandalous stories. Critics have compared his heroine Jagua Nana to Daniel Defoe's Moll Flanders, some being repulsed by her escapades, which they consider too racy and too raunchy. But so successful was the work, and so popular the heroine with readers, that Ekwensi wrote a sequel, *Jagua Nana's Daughter* (1986). It, however, fell short of the appeal of its predecessor.

Apart from city novels Ekwensi has also written about life in rural areas of the country, for example *Burning Grass* (1962), which is set in a Fulani cattle-rearing community in northern Nigeria. He has also produced a number of works for children. These include *The Passport of Mallam Ilia* (1960), *An African Night's Entertainment* (1962), and *Trouble in Form Six* (1966). Among his collections of short stories are *Ikolo the Wrestler and Other Ibo Tales* (1947), *Lokotown and Other Stories* (1966), and *Restless City and Christmas Gold* (1975). He has also written works directly related to the war, such as *Survive the Peace* (1976, 1979), *Divided We Stand* (1980), and *King for Ever* (1992).

Despite his service to Biafra during the secession effort, Ekwensi has earned praise for the pan-Nigerian inclusiveness of his sensibilities, and for his early attention to the problems adolescents face, among them teenage pregnancy and juvenile delinquency. He has also been criticized, however, for the sloppiness of his plots and his penchant for imitating foreign writers such as Daniel Defoe and Emile Zola. He was well enough thought of, though, to be given the Honors Award by the National Council for Arts and Culture in December 2001.

FURTHER READING

Emenyonu, Ernest. *Cyprian Ekwensi*. London: Evans Brothers, 1974.
———, ed. *The Essential Ekwensi: A Literary Celebration of Cyprian Ekwensi's Sixty-fifth Birthday*. Ibadan: Heinemann Nigeria, 1987.
Oku, Julia Inyang Essien. "Courtesans and Earthmothers: A Feminist Reading of Cyprian Ekwensi's *Jagua Nana* and Buchi Emecheta's *The Joys of Motherhood*." In *Critical Theory and African Literature*, ed. Ernest N. Emenyonu, R. Vanamali, E. Oko, and A. Iloeje, 225–33. Ibadan: Heinemann, 1987.

Emecheta, Buchi (1944–) Buchi (short for Onyebuchi) Emecheta was born in Yaba, Nigeria, to Igbo parents from Ibuza on July 21, 1944. Her father, an employee of the Nigerian Railways, died while she was very young, an eventuality that set in train developments that have significantly contributed to determining her career as a writer. Before her father's death she had somehow forced her parents to send her to school, but after his death she had to go and live as a servant with her maternal uncle, and although in her new home education was supposedly out of the question she again succeeded in making her will prevail. After her primary education she gained admission to the Methodist Girls' High School, Lagos, where she met Sylvester Onwordi. Emecheta was only sixteen, but seeing marriage as a means of escaping from her uncle's guardianship, which was proving was irksome for her, she married Onwordi, thus entering into a wife's role at a relatively early age and not for the most auspicious of reasons.

Soon after their marriage, Onwordi left for Britain for further studies, and Emecheta joined him two years later. Her difficult experiences due to her marriage to Sylvester and encounters with racism in London combined with her childhood remembrances of being relegated to inferiority to male siblings were rankling enough, but her husband also turned out to be as poor a student as he was an irresponsible husband to her and a father to their five children, who came in rather quick succession. Apart from being shiftless, unfaithful, and abusive, Onwordi was also intolerant of her of intelligence and impatient with her ambition to become a writer. When she let him know that she had written a novel, he fed the manuscript to the furnace when she was out of the house. The act precipitated the end of their marriage.

That life story has proved a rich quarry for Emecheta, yielding, in addition to the autobiography *Head Above Water* (1986), the novels *In the Ditch* (1972) and *Second-Class Citizen* (1975), in which the author has told and retold Ada's story (Ada being Emecheta's alter-ego). In addition to those works, which are hardly disguised autobiographies, most of Emecheta's other novels for adults are elaborate illustrations of men's seemingly pathological obsession with abusing women. In work after work she has made the case that the Igbo woman, and by extension the African woman, is the victim of institutionalized exploitation at the hands of the men to whom she is connected, including her father and her other male relatives, and certainly her husband. These include *The Bride Price* (1975), which challenges the rights of parents to determine whom their daughters may marry as well as the ostracizing of the *osu* (outcasts), *The Slave Girl* (1977), in which Emecheta gives credence to some Western feminists' contention that Africans value kinship mainly because it offers a supply of ready-to-hand potential slaves, *Double Yoke* (1982), on the obstacles a woman must contend with in her quest for a university education and a meaningful relationship, *A Kind of Marriage* (1986) and *Kehinde* (1994), both of which focus on polygamy and men's infidelity to their spouses, and *The New Tribe* (2000), which deals with issues of adoption, identity, and race.

Extending her purview to the African diaspora, Emecheta explores how, in her view, long separation from their African roots has left New-World Africans in a state of moral confusion. *The Family* (1989; earlier published as *Gwendolen*) illustrates the effects on the Jamaican family of Winston and Sonia Brillianton. Their daughter Gwendolen is raped first by a surrogate father, and later by her real father, who flies into a rage when he discovers that another man had preceded him to his daughter's favors.

The work most critics regard as her masterpiece, though, is *The Joys of Motherhood* (1994). In it the hapless heroine Nnu Ego, despite being a mother several times over, enjoys none of the bliss that, according to her culture, motherhood is supposed to confer on women, but is simply used up by the men in her life, including her children, and she dies unattended by a roadside in premature old age. Other critics, though, are apt to regard *The Rape of Shavi* (1984) as her best work, perhaps because it departs from the woman-as-victim script to deal in an allegorical way with the African encounter with the West and its deleterious consequences for Africa.

Emecheta has conceded that she has Western readers in mind when she writes, and that she writes to educate them about the situation of women in Africa. Not surprisingly, her uncompromising stance on women's issues has endeared her to Western feminists, although she sometimes tries to distance herself from them, claiming that the Igbo woman (or the African woman) is not quite the wimp that Western feminists suppose her to be. Nonetheless, she continues to be a sought-after speaker on American and European lecture circuits.

FURTHER READING

Bazin, Nancy Topping. "Feminist Perspectives in African Fiction: Bessie Head and Buchi

Emecheta." *Black Scholar* 17, no. 2 (1986): 34–40.

Daymond, M. J. "Buchi Emecheta, Laughter and Silence: Changes in the Concept of 'Woman' and 'Mother.'" *Journal of Literary Studies* 4, no. 1 (1988): 64–73.

Fishburn, Katherine. *Reading Buchi Emecheta: CrossCultural Conversations.* Westport, CT: Greenwood Press, 1995.

Kohrs-Amissah, Edith. *Aspects of Feminism and Gender in the Novels of Three West African Women Writers (Aidoo, Emecheta, Darko).* Heidelberg: Books on African Studies, 2002.

Ogunyemi, Chikwenye Okonjo. *Africa Wo/Man Palava: The Nigerian Novel by Women.* Chicago: University of Chicago Press, 1996.

Sinha, Chandrani. "Women in Protest Literature: A Study of Four Novels of Buchi Emecheta." *Africa Quarterly* 34, no. 3 (1994): 221–34.

Umeh, Marie. *Emerging Perspectives on Buchi Emecheta.* Trenton, NJ: Africa World Press, 1996.

Enekwe, Ossie Onuora (1942–) Born on November 12, 1942, in Affa in the Enugu area of eastern Nigeria, Osmond (Ossie) Enekwe graduated from the University of Nigeria, Nsukka, in 1971 before going on to Columbia University in New York for his masters and doctor's degrees. He then took a position in the English Department of the University of Nigeria, teaching literature and theater. He once served as assistant editor of *Okike*, which in its first issues (in the early 1970s) had given his creative writing welcome exposure. He assumed the editorship of the magazine at the end of 1986 when Chinua Achebe relinquished his editorship.

A writer of poetry, fiction, and drama, Enekwe has published in all three genres as well as in nonfiction. His works include the collection of poems *Broken Pots* (1977), the novel *Come Thunder* (1984), the short play *The Betrayal* (1989), the short-story collection *The Last Battle and Other Stories* (1996),

and the nonfiction work *Igbo Masks* (1987). He also collaborated with Jasper Amankulor on "Scenario for Adamma Creative Dramatic Performance" (1985), a manuscript based on the traditional Adamma masquerade performances.

Enekwe has been particularly interested in the Nigerian civil wart and its trauma, as is evident in stories like "The Last Battle," in which he depicts the impossible conditions under which Biafran foot soldiers were forced to fight. His writing on Igbo cultural performances also testifies to his keen interest in traditional verbal and performance arts.

FURTHER READING

Orabueze, F. O. "Broken Humanity: The Poetry of Osmond Ossie Enekwe." In *New Nigeria Poetry*, ed. G. M. T. Emezue, 65–84. Morrisville, NC: Progeny International, 2005.

***Famished Road, The* (1991)** In *The Famished Road* (1991), Ben Okri reaches into the rich resources of traditional African creativity and its worldview to create an allegory of the troubled state of the Nigerian nation. His tale features the Yoruba phenomenon *abiku*, a spirit child that takes periodic leaves of its companions in the spirit world to plague its mother on earth with repeated birth-and-death cycles. Okri uses the uncertainty of the child's survival to adulthood during its human phases as an analogy for the uncertainty of the survival of Nigeria. The country too, the story says, is "an abiku nation, a spirit-child nation, one that keeps being reborn and after each birth comes blood and betrayals."

The child-hero of the story is Azaro an *abiku* born to poor, struggling parents (Dad and Mum), whose love for him forces them to spend their scarce resources on keeping him from returning to his spirit comrades. Azaro himself, for all the worry he causes his parents, is captivated enough by life among the living to have decided to defy his spirit companions and break his pact to return to them. They however keep badgering him to return, and even send agents to kidnap him and force his return. His spirit part and his contacts with his spirit companions provide some of the most haunting and surreal passages in the story.

One character who features prominently in Azaro's life is Madame Koto, the corpulent bar proprietress who, apart from playing some role in keeping him from the snatches of his spirit-companions, also provided him with a second home and some sort of employment as a magnet for customers. Her bar is the locale where for the most part the assorted spirit characters and humans who populate the story gather and mingle—spirits with strange features, prostitutes, politicians, beggars, thugs, and "warriors of grass-roots politics." The assortment testifies to one of the featured activities in the story, the contest between political parties that replicates the tortuous, corrupt, and violent pattern of Nigeria's politics. The thugs and warriors battle it out in their usual bloody manner, while the Party of the Rich bribes the people with rotten powdered milk. Azaro's father eventually organizes his own party of beggars in a bid to improve his and their lives.

Further enlivening the drama of Azaro's life is his father's irrepressible ambition to become a boxer, and his secondary intention of making a killing from the wagers on his fights. His fighting name is Black Tyger, and his opponents include Yellow Jaguar, who incidentally has been dead three years, and the huge Green Leopard. Against long odds, he defeats both and takes home a good purse from betting proceeds. His final fight is against the man in the white suit, another formidable opponent whose defeat he hopes will yield enough money to enable him to build a university—a school for beggars. He does win, but at the cost of death-like exhaustion that sends him into a three-night-long sleep.

Okri's regenerative vision and hopes find expression in, among other things, Black Tyger's recuperative dream in which he redreams the world, correcting what he sees and does not like, especially the manipulation of his world by the Western world, the corruption of the rich and their exploitation of the poor, the squandering of national resources, the rule of tyrants, and the crises these all engender. He also voices the central morale of the story, "We can redream this world and make the dream real."

Okri's novel harks back to Tutuola's works, with which it shares several features, including the nature of the characters, the dissolution of the boundary between the worlds of humans and the spirits, and recourse to materials from traditional folktales. One such recourse occurs, for example, when Azaro's would-be kidnapper, a spirit with four heads, concedes that his efforts have failed but warns that a five-headed spirit will be along to try again. Okri demonstrates in this novel the possibilities of traditional African materials in the hands of an accomplished craftsman. Azaro's untroubled sleep at the end suggests an optimistic prognostication for him and for the nation.

FURTHER READING

Fraser, Robert, *Ben Okri: Towards the Invisible City*. Horndon, England: Northcote House, 2002.

McCabe, Douglas. "'Higher Realities': New Age Spirituality in Ben Okri's *The Famished Road*." *Research in African Literatures* 36, no. 4 (Winter) 2005: 1–21.

Quayson, Ato. "Harvesting the Folkloric Intuition: *The Famished Road*." In *Strategic Transformations in Nigerian Writing*, 121–56. Bloomington: Indiana University Press, 1997.

Fatunde, Tunde (1955–) Tunde Fatunde was educated at the University of Ibadan, where he received his BA degree in French before going on to France for his MA and PhD degrees. A scholar whose academic positions have included a professorship and chairmanship of the theater department at the University of Lagos, and one of the activist group that includes such writers as Harry Garuba and Tanure Ojaide, Fatunde writes and directs plays, and also writes poems as well as newspaper columns. Among his plays that have been performed and published are *Blood and Sweat* (1985), *No More Oil Boom* (1985), *No Food, No Country* (1985), *Oga Na Tief Man* (1986), *Water No Get Enemy* (1989), and *Shattered Calabash* (2002). His determination to publish his works locally militates against their being widely known elsewhere; that stricture on publication venue for his works does not extend to personal appearances, however, and he has on more than one occasion been a visiting lecturer (at, for example, Western Washington University).

His writing is addressed to the general audience with little or no formal education and is intended to foster a spirit of active rejection of oppression and exploitation. He makes his work accessible by using simple plots and simple language, very often pidgin English.

He has had his poems published in such journals as *Okike* and *The Anthill Annual* and in Harry Garuba's *Voices from the Fringe*. In such poems as "Woman Dey Suffer" (*Okike*), "Bad Belle Too Much" (*The Anthill Annual*), and "Denis Obi Don Die" (*Voices from the Fringe*) he advocates equi-table treatment of women (for example, in "Woman Dey Suffer") and deplores the deprivations that expose vulnerable people to unfortunate and tragic fates.

FURTHER READING

Garuba, Harry, ed. *Voices from the Fringe: New Nigerian Poetry*. Lagos: Malthouse, 1988.

Fyle, Clifford Nelson (1933–2006) Clifford Fyle was born in Freetown, Sierra Leone, on March 29, 1933. He had his secondary education at the Methodist Boys High School, after which he went to Fourah Bay College, receiving his BA in languages and mathematics in 1953. He later obtained a BA with honors in English and an MA in education at the University of Durham, England, in 1960. He also studied at Leeds University in the United Kingdom, and at both Indiana University and the University of California at Los Angeles in the United States. He was a schoolteacher, an education officer, and a schools inspector in the Sierra Leone civil service, as well as a lecturer in the University of Sierra Leone, heading the departments of English and education and serving as dean of faculty. After leaving the university, he joined UNESCO as world coordinator of mother-tongue languages and chief of literacy and basic education in Africa.

Clifford was the compiler (with Eldred Jones) of the *Krio-English Dictionary* (1985), the first dictionary of Krio, published by Oxford. In 1995 he founded Lekon Publishing, which produced creative works as well as textbooks. His creative trilogy *The Conquest of Freedom* (1998)—comprising *Blood Brothers, These Colonial Hills: The Odyssey of a People*, and *The Alpha*—is an allegory of the manipulation of newly independent states by the superpowers. *These Colonial Hills* explores through the story of the power-hungry Sheka Ali the manner in which the venality of leaders doom the hopes of a people struggling to emerge from the throes of colonization; the majesty of the hills around them symbolize their resilience and hope for a brighter future. In *The Alpha* (which is reminiscent of the biblical story of Job), Saithani, the embodiment of evil, tests the fidelity of the saintly Alpha, Salia, to the benevolent god Makrumasaba. Salia proves his fidelity and is appropriately rewarded by his god in the end.

Fyle also wrote short stories for both adults and children, and is the author of the lyrics of the national anthem of Sierra Leone.

G

Garuba, Harry Oludare (1958–) Harry Garuba, a poet and playwright, was born on April 8, 1958, in the Yoruba area of Nigeria. He entered the University of Ibadan in 1975, earning his BA in 1978, his MA in 1981, and his PhD in 1988. He also studied at the University of Texas at Austin from 1985 to 1986, and attended the Scottish Universities Summer School, Edinburgh, on a British Council scholarship in 1987.

Garuba taught at the University of Ibadan from 1981 until 1995 when he left to become a founding member of the editorial board of *The Post Express*, a Lagos newspaper. In 1998 he took the position of senior lecturer at the University of Zululand in South Africa, from where he moved to the University of Cape Town in 2001 as a senior lecturer in the university's Centre for African Studies, rising to associate professor in 2005. He was on the editorial advisory board of the Heinemann African Writers Series before it became defunct, and was assistant general secretary of the Association of Nigerian Authors from 1988 to 1989.

While he was still an undergraduate he had a one-act play, "Pantomime for Saint Apartheid's Day," published in the *Festac Anthology of Nigerian New Writing* (1977). It is in the genre of poetry, though, that he has established himself as a major force, although he has published only one volume of poetry, *Shadow and Dream and Other Poems* (1982). He is considered a member of the generation of "new" poets, a generation that includes his fellow Nigerians Tanure Ojaide and Funso Aiyejina, the Ghanaian Kofi Anyidoho, and the Gambian Tijan Sallah. His poetry, like theirs, is marked by the influence of such early writers as Christopher Okigbo in its musicality, while at the same time evincing a reaction against their opacity. Garuba also shares with the "new" poets a concern with both the lingering effects of colonialism and the civil strife that continues to plague African societies.

Garuba's poems have been published in *The Fate of Vultures: New Poetry from Africa* (1989) edited by Kofi Anyidoho, Peter Porter, and Musaemura Zimunya, the *English Academy Review*, and elsewhere.

FURTHER READING

Ojaide, Tanure. *Poetic Imagination in Black Africa: Essays on African Poetry.* Durham, NC: Carolina Academic Press, 1996.

Habila, Helon (1967–) Helon Habila was born in November 1967 in Kaltungo in northeastern Nigeria. His schooling, both primary and secondary, was at Gombe, where at the age of four he had moved with his father, a civil servant. Growing up, he developed a reading habit as an escape from reality in a country just emerging from civil war, still under military rule and awash in oil money and official corruption, and also because he was something of a loner, with minimal interaction with his siblings. His reading fare, supplied by his father, included romance novels and Hausa translations of Arabic classics. To these he added on his own the Bible and English popular fiction, but also Nigerian writers such as Chinua Achebe, Ben Okri, and Wole Soyinka. After high school he enrolled briefly at the Bauchi University of Technology and the Bauchi College of Arts and Science in pursuit of his father's wishes that he become an engineer. Finding that he had no aptitude in that direction, he dropped out of the college in the mid-1980s. He returned to his studies later at the University of Jos, but this time to study English and literature, and he received his degree in 1995.

Habila took a job as an assistant lecturer in English at Federal Polytechnic in Bauchi and wrote a collection of related stories that he gave the title *Prison Stories*, about the experiences of Lomba, a young journalist in Lagos during the dictatorship of General Sani Abacha. After two years at the job he moved to Lagos and wrote romances for the popular magazine *Hints*, and later took another job as the arts editor for the *Vanguard*, a Lagos newspaper. He continued to write, both poetry and prose, winning the Musical Society of Nigeria (MuSon) Poetry Festival Prize for the poem "Another Age" and the Liberty Bank Prize for the short story "The Butterfly and the Artist," both in 2000. His short story "Love Poems," from the collection "Prison Stories," won the Caine Award in 2001. He reworked the material as a novel and published it as *Waiting for an Angel*, which won him the Commonwealth Prize for Best First Book, African Region, in 2003.

His second novel, *Measuring Time*, was published in 2007. Set in the small Nigerian village of Keti, the story is about the lives and experiences of the twins Mamo and LaMamo, whose mother dies giving them

birth, leaving them to be raised by their Aunt Marina and their indifferent father Lamang. Mamo suffers from sickle-cell anemia and is not expected to live long, with the result that he receives even less attention from his father than his twin brother LaMamo. But he defies expectations and lives into adulthood long enough to go to the university and become a teacher and writer of history. LaMamo goes off at sixteen to join freedom (or rebel) fighters in African countries in need of liberation from the forces of neocolonialism and from externally manipulated rulers. Mamo's writings and experiences expose the corruption in private and official lives in Nigeria in the years spanning the 1960s and the 1990s, while LaMamo's letters home illustrate the problems African countries confront, both self-induced and externally imposed.

Habila enjoyed a two-year writing fellowship at the University of East Anglia, at the same time working toward a doctorate in the university's creative writing program. He is currently a fellow at African Global Studies, Bard College, New York.

Healers, The (1978) *The Healers* is a historical novel by Ayi Kwei Armah, set in the time of the Asante War of 1873 to 1874. While the Asante kingdom is being threatened by British forces, an internal and personal drama is unfolding in the Fante village of Esuano, where the story's protagonist Densu is accused of murdering the prince Appia. Densu seeks refuge with the healer Damfo, who is both healer and spiritual mentor to Appia's mother and to the leader of the Asante Army, Asamoa Nkwanta. Consistent with Armah's portrayal of kings and rulers in his works, members of the royal clan collude with the British army, which defeats the Asante forces and takes Kumasi. When Densu is brought to trial for Appia's murder the victim's mother defends and exonerates

Densu while exposing the Ababio. Because of his disillusionment with power, Densu is able to resist the temptation that confronts him when he is offered the throne.

The story is a mixture of fiction and history, inasmuch as the British conquest of the Asante and capture of Kumasi in 1874 are historical, and Asamoa Nkwanta is a historical figure. The author's intention in the book, according to the blurb, is to teach the lesson that the cause of Europe's conquest of Africa was African disunity: "divisions among kindred societies; divisions within each society between aristocrats, commoners, slaves." As usual, Armah proposes traditional spiritual figures, visionary champions of African unity, as the "healers."

The novel's style is far more conventional and less trying than that of its predecessor, *Two Thousand Seasons*, and critics have noted its optimistic tone, which contrasts with the pessimism of much of the author's previous works. But praise for it has not been universal, Bernth Lindfors describing it as "basically … juvenile adventure fiction of the *Treasure Island* or *King Solomon's Mines* sort."

FURTHER READING

Ola, Virginia U. "The Feminine Principle and the Search for Wholeness in *The Healers*." *Sage* 5, no. 1 (1988): 29–33.

Wright, Derek, ed. *Critical Perspectives on Ayi Kwei Armah*. Washington, DC: Three Continents Press, 1992.

Henshaw, James Ene Ewa (1924–) James Ene Henshaw was born in Calabar in the eastern part of Nigeria in 1924. He attended Christ the King College, Onitsha, for his secondary education and later studied medicine at National University, Dublin, receiving his MD in 1949. On returning to Nigeria he worked variously as a medical consultant, controller of medical services, a member of the National Councils on Health, and in other capacities.

Henshaw was one of the earliest playwrights in the country, publishing his first collection of plays, *This Is Our Chance: Three Plays from West Africa*, in 1956. Included in the volume were *This Is Our Chance* (which he had written for the Association of Students of African Descent), *The Jewel of the Shrine*, and *A Man of Character*. *The Jewel of the Shrine* had won the Henry Carr Memorial Cup in the 1952 All Nigeria Festival of the Arts. *Children of the God and Other Plays*, comprising the title play, *Companion for a Chief*, and *Magic in the Blood*, was published in 1964. The first is a three-act drama in which Christianity is pitted against traditional religion; the other two are one-act comedies, and all were designed for school and amateur production. In the same year Henshaw published *Medicine for Love: A Comedy in Three Acts*, in which polygamy, politics, and bribery receive some comical going over. *Dinner for Promotion*, another three-act comedy involving a young man's efforts to fulfill his ambition, was published in 1967. His other works include the post-Biafran *Enough Is Enough* (1976), which took up the problems of people caught up in the civil war, and *A Song to Mary Charles* (1985), a tribute to an Irish nun.

Henshaw's early plays characteristically dwelled on social and political issues facing the country at independence, for example interethnic stresses and individual morality, as well as the conflict of cultures. They were popular choices for school performances in the 1960s and 1970s. Although critics found them somewhat deficient in dialogue, characterization, and dramatic intensity, Henshaw showed marked improvement in the latter ones, like *Medicine for Love* and *Dinner for Promotion*, and most especially in *A Song to Mary Charles*.

FURTHER READING

Omobowale, B. "Ageing in Nigerian Literature: James Ene Shaw's *The Jewels of the Shrine*." *Lancet* 354 Suppl. 3: SIII2 (November 1999): 1–3.

Heroes (1986) Festus Iyayi's third novel, *Heroes*, is set during the Biafran War, which raged between 1966 and 1970. The hero is the reporter Osime Iyere, a political correspondent for the *Daily News* stationed in Benin. At the outbreak of hostilities he is a staunch believer in the federal cause and the professionalism of Nigerian soldiers. He is also convinced that the Biafrans' case is without merit and their soldiers undisciplined and bloodthirsty as well as poorly clad and equipped. By the end of the story, however, his experiences have left him questioning the necessity of the war and wondering if either side is better than the other. His conversion is effected by his witnessing the atrocities committed on a community during the early stages of the conflict, first by Biafran forces then by the Nigerians. He thereafter strives to work to protect the enlisted men from their self-serving, self-aggrandizing commanders. He uses as the main illustration of the perfidy of the officers a disastrous military engagement in which thousands of Nigerian soldiers die in a Biafran ambush, because of their commander's carelessness and his wish to make a good impression on his supreme commander by winning a spectacular victory. It is based on an actual military disaster during the war resulting from a commanding officer's poor judgment.

In the novel, Iyayi returns to his familiar thesis that the problems in society derive from class inequities. The war, he argues, stems from rivalry within the ruling class and not between ethnic groups as the leaders on both sides had claimed, the rivals using the lower classes as surrogate fighters. In a discussion with a fellow journalist who sees two sides to the conflict—the Nigerians and the Biafrans—Osime insists that there is a third side, made up of the workers (both Biafran and Nigerian) who represent a "third army" that will arise to engage the exploiting army of generals, traditional rulers, bishops, politicians, police chiefs, businessmen, and professors and usher in a more equitable dispensation.

The novel was awarded the Commonwealth Writers' Prize in 1988.

FURTHER READING

Owomoyela, Oyekan. "Festus Iyayi." In *Twentieth-Century Caribbean and Black African Writers*, ed. Bernth Lindfors and Richard Sander, 113–22. Detroit: Gale Research, 1996.

I

Icarus Girl, The (2005) *The Icarus Girl* is Helen Oyeyemi's first novel, written when she was eighteen and studying for her A-levels in England. It is the story of Jessamy Harrison, an eight-year-old girl who lives in suburban Kent with her English father and Nigerian mother. Jess is an extremely bright young girl with the unusual (for her age) pastime of composing haiku poetry. But she also has psychological problems that cause her to hide in cupboards and succumb to screaming fits. Her worried mother decides to take her to visit her Nigerian family with the hope that the change will help. There she meets Titiola, alias Tilly Tilly, a girl her age; they become fast friends, Tilly Tilly introducing Jess to risky adventures.

Soon after she return to England she is surprised to see Tilly Tilly at her door, announcing that she has moved to England. Jess is happy to have someone to play with other than her perfect cousin Dulcie, and someone who promises to take care of the bullies who have always tormented her. The happy reunion quickly turns disastrous, though, because Tilly Tilly proves to be a bad influence on Jess and an invisible disaster for others. Most upsetting for Jess is Tilly Tilly's revelation that Jess, actually had a twin sister who died at birth, an eventuality that her parents should have addressed by carving an *ibeji* doll for her, as Yoruba custom dictates, as a stand-in for her dead twin. Because Tilly Tilly is invisible, she can be taken to be an unseen double who exists only in Jess's imagination. She has been compared to the *abiku* ("spirit child") in Ben Okri's *The Famished Road*, and Tilly Tilly's description of her as a "half-and-half child" also recalls the half-child of Wole Soyinka's *A Dance of the Forest*.

Critics have been most impressed by this remarkable debut by Oyeyemi, praising her control of language and characterization, although some find fault with her forays into her characters' consciousness.

Ike, Chukwuemeka (1931–) Vincent Chukwuemeka Ike was born on April 28, 1931, in Ndikelionwu in the present-day Anambra State of Nigeria. He attended Government College, Umuahia, from 1945 to 1950 for his secondary education, and after teaching for a year at Amichi Central School, Amichi he gained admission to the University College, Ibadan (now University of Ibadan) and earned his BA in 1955. From 1955 to 1956 he taught at the Girls' Secondary School, Nkwere, in eastern Nigeria before returning to his alma mater at Ibadan in 1957 to work as an administrative assistant and registrar of students. In 1960, he moved to the University of Nigeria, Nsukka, to serve as deputy registrar and was elevated to the post of registrar three years later. He took some time off to study at Stanford University for his master's degree, which he received in 1967. When the Nigerian civil war broke out he took charge of refugees in Umuahia Province, and after the war he returned to Nsukka and briefly served as the interim head of the university.

Both at Government College, Umuahia, and at University College, Ibadan, Ike had had his stories published in the students' magazines, and his first full-length fiction *Toads for Supper* appeared in 1965. It deals with the complications in the love life of a university student, arising partly from the differences in the lovers' ethnic backgrounds. His second novel, *The Naked Gods* (1970), is also set in a university, the mythical University of Songhai, and deals with the contest between two candidates, Dr. Okoro and Professor Ikin (with American and British backing respectively) for the post of vice chancellor. The contest is enlivened with the deployment of juju and sexual incentives. Ike's third work, *The Potter's Wheel* (1973), is a realistic and upbeat story about the youthful experience of a schoolboy, while *Sunset at Dawn: A Novel about Biafra* (1976) deals with the devastation caused by the civil war.

Ike's early works are marked by cheerful humor, which had become out of place, though, by the time of *Sunset at Dawn*, his later works addressing and reflecting the chronic state of corruption and chicanery in the country after the war. These include *The Chicken Chasers* and *Expo '77* (both 1980), and a number of others published in Nigeria. His *To My Husband from Iowa* (1996), however, departs from such themes. It is the account of the Nigerian Ify, a happily married young mother of two young children, who has undergone a three-month residency at the Iowa University International Writing Program. It recounts her experiences at different locales during the stint (on farms, in factories, and so on), her conversations with other participants in the program from other countries, her observations on American life (television shows, televangelists, electioneering campaigns), and comparisons of all of these with Nigerian life. Ify serves as a vehicle for the author to voice his disapproval of homosexuality and acceptance of polygamy as well as the notion of women's subservience to their men.

Ike has been active in promoting writing in the country; he was on the editorial committee of *The African Writer: Journal of the African Authors Association* from 1961 to 1962, and in 1970 he participated in the founding of *Okike: An African Journal of New Writing*. From 1986 to 1991 he served as the chairman of the Culture Sector of the National Commission for UNESCO. In an awards ceremony at the end of 2001 the National Council for Arts and Culture cited him for his efforts to create "an enabling environment for the growth of Nigerian Literature and the entire book industry," noting both his long years of service as chairman of the West African Examinations Council and president of the Nigerian Book Foundation.

FURTHER READING

Ezenwa-Ohaeto. "Chukwuemeka Ike." In *Twentieth-Century Caribbean and Black African Writers*, ed. Bernth Lindfors and Reinhard Sander, 96–104. Detroit: Gale Research, 1996.

Interpreters, The (1965) In *The Interpreters*, Wole Soyinka accurately captures the ambiance of the early 1960s scene among the country's young intellectuals, in the glow of the early days of Nigerian independence. Members of a small university-educated elite class, their ears had been filled during their student days with the constant reminder that their pampered education, whether in the country's one university or on government scholarship in some university abroad, was in preparation for taking over the leadership of the country from the colonizers. Concomitant with the education and the promise was an assumption on their part of privilege, entitlement, and license, or at least exemption from certain behavioral constraints that less special people might be subject to.

The story depicts the experiences (principally) of five young men—Egbo (a For-

eign Office bureaucrat), Sagoe (a journalist), Kola (a university lecturer and artist), Bandele (a university lecturer), Sekoni (an engineer)—as they flounder in search of some meaning and purpose to their existence. Seemingly lacking the will and wherewithal to affect their present, they make do with carousing, exchanging clever witticisms, exposing and mocking the failings of others, and generally indulging in desultory living. At the opening of the novel they are drinking in a nightclub on a sodden night, where Sagoe, one of their number, obsesses with his "drink lobes," a favorite subject, along with his scatological philosophy of Voidancy, with which he will later regale his reader at some considerable length.

The story reflects some of the effects of the disparity between expectation and reality for these young men, for whom reality turned out, in contrast to their expectations, to entail contending with holdovers from the ancient regime who lacked the drive, sophistication, and integrity the elite claimed for themselves. Through the story Soyinka argues the necessity to temper visionary impulses with some dose of realism, to guard against expecting events to pan out as one plans or wills them, especially when one has no decisive control over them. It is, for example, Sekoni's failing in this regard that precipitates his dementia and ultimately causes his early death. He had returned home from his study abroad with dreams of using his engineering genius to transform his society, but his superiors frustrated his ambition, reducing him to a deskbound bureaucrat. He subsequently loses his mind and dies in an accident.

The quest for meaning and purpose is symbolized in Kola's ambitious project, a painting of the Yoruba pantheon in which the members of his circle would be stand-ins for the gods (and such other natural manifestations as the rainbow), each human paired with a supernatural entity on the basis of temperamental affinity. The composition of the painting and the spatial relationship of the figures on the canvas itself serve as Soyinka's own statement of his perception of the African (specifically the Yoruba) universe. The completion of the painting and the celebration that marks the event constitute the climax of the novel.

The Interpreters is also a vehicle for Soyinka to expose the various forms of corruption that were eating away at the core of the country and society, and that confounded the aspirations of the young intellectuals. For example, Sir Derinola, an ex-judge and chairman of the board of the news publication *Independent Viewpoint*, conspires with his fellow board member Chief Winsala to demand a bribe from Sagoe before they will offer him employment. Another example is Professor Ogwuazor, the hypocrite who dotes on his illegitimate daughter by an illicit affair but rails against the moral turpitude of a female student who was impregnated by Egbo. Yet another is Dr. Lumoye, a physician and another hypocrite, who joins Ogwuazor in the denunciation of the student, having earlier refused her request for an abortion because she would not first sleep with him.

Among the other issues Soyinka addresses are, first, the complementarity of past and present, and the necessity to forge a connection between both, a necessity powerfully evoked in the conception of a bridge that leads not in one direction only but in two opposite ones. The story witnesses to the presence of the past, that is, of the past reaching out from its supposed grave to affect events in the present, an idea that Soyinka had earlier elaborated in the play *A Dance of the Forests*. It is articulated in *The Interpreters* with particular regard to Egbo, who is troubled by his apostasy: when he had the opportunity to assume the traditional throne

of his village (that was his inheritance), he had instead drifted with the tide back to his modern Foreign Office drudgery.

Another issue centers on the questions of identity and self-acceptance, especially in the character of Joe Golder, much about whose life is interstitial. He looks white but hates his whiteness, loves the one-quarter of him that is black, and laments not being blacker. Besides, he has the body of macho bodybuilder but is a homosexual and an accomplished singer; his theme song is "Sometimes I Feel Like a Motherless Child." Golder's presence in the story also permits Soyinka to reveal some of the local attitudes to homosexuality: Sagoe's reaction when Golder makes a play for him is calm, somewhat nonjudgmental rejection and dismissal of the advance; the young boy Noah is so terrified by Golder's attempt at seducing him that the boy falls to his death from Golder's balcony; Egbo springs away from Golder with absolute disgust and revulsion, as from someone who had the plague, when Bandele reveals Golder's queerness to him.

Soyinka's first major prose work came after he had achieved considerable success as a dramatist and a poet, and it further confirmed the reputation he had established for himself in those two media as an artist with prodigious talent and a penetrating insight into the human condition, an unrelenting assailant of personal and social errancy, and, above all, a daring experimenter with literary diction and form. The novel is packed with clever and unusual usages of English, a Soyinka trademark and one that sometimes (in this work) threatens to get out of hand, as (to take a random example) in the later part of Sagoe's dyeing-pit reverie at Golder's recital. The novel is also unconventional in having no identifiable hero—each of the principal characters claiming the role for a while and then relinquishing it—and in its abrupt shifts in time, from the present to the past and to the future, the past to rationalize the present, the future to offer a glimpse of its culmination.

Finally, *The Interpreters* offers further evidence of Soyinka's fascination with a certain type of woman—independent-minded, self-assured, feisty, and alluring, like the student who became pregnant by Egbo, and like Dehinwa, Sagoe's girlfriend.

FURTHER READING

Kinkead-Weekes, Mark. "*The Interpreters*: A Form of Criticism." In *Critical Perspectives on Wole Soyinka*, ed. James Gibbs, 219–38. Washington, DC: Three Continents Press, 1980.

Iroh, Eddie (1946–) Eddie Iroh says that he was "born on banana leaves and partially orphaned at eight," and that he learned to fend for himself very early. He was raised in Ikenanzizi in Imo State in eastern Nigeria, and he has had a varied professional career. He was serving in the Nigerian Army when the Biafran War broke out, and when he transferred his allegiance and services to the Biafran army he was assigned the command of the war-reports desk of the Biafran War Information Bureau, an assignment that gave him ample opportunities to visit the front to cover some of the fighting. Along with reporting on the war he also drafted speeches for the secessionist leaders. After the conflict he worked for the Reuters news organization, and later for the publisher Evans before joining the Nigerian Television Corporation, Enugu, as a producer. In 1979 he moved to the Nigerian Television Authority in Lagos as the head of its features and documentary department. He also served for a while during the Buhari-Idiagbon regime as the managing editor of the Lagos newspaper *Guardian* before moving to London as the editor of the magazine *Chic*. In 1999 Nigeria's President Olusegun Obasanjo invited him to head the Federal Radio Corporation of Nigeria, a post he currently occupies.

He began writing his impressions of some aspects of the civil war shortly after the conflict, and in 1976 he published what would be the first of a trilogy, *Forty-Eight Guns for the General*, a work that revealed the cold and cynical attitude of the white mercenary soldiers the Biafran side employed, as well as the conflict between the mercenary leader, Colonel Rudolf and the Biafran Colonel Chumah. In *Toads of War* (1979) he continued to expose the way people in positions of authority took advantage of the tragedy to advance their personal interests. Set in the bureaucracy behind the fronts, it also features a love triangle involving the war hero Kalu, the civil servant Chima, and the attractive Kechi. *The Siren in the Night* (1982) is set after the end of the war but is a hangover from it, as it pits an ex-Biafran colonel against a colonel in the Federal Security and Intelligence Directorate. All three works are aptly characterized as in the thriller tradition.

Iroh has also written a children's book, *Without a Silver Spoon* (1984), about a child's poverty-stricken upbringing.

FURTHER READING

Ezeigbo, Theodora Akachi. "War, History, Aesthetics, and the Thriller Tradition in Eddie Iroh's Novels." *African Languages and Cultures* 4, no. 1 (1991): 65–76.

Iweala, Uzodinma Chukuka (1982–) Uzodinma Chukuka Iweala was born on November 5, 1982, in Washington, D.C., and grew up in the United States, where his mother was an executive of the World Bank and his father a surgeon. Apart from living with his mother in Abuja, Nigeria's capital, when she served as the country's finance minister and then briefly as foreign minister between 2003 and 2006, Uzodinma's experience of Nigeria was limited to brief annual summer visits.

After receiving his high-school education at St. Albans School in Washington, he enrolled at Harvard University on a Mellon Mays scholarship as a premed student, but he found himself drawn to creative writing, although no such major existed at the university. His student writing won him such prizes as the Eager Prize for Best Undergraduate Short Story (2003), the Horman Prize for Excellence in Creative Writing (2003), the Le Baron Briggs Prize, and both the Hoopes Prize and Dorothy Hicks Lee Prize for Outstanding Undergraduate Thesis (2004).

His hugely popular maiden novel *Beasts of No Nation* (2005), which has won the John Llewellyn Rhys Prize for 2005 and the Barnes & Noble Discover Award for 2006, grew out of the undergraduate thesis. It tells the harrowing story of Agu, a child forced into the life of a soldier by rebels fighting against the government of an unnamed African country. Iweala was inspired to write the story because once he learned about the life and ordeal of child soldiers in Sierra Leone from reading a *Newsweek* article, he found he could not walk away without taking some action. His resolve to act was further strengthened by his encounter with a woman who had been a child soldier herself in Uganda, and by working at a rehabilitation camp for ex-child soldiers when he lived in Nigeria.

The story, told in Agu's voice and in a form of pidgin English, highlight's the boy's innocence and naiveté, which lend even more impact to the horrible acts he is made to commit by Commandant, such as indiscriminately killing people, and the equally horrid abuse he endures at Commandant's hands, such as being subjected to repeated sodomy. The book's indebtedness to Ken Saro-Wiwa's *Sozaboy: A Novel in Rotten English* (1985) is unmistakable, although Mene, Saro-Wiwa's protagonist, is older than Agu. Like Agu Mene is also naive about what war means, and much of the time either does not know why or who he is fighting, a fact underscored by his switching from one side to the other. Agu's brand of pidgin English is also quite reminiscent of Mene's, and Iweala's characterization of it similar to Saro-Wiwa's.

Capturing the Llewellyn Rhys Prize at the age of twenty-three makes Iweala one of the youngest winners of the award, and he has credited the nurturing and encouragement he received from Jamaica Kincaid, his teacher and adviser at Harvard, for much of his success as a writer.

Iyayi, Festus (1947–) Festus Iyayi was born on September 29, 1947, at Eguare-Ugbegun in modern-day Edo State, part of what was at the time the Western Region of Nigeria. He attended the CMS (Anglican) primary school and Annunciation Catholic College, where he adamantly refused conversion to Catholicism, and in 1970 he went to the Ukraine to read economics and business management at the Kiev Institute of Economics. In the process he learned Russian and became familiar with the works of writers like Leo Tolstoy and Fyodor Dostoyevsky, having already acquainted himself with John Steinbeck and *The Grapes of Wrath* in his high-school days. After a brief return to Nigeria, he left for Bradford University in Great Britain to study for a doctorate in management and business administration. On completing the degree in 1980, he took a job as a lecturer in the department of business administration in the University of Benin. He served as chairperson of the Academic Staff Union from 1984 to 1986 and the national president of the Academic Staff Union of Nigeria from 1986 to 1987. In the fulfillment of those offices, he incurred the ire of the Nigerian military government under General Babangida, which fired him in 1987.

Iyayi began his writing career at a time when Nigeria was in deep crisis; the country had emerged from a bloody civil war whose effects were still quite obvious, and had entered into a period of monumental corruption fueled by a deluge of petronaira. For him and others of his generation, the immediate problems connected with colonialism had given way to the shambles Africans were making of the countries they took over from the colonizers, and the unconscionable exploitation of the weak and vulnerable by the powerful and well placed.

Violence (1979), Iyayi's first published novel, explores the impossible struggles of a destitute young couple, Idemudia and Adisa, to make an honest living in a callous and corrupt society like Nigeria in the oil boom years. At every turn, they suffer exploitation at the hands of corrupt and greedy employers like Obofun and his wife Queen; their experiences eloquently corroborate the author's point that the oppressed workers suffer social violence at the hands of their exploiters and of the society that makes the conditions of their exploitation possible.

The Contract (1982), though published after *Violence*, was actually Iyayi's first, written when he was a student in the Soviet Union. He had placed it with Longman after completing it, but they had neglected to publish it. It is about the blatant corruption that attended the award of contracts in Nigeria at the time, according to which the contract amount for a project was routinely inflated as much as tenfold, with the understanding that the contractor and all the officials involved in the negotiations would share the excess. In a Brechtian touch, and reminiscent of Ngugi wa Thiong'o in *Devil on the Cross* (1982), Iyayi gives each major character a name that proclaims his corrupt nature.

Iyayi's third novel, *Heroes* (1986), set during the Nigerian civil war, is the story of war correspondent Osime Iyere, whose experiences disabuse him of the simplistic notion that there is a good side and a bad in the war. Both sides are equally capable of atrocities, he learns, and on both sides the generals and other highly placed functionaries enjoy luxury in safety while the foot soldiers and ordinary people suffer and die. Iyayi won both the Commonwealth Prize for Literature for the Africa Region and the Association of Nigerian Authors Prize in 1988.

In his collection of fifteen short stories, *Awaiting Court Martial* (1996), he continues his assault on corruption, violence, and inhumanity during the dark years of dictatorial rule in the country. Another collection, *The Rainbow Has Only One Colour: A Collection of Short Stories*, is in progress.

FURTHER READING

Fatunde, Tunde. "Images of Working People in Two African Novels: Ouologuem and Iyayi." In *Marxism and African Literature*, ed. Georg M. Gugelberger, 110–17. Trenton, NJ: Africa World Press, 1986.

Udumukwu, Onyemaechi. "Ideology and the Dialectics of Action: Achebe and Iyayi." *Research in African Literatures* 27, no. 3 (Fall 1996): 34–49.

J

Jagua Nana (1961) Cyprian Ekwensi's *Jagua Nana* (1961) is one of the most popular novels with Nigerian readers. It epitomizes what critics have described as the city novel, because its main setting is the city, which might justifiably be regarded as itself a major character in the story, although the plot also includes forays into the village.

The name of the heroine, Jagua, testifies to her class and exclusiveness, qualities that Nigerians associated with the British automobile of the same name, Jaguar, in the 1960s. A flamboyant and much sought after prostitute, Jagua had moved to Lagos from her village of Ugabu in the eastern (Igbo) region of the country, and in anticipation of the time when she would have to retire from her profession, she takes on the much younger Freddie as a lover. He already has a girlfriend Nancy who is closer to his age, but Jagua is intent on displacing her with the hope of marrying Freddie. To strengthen her hold on him, she sends him to England to study law.

The plot is typically busy with numerous twists and turns: Jagua fights Nancy while Freddie is away in England; she becomes involved with Chief Ofubara in the Delta area of the country, with the politician Uncle Taiwo, and with the Lagos thug Dennis. In time Dennis returns from England, marries Nancy, and challenges Uncle Taiwo in the elections, a move that places him and Jagua in opposite camps, and that leads to his death at the hands of Uncle Taiwo's thugs. Uncle Taiwo loses the election and is murdered by members of his own party. After a host of other twists, Jagua is able to retire from prostitution and, thanks to a bag of money Uncle Taiwo had given to her for safekeeping, embark on another career as a trader, a "real Merchant Princess," in Onitsha.

The plot, which takes Jagua from Lagos to her village, to Onitsha, and to Chief Ofubara's village of Krinameh, enables Ekwensi to explore the character of the city in contrast to the village, highlighting its high-life vibrancy, fast pace and glitter, as well as its violence and corruption. It thus offers a representative illustration of the transformation the entire society had undergone since the arrival of European influence, as the forays into the villages offer vignettes of the prior conditions, communities in which life was slow but secure, in which there was no prostitution, no violence, and no corruption. The picture Ekwensi presents is however not one of rural utopia versus urban dystopia, for the city is also associated with the educational and other opportunities to which even the people of the villages aspire.

FURTHER READING

Oku, Julia Inyang Essien. "Courtesans and Earthmothers: A Feminist Reading of Cyprian Ekwensi's *Jagua Nana* and Buchi Emecheta's *The Joys of Motherhood*." In *Critical Theory and African Literature*, ed. Ernest N. Emenyonu et al., 225–33. Ibadan: Heinemann, 1987.

Johnson, Lemuel (1941–2002) Lemuel Johnson was born in Sierra Leone in 1941. After a brilliant finish to his high school education he went to do his undergraduate studies at Oberlin College, earning an AB in 1965. From Oberlin he went on to Pennsylvania State University, where he received his MA in 1966, and thereafter he enrolled in the Comparative Literature program of the University of Michigan, taking his PhD in 1968. Joining the faculty of the university that same year, he rose to become a professor of English and director of the Center for Afroamerican and African Studies from 1985 to 1991. He was a visiting professor at a number of universities, including the Colegio de Mexico, the University of Sierra Leone, the Salzburg Seminar, and Oberlin College. He was also the president of the African Literature Association from 1977 to 1978 and vice president of the Association of Caribbean Studies from 1983 to 1985.

Johnson was an exquisite poet. His *Sierra Leone Trilogy* (comprising *Highlife for Caliban*, 1973; *Hands on the Navel*, 1978; and *Carnival of the Old Coast*, 1995) covers the African experiences from the time of the transatlantic slave trade to the postindependence period, including those of the colonial period when Africans were drawn into conflicts among European nations, especially during the Second World War. The works are a triumph of the integration of traditional resources, poetic sensibility, and scholarly erudition, all expressed with wit and passion.

Johnson's scholarly works include *The Devil, the Gargoyle and the Buffoon: The Negro as Metaphor in Western Literatures* (1970), *Toward Defining the African Aesthetic* (1983), and *Shakespeare in Africa and Other Venues: Import and the Appropriation of Culture* (1998). Fluent in several languages—including Spanish, Portuguese, French, Italian, and German, as well as Krio (his national language), Yoruba, Hausa, and Igbo—Johnson translated Rafael Alberti's play, *Night and War in the Prado Museum* (1969) from Spanish.

He died on March 12, 2002.

FURTHER READING

A Tribute to Professor Lemuel Johnson. *GEFAME: Journal of African Studies* 1, no. 1 (November 2004). www.hti.umich.edu/g/gefame.

Joys of Motherhood, The (1994) Buchi Emecheta's fifth novel, *The Joys of Motherhood*, returns to a subject that readers of her earlier works perhaps expected of her: the terrible fate that misogynous African patriarchies impose on women. In this work she takes aim at the supposedly sacred concept of motherhood, which according to Africans and Africanists confers honor, prestige, and privilege on women, especially women as mothers. The heroine is Nnu Ego, daughter of the powerful chief Agbadi and his beloved Ona. Her first marriage to Amatokwu is childless, a plight for which Nnu Ego bears the blame and stigma, and it is eventually terminated. She subsequently marries Nnaife Owulum, a washerman for an English couple in Lagos, and finally has the good fortune of becoming a mother. Although she loses her first son, her later births are fortunate, and she winds up with five children who survive and thrive.

The title is hugely ironic, because the novel is a documentation of the curse motherhood turns out to be for Nnu Ego. It imposes upon her the obligation to ensure that her children are well fed and well provided for when their father's earnings are inadequate or when he is away for long spells. It is in fact from her earnings as a trader that the fees for the children's education are paid. The consequence is that her life is so consumed with caring for her family that she has no time to make friends. Motherhood, the novel thus argues, is simply another prison into which women are lured by deceptive misrepresentations. The joys that accrue to a mother are only those that come from knowing that her children have turned out well, for motherhood brings no tangible benefits or rewards. By the end of the story Nnu Ego is back in her village; she has been abandoned by Nnaife, who has long since taken another wife, her two oldest sons have moved to the United States and Canada respectively, while her caring daughters have remained in Lagos. In the village the news reaches her that her eldest son has married a white woman in the United States, and the news is so devastating that she loses her mind and dies unattended at a roadside.

Emecheta's admirer's consider *The Joys of Motherhood* her best work, her best presentation of the institutionalized victimization of women by the male members of her family, including her own sons. It also vindicates critics' description of Emecheta's vision as iconoclastic, especially with regard to the status of women in African societies, and inasmuch as it is consistent with her efforts to explode whatever arguments might be advanced to the effect that African cultures are characterized by regard for women and their well-being. A debunking of the sacredness of African motherhood is certainly a daring attack on one of the mainstays of the African social structure.

The book also contains arguments against the picture of general male misogyny: Agbadi's relationship with Ona was tender and loving, and he also doted on his daughter Nnu Ego, for whose happiness he was willing to do practically anything. The sentiment he expressed at Nnu Ego's birth, "This child is priceless, more than twenty bags of cowries," belies the common assertion (by Western and some African feminists alike) that in African societies girl-children were (are) regarded as worthless. Nnu Ego (twenty bags of cowries) is evidently not a quantification or commodification of the child, but a shortened assertion of her pricelessness.

Moreover, the joys (or plagues) of motherhood are not much different from those of fatherhood, inasmuch as Nnaife fares no better than Nnu Ego, and arguably even worse, with regard to how much affection and consideration he receives from their children. Their oldest son Oshia does not hide his contempt when he talks back to his father, and the rest of the children pay little attention to his wishes about their lives, let alone what he expects them to do for him. He is better off, of course, in having another wife to move in with after the estrangement from Nnu Ego, who is condemned to a lonely death.

FURTHER READING

Oku, Julia Inyang Essien. "Courtesans and Earthmothers: A Feminist Reading of Cyprian Ekwensi's *Jagua Nana* and Buchi Emecheta's *The Joys of Motherhood*." In *Critical Theory and African Literature*, ed. Ernest N. Emenyonu et al., 225–33. Ibadan: Heinemann, 1987.

1951, working as a reporter, and also worked for the Gold Coast Broadcasting Service. In 1956 the Ghanaian government sent him first to London for further training, and then to Strasbourg University to study journalism. On returning to Ghana in 1957 he joined the Ghana News Agency and also reported for several government news publications. Beginning in 1963 he began to study traditional customs and to write on these and other matters, his first published novels being *Wizard of Asamang* (1964), *The Lawyer Who Bungled His Life* (1965), and *Come Back Dora!* (1966).

His novels and short stories, which are aimed primarily at the popular reader, employ simple English and focus on life in rural Ghana, depicting the customs and dealing with common problems. These include those resulting from childlessness, which constitute the subject of *A Woman in Her Prime* (1967), the validity of traditional beliefs and practices, which he addresses in *Ordained by the Oracle* (1969), and official corruption, his focus in *Shadow of Wealth* (1966). Konadu has also written under the pseudonym Kwabena Asare Bediako specifically for the popular market. The works under this pseudonym are published by Konadu's own imprint, Anowuo Educational Publications. The titles include *Don't Leave Me MERCY* (1966) and *A Husband for Esi Ellua* (1967).

Konadu, Samuel Asare (1932–94) Asare Konadu was born in 1932 at Asamang in the Asante area of Central Ghana. He attended the local primary and middle schools before going on to the Abuakwa State College. He joined the Ghana Information Service in

Laing, B. (Bernard Ebenezer) Kojo (1946–) Kojo Laing was born in Kumasi on July 1, 1946, to Darling Laing (née Egan) and George Ekyem Ferguson Laing, an Anglican minister. His parents sent him to Scotland in 1957 after he had attended the Bishop's Boys' School in Accra. There he lived with his father's family friend, Richard Holloway, bishop of Edinburgh, and continued his education at Bonhill Primary School and the Vale of Leven Academy in Alexandria, Dunbartonshire. He went on in 1964 to study political science and history at Glasgow University, earning his MA 1968. He returned to Ghana the same year to work for the Ghanaian civil service, and had opportunities to learn a great deal about the Ghanaian countryside as a result of postings to a succession of rural locations. The experience has infused his writings with a palpable feel for Nature and natural phenomena. He moved to Accra in 1978 and served at the Castle, the official residence and office of the Ghanaian president, and from there he went on in 1979 to the University of Ghana, Legon, to work as secretary to the Institute of African Studies, leaving the position in 1984 to run a school in Accra.

Using the name Kojo rather than his given names, Bernard Ebenezer, he scored his first literary success with the novel *Search Sweet Country* (1986), which also established his credentials as a writer in the surrealist or magical realist tradition (along with the Nigerian Ben Okri and the Sierra Leonean Syl Cheney-Coker). Set in Accra in 1975, at a time of military rule rife with corruption and hardship for the populace, the novel decries exploitative self-interest and promotes cooperation among people as the path to a better future. It won a number of awards, including the VALCO Award and the Ghana Book Award.

Laing's next novel, *Woman of the Aeroplanes* (1988), is set in a mythical place and time, although the details of the locale and the referenced history indicate Ghana. It pits modern technology against traditional spiritualism, suggesting that neither can be whole without the other. His historical reconstruction has been compared to his compatriot Ayi Kwei Armah's, although he is less intense than Armah. His third

novel, *Major Gentl and the Achimota Wars* (1992), is set in the future, in 2020. It is a military confrontation between European powers, represented by the evil mercenary Torro the Terrible, and African countries, championed by Major Amofa Gentl, one side deploying rats and computers and the other snakes. The good snakes triumph in the end, and the novel won Laing another VALCO Award in 1993.

Godhorse (1989), Laing's poetry collection, shares the magical and mystical qualities of his novels, qualities that are also evident in his short stories, for example "Vacancy for the Post of Jesus Christ," which is included in *The Heinemann Book of Contemporary African Short Stories* (1992), edited by Chinua Achebe and C. L. Innes.

FURTHER READING

Cooper, Brenda. *Magical Realism in West African Fiction: Seeing with a Third Eye*. London: Routledge, 1998.
Maja-Pearce, Adewale, "Interview with Kojo Laing." *Wasafiri* 6–7 (Spring–Autumn 1987): 27–29.
Rohrberger, Mary. "*Woman of the Aeroplanes*." In *Magill's Literary Annual 1991*, ed. Frank N. Magill, 2:914–18. Englewood Cliffs, NJ: Salem Press, 1991.

Last Harmattan of Alusine Dumbar, The (1990) Syl Cheney-Coker's novel *The Last Harmattan of Alusine Dumbar* opens with a prologue in which General Masimiara, the leader of Malagueta's army, contemplates the events that led to his arrest and imprisonment in an island prison that used to be a holding pen for slaves about to be shipped to the Americas. He had felt betrayed by the policies and actions of President Sanka Maru and his circle, their pretensions and aping of Western manners and ways. These were all actions and behavior that soiled Malagueta's heritage as a shining star. The last straw for Masimiara was learning, while on a visit to the United States, that Sanka Maru had taken a bribe of twenty-five million dollars from a company in the United States as a price for permitting the company to dump nuclear waste into the waters off Malagueta.

Malagueta had been settled in the land of Kasila by ex-slaves from Canada, who had had enough of being ill treated by white men after the king they had sided with in the colonial war had reneged on the reward he promised them. The first wave of settlers on the West African coast under Jeanette and Sebastian Cromantine had lost their new home when the nearby residents of Kasila, blaming them for a deadly plague that had begun in Malagueta and spread to Kasila, burned their settlement and chased them into the hills. Eight years later a new group arrived under the one-eyed Thomas Bookerman, whose leadership gave the new Malagueta prosperity, until Captain Hammerstone arrived and imposed a British colony on the people. It however took many years of resistance before the colonizers eventually prevailed, with the collusion of the Malaguetans.

The plot parodies the sequence of events that in reality played itself out in several West African colonies. After the colonial presence and its policies had replaced the once idealistic and communal character of the Malaguetans with an individualistic and materialistic ethos, the British came to realize that their eventual departure was inevitable, and they hurriedly promoted junior African officers in the security forces to the senior ranks, leaving Masimiara as brigadier general and commander of the army. The civilian administration, which was left in the hands of Ali Baba and the Forty Thieves, was so corrupt that the soldiers toppled it in a coup and gave the reins of government to Masimiara. His new mistress Sadatu, a descendant of Sebastian and Jeanette Cromantine, leaders of the original Malagueta

settlers, made him realize that he was not cut out to administer a country, and after trying without success to hand over civilian power to his second-in-command Colonel Lookdown Akongo, he invited the Labor leader Sanka Maru to take over as premier. Sanka Maru proceeded to pack the ruling assembly with cronies who granted him more and more powers and enabled him to set up a personal security force that was more powerful than the army, and that gave him the confidence to, among other abuses, sell off public assets, and muzzle both the press and the critical students.

The novel ends with an epilogue announcing the hanging of Masimiara a year after he had been arrested. It covers Masimiara's yearlong solitary confinement and reflection on the dream that was Malagueta and a montage of its history with remembrances of the memorable characters involved: the Cromantines, Thomas Bookerman, and such heroic women as Phyllis, who disguises herself as a man in order to join in the defense of Malagueta against Hammerstone's forces.

The "magical" aspect of the novel centers on the figure of Suleiman the Nubian, alias Alusine Dunbar, who makes his first appearance in Kasila long before the founding of Malagueta. He in fact sired the woman Fatmatta, who after being captured and transported as a slave to America begins the voyage back with the Cromantines but dies during the voyage. He had foreseen and foretold the events that would later unfold, and at critical points in the story he made an appearance in Malagueta, announced by atmospheric disturbances. The epilogue recounts his final advent in his last harmattan on the morning of Masimiara's execution, when he, through the device of a cosmic gale, bodily lifts Sanka Maru from his palace and hauls him to his death in the Malagueta streets, and also makes an end of both Lookdown Akongo and his mistress, locked in each other's embrace.

The novel lays the blame for the destruction of the Malagueta experiment on the people's abandonment of the principles of communalism in preference for the philosophy of individualism, their captivation by Western habits, and their hunger for wealth and power. The events it chronicles closely mirror the real-life confrontation between Brigadier-General John Ahmadu Bangura (1930–71), and President Siaka Steven (1905–88). Bangura was arrested for plotting a coup against the corrupt rule of Stevens, and he was executed in 1971.

Maddy, (Pat) Yulisa Amadu (1936–) Yulisa Ammadu Maddy was born in Sierra Leone in 1936. After his early education in his home country he attended Rose Bruford College and London University. During the 1960s he worked in the United Kingdom and Denmark, where he produced plays by African playwrights for broadcast on Danish radio. He also taught and worked in theater in Nigeria and Zambia, as well as in the United States.

Maddy's first collection of plays was published in the Heinemann series in 1971. In addition to the title play *Obasai* the volume contained three other plays: *Alla Gbah*, *Gbana-Bendu*, and *Yon-Kon*. The first two feature traditional ritual, song, and drama, and in the third the playwright shifts gear to a melodramatic treatment of contemporary issues, and thence to the satirical consideration of money and its effects on people in his society. Other plays include *Big Breeze Blow* (1984), *Take Tem Draw Di Rope* (1975), *Naw We Yone Dehn See* (1975), *Big Berrin*

(1984), *A Journey Into Christmas* (1980), and *Drums, Voices and Worlds* (1985), the radio play *If Wishes Were Horses* (1963), and the television play *Saturday Night Out* (1980). He is also the author of the novel *No Past, No Present, No Future* (1973), and of the critical works *Apartheid and Racism in South African Children's Literature, 1985–1995* (2001), *African Images in Juvenile Literature: Commentaries on Neocolonialist Fiction* (1995), and *Ambivalent Signals in South African Young Adult Novels* (1998), all in collaboration with Donnarae MacCann.

Cosmopolitan in education and influenced by European theatrical practice, Maddy nonetheless reaches out to local African audiences, as is evident in his treatment of relevant social issues and his use of pidgin English in several of his plays. His artistry was rewarded with a national award at the Sierra Leone National Arts Festival in 1973, and he later won a Gulbenkian Grant in 1978, and an Edinburgh Festival Award in 1979.

Madmen and Specialists **(1971)** Conceived when the playwright was in detention between 1967 and 1969 for alleged involvement with the Biafran secessionists during the Nigerian civil war, Wole Soyinka's *Madmen and Specialists* depicts a mad world pervaded by anomie, in which spiritual deformity and moral depravity are the norm. Those to whom the affairs of the state are entrusted have turned predators and exterminators, and even filial bonds have not escaped the general corruption. Bero and his father, Old Man, are both the specialists and the madmen of the play, whose major action is the conflict between the two. Both are physicians; Dr. Bero had enlisted in the war as a member of the medical corps, but after the mysterious death of the head of intelligence services (there is a suggestion that Bero might have had something to do with it), Bero's aptitude made him the ideal candidate to succeed him. In that office he enjoyed unlimited license in devising means of forcing information out of recalcitrant witnesses, and unlimited opportunities to gratify his homicidal inclinations.

Apparently, reports reaching Old Man about the war's carnage and his son's role in it persuaded him to join the war effort, but with a sinister purpose. "All intelligent animals kill only for food, you know," he reasoned with the officers, having placed human flesh before them without their knowing the nature of the meal, "and you are intelligent animals. Eat-eat-eat-eat-eat—Eat!" He somehow escaped the later murderous vengeance of the officers with Bero's help, but now he is in the equally vengeful clutches of his son who wants to get to the bottom of the subversive doctrine of As—"As Was, Is, Now, As Ever Shall Be …"—with which Old Man had infected the underlings in the war.

The other characters in the story are veterans of the war who had come under Old Man's influence during the conflict. They are Aafaa, a sort of priest afflicted with St. Vitus spasms that he can switch on or off to serve his purposes, Cripple, Goyi, and Blindman. They all use mendicancy as a cover for spying on Bero's behalf on his sister Si Bero, her two instructors in the mysteries of herbal powers (Iya Agba and Iya Mate), and Old Man, whom Bero had secretly spirited into the basement of the family home. They have been converted to Old Man's doctrine of As, and sing its refrain, in Yoruba:

> *Bi o ti wa*
> *Ni yio se wa*
> *Bi o ti wa*
> *Ni yio se wa*
> *Bi o ti was l'atete ko* [*se*].

First performed at the Eugene O'Neill Theater Center in Waterford, Connecticut, in August 1970, the play had its Nigerian premiere at the Arts Theatre, University of Ibadan, in March 1971. Although set against the backdrop of the Nigerian civil war, the play is intended to have universal application, and Soyinka accordingly instructs directors that a pivotal speech assigned to Blindman toward the end of part two be "varied with the topicality and locale of the time."

The play also testifies to Soyinka's powerful sense of theater, as well, though, as to his propensity to be opaque and problematic with regard to a moral vision. The discussion of As and its philosophy (by Old Man and the mendicants) is sometimes difficult to fathom, and in the end Old Man, presumably the advocate of the good (such as it is), is murdered by his son Bero.

Marriage of Anansewa, The (1975) *The Marriage of Anansewa*, a play by Efua Sutherland, is one of the earliest in the Anglophone West African theater repertoire, and had been popular both in performance and in manuscript form long before its eventual publication. It is based on the antics of Anansi, the Akan trickster, whose stories are employed for entertainment as well as social commentary.

In throes of poverty, Ananse offers his daughter Anansewa in marriage to four suitors, encouraging each to believe that there is no obstacle to his success, and receiving gifts from all of them. When the danger of exposure looms he announces that his daughter has died, and he receives even more gifts from the sympathetic and solicitous suitors. When Chief-Who-Is-Chief, the suitor whom Anansewa truly loves, comes to visit, Anansi proclaims that the suitor's love has wrought the miracle of restoring the prospective bride to life, and preparations begin for the wedding.

The play was an important vehicle in the story theater *anansegoro* that Sutherland established in the 1960s.

Mbari Club The famous Mbari Artists and Writers Club played a central role in encouraging artists and popularizing their works in the exciting decade of the 1960s. Ulli Beier, the German visionary who profoundly influenced Nigerian creative endeavors in diverse media during the period, collaborated with Wole Soyinka and Ezekiel Mphahlele to found the club in 1961. Soyinka had only recently returned from his studies in England, and Mphahlele, the South African teacher and writer, was in the early years of his exile from apartheid in his country. Also in on the founding of the club were a number of people with disparate artistic interests, such as the actress Frances Ademola, the novelist Chinua Achebe, the poets John Pepper Clark (Bekederemo), Arthur Nortje, and Christopher Okigbo, the sculptor Bruce Onobrakpeya, the painter Demas Nwoko, and poet-painter Uche Okeke, and other talented artists, all united in the desire to give greater visibility to native African creativity at a time that the continent was emerging from colonialism. Mphahlele served as the first chairman of the club, and Begum Hendrickse as the first secretary.

At its premises in the commercial area of Ibadan, the Mbari Club maintained a library and an office, as well as an open-air theater where local musicians and theater groups performed. The club also invited internationally renowned artists to perform or exhibit their works. The African American poet Langston Hughes, the African American painter Jacob Lawrence, and the folk singer Pete Seeger were just a few of such artistes to grace the Mbari stage. The works of the members were also featured at the club, including the premiere of Soyinka's farce *The Trials of Brother Jero* and that of J. P. Clark's tragedy *Song of a Goat*.

In addition to staging plays and other live performances, and exhibiting paintings, the Mbari Club also established its own publishing house and issued some of the important works by Africans from across the continent during those formative years of modern African literature—works by Kofi Awoonor, Dennis Brutus, J. P. Clark, Alex La Guma, Christopher Okigbo, Lenrie Peters, and Wole Soyinka, among others, along with works by Ulli Beier (who often wrote behind a pseudonym).

Although the word Mbari is Igbo, the name for the traditional mud structures in which Igbo people collectively create artistic objects, it also has a meaning in the Yoruba language, "Were I to see." It is in that sense that Beier adopted it as the name for the offshoot Club at Oshogbo, Mbari Mbayo (meaning "Were I to see, I would rejoice"), where he spent many years mentoring Duro Ladipo and collaborating with him in the development of his "opera" company. There also, Beier collaborated with his wife Suzanne Wenger to nurture the artists of the famous Oshogbo school of German impressionism. Another offshoot, Mbari Mbayo, was later established in Lagos, and it formed the model for the Chemchemi Center that Mphahlele later founded in Nairobi and the Iwalewa House that Beier later established at Bayreuth.

Mezu, Sebastian Okechukwu (1941–) Sebastian Okechukwu Mezu was born on April 30, 1941, at Emekuku, Owerri, in Nigeria. He had his early education at the Holy Ghost School, Owerri, and the Upper School of the Holy Family at Abak. He taught for a short while at the Saint-Rosary College, Port Harcourt, and in 1961 left for the United States to study at Georgetown University, from which he received a BA in French and German in 1964. He also received an LLB from La Salle Extension University in 1966, and a PhD in romance languages from Johns Hopkins University in 1967, with a dissertation on Léopold Sédar Senghor. Mezu was for some time a UNESCO fellow at the Sorbonne and has been a director of African studies at SUNY Buffalo. He is the founder of Black Academy Press, the publishers of several of his books. He was an official of the breakaway republic of Biafra during the Nigerian civil war.

In 1966 Mezu published his collected poems, *The Tropical Dawn*, which he opened with the long essay, "Poetry and Revolution in Modern Africa," and in 1970 he published the novel *Behind the Rising Sun*, a work in which through the experiences of the hero Freddy Onuoha he told the story of the conflict from a Biafran perspective, but in which he was critical of some of the rebel leaders, as well as profiteering foreigners and Nigerians. His critical works include *Léopold Sédar Senghor et la défense et illustration de la civilisation noire* (1968), *The Poetry of Léopold Sédar Senghor* (1973), and *The Philosophy of Pan-Africanism: A Collection of Papers on the Theory and Practice of the African Unity Movement* (1965), which he edited.

In 1973 Mezu returned to Nigeria and engaged in politics, but military intervention in public affairs persuaded him to leave the country and concentrate on his commercial activities in the United States, part of which is his editorship of the *Black Academy Review*.

Moore, Bai T. J. (1920–88) Bai Tamia Johnson Moore, a Liberian poet and folklorist, was born in Dimeh near Monrovia. He studied agriculture at the Virginia Union University, and on returning home in 1941 he joined the Liberian civil service, once serving as undersecretary of state for cultural affairs in President William S. Tubman's administration. He also served for some time in the education section of UNESCO's Liberia office.

In 1947 he coedited with Ronald T. Dempster and T. H. Carey *Echoes from the Valley:*

Being Odes and Other Poems, a volume in which several of his own poems appeared. In 1962 he published another volume of his poems, *Ebony Dust*, and in the following year came his novella *Murder in the Cassava Patch*, an expanded version of a short story with the same title, which was based on an actual murder. The novel *The Money Doubler* followed in 1976. Moore also contributed a story to the book *Four Stories by Liberian Writers* (1980), edited by Wilton Sankawulo.

Munonye, John (1929–99) John Okechukwu Munonye was born in Akokwa in the Igbo area of eastern Nigeria on April 28, 1929. He attended Christ the King College in Onitsha from 1943 to 1947 for his secondary education, and went on to study the classics at the University College, Ibadan (now University of Ibadan), graduating in 1952. In 1954 he did graduate studies at the London Institute of Education and returned to Nigeria to serve as an inspector of education in the Nigerian civil service. He also worked for a while as the principal of the Advanced Teaching Training College, Owerri, and later as chief inspector of education in the Imo State ministry of education.

His first novel, *The Only Son* (1966), deals with a young boy's desire for Western education, and his consequent alienation from his widowed mother and his relatives. The contest between traditional ways and beliefs and new influences is also the subject of its sequel, *Obi* (1969), in which a couple's returning from the city to their village causes friction between them and their extended family. Western education and its demands on family resources is the subject of another Munonye novel, *Oil Man of Obange* (1971), in which a palm-oil trader becomes estranged from his family and sacrifices everything, including his life, to pay for his children's education. The problems attendant on moving from traditional ways to modernity and the crucial role of education in negotiating the passage, which resurface repeatedly in Munonye's writings, are also present in *A Wreath for the Maidens* (1973), which touches on the effects of the civil war; *A Dancer of Fortune* (1975), which is about modern business practices; and *Bridge to a Wedding* (1978).

Munonye has won the praise of critics for his sympathetic portrayal of rural characters and his fidelity to Igbo culture, which some compare favorably with Chinua Achebe's. He devotes his attention to individuals and their struggles, leaving aside such issues as colonization, cultural imperialism, economic exploitation, and political upheavals that have preoccupied most other Anglophone West African writers.

Munonye died on May 10, 1999, and after his passing his admirers lamented that he had not received, during his lifetime, the recognition and attention that he deserved.

FURTHER READING

Griswold, Wendy. *Bearing Witness: Readers, Writers, and the Novel in Nigeria.* Princeton: Princeton University Press, 2000.

Ndibe, Okey (1960–) Born in Yola in northern Nigeria in 1960, Okey Ndibe earned a diploma from the Institute of Management and Technology, Enugu. He worked in Nigeria for several years as a journalist and columnist before moving to the United States in 1988 to become the editor of *African Commentary*, a new magazine that Chinua Achebe was launching. He later enrolled at the University of Massachusetts, Amherst, where he earned an MFA. In 1993, while studying at Amherst, he became the inaugural editor of the newly founded

African World: The Forum of People of African Descent, founded and published by Bartholomew Nnaji, a former government minister in Nigeria who was then a professor of industrial engineering and operations research at Amherst. Among his journalism-related experiences was a stint as a member of the editorial board of the *Hartford Courant*. Ndibe was a visiting assistant professor of English and creative writing at Connecticut College from 1997 to 2000, and he has also been a Fulbright lecturer in English at the University of Lagos. In 2002 he moved to Simon's Rock College, Great Barrington, Massachusetts, where he is an associate professor of English.

Apart from contributing poems to Tijan Sallah's *An Anthology of New West African Poets*, Ndibe is the author of the novel *Arrows of Rain* (2000), a condemnatory expose of crime and corruption in an African state. It is set in the fictional state of Madia ruled by the despotic General Isa Palat Bello, but few readers will have any difficulty identifying the referents as Nigeria and the bloody tyrant General Sani Abacha, respectively. The novel continues in fictional form the uncompromising criticisms Ndibe has leveled at Nigeria's military dictators and the civilian administration of Olusegun Obasanjo. The story takes off from a young woman's death by drowning in which the dictator is implicated, with the connivance of corrupt law enforcement and judiciary systems, and documents the remorseful suicide by hanging of a man who chose silence over speaking truth to tyrannical power. Ndibe acknowledged his debt to Wole Soyinka, especially to his *The Man Died*, in which he argues that silence in the face of tyranny is moral death.

In its October 2001 special edition on "New Fiction from the South," the British magazine *New Internationalist* named *Arrows of Rain* as one of the most remarkable novels published the previous year.

Ndu, Pol Nnamuzikam (1940–76) Pol Ndu, an Igbo poet was born on November 14, 1940, in Eastern Nigeria. He attended the University of Nsukka, where he later taught until 1967. After the Nigerian civil war he worked for his PhD in Afro-American Literature in the SUNY system, and on obtaining his degree he taught at the University of Vermont, where he served as director of the Living and Learning Center from 1975 to 1976. He returned to Nigeria later that year, but he died shortly thereafter in an automobile accident.

First published in *Black Orpheus*, his poetry was also included in the revised edition of *Modern Poetry from Africa* (1968), edited by Gerald Moore and Ulli Beier. He authored two poetry collections, *Golgotha* (1971) and *Songs for Seers* (1974), whose title poem he dedicated to Christopher Okigbo. His poetry shows the marked influence of the older poet, and many believe both poets to have been cast in the same mold. In 1964, while teaching at Nsukka, he appeared briefly in David Schickele's film about the Peace Corps, *Give Me a Riddle*.

Noma Award The Noma Award for Publishing in Africa was established in 1979 by Shoichi Noma (d. 1984), president of the Japanese publishing house Kodansha as a means of alleviating what he perceived as the acute book needs of Africa and of encouraging the publication of works by African authors and on the African continent. The Noma Award attracts hundreds of entries each year, and the high standard it has maintained has made its endorsement of any work a guarantee of that work's international success. One of the most prestigious prizes any African writer could covet, it is administered from a secretariat in Oxford through an endowment registered with the UK Charities Commission as a charitable trust. The jury, which meets annually, is assisted by a panel of scholars on the basis of whose advice it determines the winner, as well as works worthy of special commendation and honorable mention. The presentation of the Noma Award takes place annually at a special ceremony, usually in Africa, at appropriate book-related forums such as book fairs, and enlisting distinguished African personalities to make the presentation.

Works in three categories are eligible for the competition, which carries a monetary prize of $10,000: scholarly or academic books, books for children, and literature and creative writing. These may be written in any of the languages in use in Africa, both African and European. The winner (sometimes joint winners) and the publisher receive commemorative plaques. The first award of the Noma was made in 1980; it went to the Senegalese novelist Mariama Bâ for *Une si longue lettre* (1979; *So Long a Letter*, 1981), the first of her two published works.

Nwankwo, Nkem (1936–) Nkem Nwankwo was born in 1936 in Nawfia-Awka, a village near the Igbo metropolis of Onitsha. He studied English at the University of Ibadan, earning a BA in 1962. After graduation he took a teaching job at the Ibadan Grammar School, but he soon moved from teaching to working in the media, for *Drum* magazine and the Nigerian Broadcasting Corporation. He spent the civil war years in the rebel Biafran area, serving on the rebel republic's Arts Council, and in 1968 he wrote *Biafra: The Making of a Nation* in collaboration with Samuel X. Ifejika. At the end of the conflict he returned to Lagos and took a job with the national newspaper *Daily Times*. In 1973 he visited the African Studies Center at Michigan State University as writer-in-residence, and afterward enrolled at Indiana University, where he studied for his MA and PhD. He teaches at Tennessee State University, in Nashville.

While a student at the University College, Ibadan (now University of Ibadan), in 1960, Nwankwo won a prize from *Encounter* for a play he had written. Thus encouraged, he wrote several stories for children that were published in *Tales Out of School* (1963) and *More Tales Out of School* (1965). His biggest success came, though, with the publication of his novel *Danda* in 1963 by African Universities Press in Lagos. It was such a popular success that André Deutsch picked it up the following year. The story, told in lively and witty language, is about the irrepressibly gay but irresponsible Danda, a chief's son who would rather drink and frolic than do an honest day's work. The hero is so engaging, for all his foibles, that the story was made into an equally popular musical that has seen wide performances in Nigeria, and it was entered in the Festival of Negro Arts in Dakar in 1966. A second novel, *My Mercedes Is Bigger Than Yours* (1975), satirizes the new elite and their obsession with the automobile as status symbol, although a most precarious one. His third novel, *The Scapegoat*, a critique of life in modern Nigeria, was published in 1984.

FURTHER READING

Ezenwa-Ohaetu. "Nkem Nwankwo." In *Perspectives on Nigerian Literature: 1700 to the Present*, ed. Yemi Ogunbiyi, 2:106–11. Lagos: Guardian Books, 1988.

Taiwo, Oladele. *Culture and the Nigerian Novel.* New York: St. Martin's Press, 1976.

Nwapa, Flora (1931–93) Florence Nwanzuruahu Nkiru Nwapa was born on January 18, 1931, in Oguta in eastern Nigeria. Both of her parents were teachers. She was one of the early graduates of the University College, Ibadan (now University of Ibadan), earning a BA in 1957. Nwapa also received a diploma in education from the University of Edinburgh before embarking on an educational career in 1958.

On her return to Nigeria from Edinburgh she worked for a year as an education officer in the ministry of education at Calabar, and in 1959 she was transferred to Queen's School, Enugu, where she taught English and geography. She became the assistant registrar in charge of public relations at the University of Lagos in 1962. After the Nigerian civil war she was the commissioner for health and social welfare for the East Central State from 1970 to 1975, and later commissioner for lands, survey, and urban development.

When Heinemann published her first novel *Efuru* in 1966, Flora Nwapa became the first woman on its list. Historians of African literature often see her as the female counterpart to her fellow Igbo writer, Chinua Achebe—that is, as the female pioneer of modern African literature, although some dispute her claim to that honor. Nonetheless, as the first major female writer she set the pattern for later women authors, especially with her concentration on women's experiences, which early male writers have been accused of ignoring. Indeed, critics often cite her representation of women engaging in dialogue with one another rather than working through problems in isolation, for example in her early fiction *Idu* (1969), as an approach that distinguishes African women's writing from male writers.

Both *Efuru* and *Idu* are named for their heroines, beautiful, industrious, and successful women who have the misfortune of being barren in a society that places a great store on having children. Efuru, childless after two unhappy marriages, abandons the married life and finds happiness and fulfillment in her dedication to the childless goddess of the lake, Uhamiri. Idu is similarly beset with barrenness after her first child, but even after the misfortune ends, she shows that her attachment to her husband transcends motherhood and survives his death.

Nwapa, who would not accept descriptions of her or her work as feminist, differed markedly from some of the women writers who came after her in representing women as powerful agents rather than as doormats for men. Her female characters, both the ones drawn from folkloric models and the ones she created in her own imagination, are independent and capable of achieving success outside the roles conventionally assumed for women.

Although her first works followed the pattern Achebe set in his early novels, that of locating stories in traditional Igbo communities, the better to explore traditional ways, beliefs, and relationships, Nwapa also wrote works set in urban areas, such as the novels *One Is Enough* (1981) and *Women Are Different* (1986), and the short-story collection *This Is Lagos and Other Stories* (1971). In such works she dealt with the debilitating impact of modernity on mores and morals, which result in such things as official corruption and promiscuity. She also wrote about the civil war and its impact on women in *Never Again* (1981) and *Wives at War and Other Stories* (1980).

Nwapa became involved in publishing because of her dissatisfaction with the efforts that Heinemann, who published her earliest works, devoted to publicizing and marketing them. She founded her own publishing company, Tana Press, in 1974. Three years later she established another, Flora Nwapa Books, which specialized in works for children, for example *Mummywater* (1979). In these she drew upon folk materials for the entertainment and instruction of children. She also wrote poems and stories for children, such as *Cassava Song and Rice Song* (1986) and *The Adventures of Deke* (1980), respectively.

Beyond her accomplishments as a writer, Nwapa also contributed to our understanding of the woman's place and role in traditional communities as well as in modern society. Apart from her insistence that traditional women had viable agency in their own right, she also differed from later women writers and critics with regard to some of their assertions about their plight. Whereas some explain the relative sparseness of women's writing in comparison with men's during the early stages of African literature as resulting from women's inability to find the time to write, Nwapa said by contrast that she took up writing because on her first job she found herself with little to do after the workday, and she needed to do something to fill the idle hours. That assertion would not deny that some women might indeed have too much to do to find the time for writing, but it would suggest that, even if such a plight was peculiar to women, it was not a general condition.

In 1982, the Nigerian government honored Nwapa with the Order of the Niger, one of the country's highest honors, and her native town of Oguta conferred on her the ultimate chieftaincy title Ogbuefi, a title that traditionally recognized men of the highest achievement. She died on October 16, 1993.

FURTHER READING

Ezeigbo, Theodora Akachi. "Traditional Women's Institutions in Igbo Society: Implications for the Igbo Female Writer." *African Languages and Cultures* 3, no. 2 (1990): 149–65.

Ikonné, Chidi. "The Society and Woman's Quest for Selfhood in Flora Nwapa's Early Novels." *Kunapipi* 6, no. 1 (1984): 68–78.

James, Adeola. "Flora Nwapa." *In Their Own Voices: African Women Writers Talk*, 111–17. London: James Currey, 1990.

Ogunyemi, Chikwenye Okonjo. *Africa Wo/Man Palava: The Nigerian Novel by Women*. Chicago: University of Chicago Press, 1996.

Umeh, Marie. *Emerging Perspectives on Flora Nwapa: Critical and Theoretical Essays*. Trenton, NJ: Africa World Press, 1998.

O

Obafemi, Olu (1948–) The dramatist Olu Obafemi was born in Akutukpa Bunu, Kabba, in Kogi State, Nigeria. His elementary education was in Kabba, after which he went to the Provincial Secondary School in Dekina, and later to the Pitkum College, Egbe. He studied English for his BA at Ahmadu Bello University, Zaria. After teaching for a while at the University of Ilorin he proceeded to the University of Sheffield for an MA in English, and thence to the University of Leeds for his PhD, returning to Nigeria in 1981. He teaches at the University of Ilorin and is the founder of the Ajum Players. He held the office of chairman of the Association of Nigerian Authors (ANA) Kwara State, and in 2004 he became the national president of the association.

Obafemi began writing seriously as an undergraduate at Ahmadu Bello, and also was the editor of a literary magazine. His first play, *Pestle on the Mortar*, was produced in 1974 and also broadcast by the Kaduna Broadcasting Corporation. He has published a number of plays, among them *Nights of a Mystical Beast* and *The New Dawn* in 1986 and *Suicide Syndrome* and *Naira Has No Gender* in 1993. The first of these employs mythological devices to address the social problems confronting postindependence Nigeria, while the second looks forward to their amelioration. His works all reflect the social consciousness and activist tendencies that have characterized the writings of the generation of writers and scholars who came to the fore in the country in the 1980s. His writing, according to him, has been an exploration of the question, "Why should the society be organized in such a way that so many people can be suffering while a few have so much to waste?"

Although his works have been performed in Britain as well as in Nigeria, he writes primarily for Nigerians, seeking not to denounce those responsible for the country's privations but to explore ways to correct the problems. And although he considers himself a dramatist, he has also published a volume of poems, *Songs of Hope*, two of its poems being included in the Joint Admission and Matriculation Board (JAMB) syllabus. His scholarly works include *Nigerian Writers on the Nigerian Civil War* (1992), and *Contemporary Nigerian Theatre: Cultural Heritage and Social Vision* (1996). He also edited *New Introduction to Literature* (1994), and, in collaboration with Wole Ogundele and Femi Abodunrin, *Character Is Beauty: Redefining Yoruba Culture & Identity* (2001).

Ofeimun, Odia (1950–) Odia Ofeimun was born in Irhukpen, Nigeria, on March 15, 1950. He studied political science at the University of Ibadan and once served as private secretary to the late statesman and politician Chief Obafemi Awolowo. He is credited with inaugurating of the pattern of giving substantial attention and coverage to serious poetry in the nation's newspapers during his tenure as the editor for the culture page of the *Guardian* (Lagos). He has also served both as secretary-general and president of the Association of Nigerian Authors.

The group of writers that includes him, the poets Niyi Osundare and Funso Aiyejina, and the dramatist Femi Osofisan, constitutes the generation that according to critics immediately succeeded that of Wole Soyinka, Christopher Okigbo, and John Pepper Clark-Bekederemo, while others place him in a younger generation than Osundare's. The influences that formed his consciousness include the civil war, which soured the promises of independence for his generation, his difficult experiences as a factory laborer and clerk, and later as a party functionary. Such experiences explain his radical politics, and the commitment of his poetry to championing the cause of the underclass. Inasmuch as he is not a Yoruba, his alignment with, and service under, Awolowo, who was a prominent Yoruba (and national) politician in the heyday of ethnic consciousness in Nigerian politics, both testified to and reinforced his commitment to the Nigerian nation, above any parochial allegiance.

His first collection of poems, *The Poet Lied* (1980), was a direct response to the civil war and its attendant civil and political strife, the succession of devastating military dictatorships and the corruption that the country's oil boom fueled. It addresses the collective trauma without indulging in personal or solipsistic sentiments, and it acknowledges the pain and suffering on both sided of the Biafran conflict. The title poem was widely believed to be a chastisement of Clark-Bekederemo's *Casualties*, itself a response to the civil war, but full of the poet's lamentation about personal losses. Clark-Bekederemo lent credence to the supposition by threatening to sue the book's publisher, because he claimed that the title poem referred to him and damaged his reputation. The effect was to have the book withdrawn from circulation. Other volumes by Ofeimun are *A Handle for the Flutist and Other Poems* (1986), *Under African Skies* (1990), and *London Letter and Other Poems* (2000).

Ofeimun has lately been appointed the chairman of the editorial board of the Independent Communications Network.

FURTHER READING

Amuta, Chidi. *The Theory of African Literature: Implications for Practical Criticism*. London: Zed Books, 1989.

Oguibe, Olu (1964–) Olu Oguibe is by training and profession an artist—a painter, sculptor, and photographer—who enjoys an enviable international reputation in that pursuit. Literature is a sideline for him, but one in which he has also earned some distinction.

Born on October 14, 1964, in Aba, Nigeria, he studied at the University of Nigeria, Nsukka, receiving his BA in fine and applied arts in 1986, after a brief suspension from university for his activities as secretary general of the University of Nigeria Students Union from 1983 to 1985. After graduating he taught painting and drawing at the Ogun State College of Education, Abeokuta, and in 1987 he passed up an offer to study at Harvard, returning instead to the University of Nigeria to undertake a combined master's and doctoral program with a concentration in art history. He quit the program, though, after a year and a half, and soon thereafter, in 1989, accepted a potential leaders' scholarship from the British Foreign and Commonwealth Office to pursue a PhD in contemporary and African art at London University's School of Oriental and African Studies. He earned the degree in 1992 and has since held several teaching appointments in universities and colleges, including the School of Oriental and African Studies, where he taught African literature. He joined the art history faculty of the University of Illinois in 1995, and later moved to the University of Connecticut.

Oguibe's versatility is remarkable, and both his tone and style have led critics to compare him to Christopher Okigbo. His poetry publications include *A Song from Exile* (1990), *A Gathering Fear* (1992), and *Songs for Catalina* (1994). He wrote *A Song from Exile* in London during the fall and early winter of 1989 shortly after arriving in England. It is about the poet's anguish as a result of his exile, his yearnings for home, and his concerns about the troubled state of affairs in his country. The poems collected in *A Gathering Fear* were written between 1988 and 1992, partly in Nigeria and partly in

England. The most celebrated piece is "I am bound to this land," which according to the poet has become a generational anthem in Nigeria. The collection won the All-Africa Chris Okigbo Prize for 1992 and an honorable mention in the Noma Awards competition the following year. The poems in *Songs for Catalina* were all composed during a two-week spell in London during the summer of 1993 after the poet returned from a trip to Mexico. They are in celebration of Catalina Ferrera, a young woman he met in Guadalajara during the trip. In addition to those in his books, his poems have also appeared in numerous journals, including *Poetry Wales*, *Wasafiri*, and *West Africa* magazine.

Oguibe is the editor of *Sojourners: New Writing by Africans in Britain* (1994), and in 1995 his interview by Pitika Ntuli was published as *The Battle for South Africa's Mind: Towards a Post-Apartheid Culture*. He also serves on the boards of *Third Text*, *Social Identities*, *Atlantica*, and the literary journal *Wasafiri*. His collection of critical essays, *The Culture Game*, was published in 2003.

Ogundipe, Omolara (1941–) Abiodun Molara Ogundipe, who started her professional life as Omolara Ogundipe-Leslie, was born in 1941 at Abeokuta in the Ogun State of western Nigeria. She attended Queen's School, Ede, for her secondary education, and in 1958 she was admitted to University College, Ibadan (now University of Ibadan), where she earned a BA with first-class honors in 1963. She lived and taught in universities in the United States for a few years before returning to Nigeria in 1973 as a lecturer and assistant professor of English at the University of Ibadan. She remained at the university, with brief interruptions to accept visiting appointments in the United States, until 1983, when she was called upon to inaugurate the English department of the newly created Ogun State University. Beginning from 1990

she again took a variety of university professorships in the United States, Canada, and South Africa, while also working for a PhD in literary theory and comparative literature from Leiden University in the Netherlands. She has continued to share her time among universities on different continents.

Although a well regarded poet whose poems have been widely anthologized, Ogundipe is better known as an activist on behalf of women's empowerment, a subject on which she has written and spoken widely. She is committed to Marxism and has no reticence about identifying herself as a feminist. Her one anthology of poems thus far, *Sew the Old Days and Other Poems* (1985), is an excellent record of her dedication to the woman's cause. He overriding preoccupation in the poems is the plight of women, specifically Nigerian women—their treatment by Nigerian men, and the restricted opportunities available to them for participating in nation building. In making her case she takes advantage of her close knowledge of Yoruba rhetorical and cultural resources, proverbs for example, and her mastery of literary form and style.

In 1995 she published a collection of her essays, *Recreating Ourselves: African Women and Critical Transformation.*

FURTHER READING

Maduakor, Obi. "Female Voices in Poetry: Catherine Acholonu and Molara Ogundipe-Leslie." In *Nigerian Female Writers*, ed. Henrietta Otokunefo and Obiageli Nwodo, 75–91. Lagos: Malthouse Press, 1989.

Ohaeto-Ezenwa. "The Other Voices: The Poetry of Three Nigerian Female Writers." *Canadian Journal of African Studies* 22, no. 3 (1988): 662–68.

Ojaide, Tanure (1948–) Tanure Ojaide was born on April 24, 1948, in Okpara Inland in what used to be Midwest of Nigeria, now Bendel State, and was raised by his mother

Amreghe. He did his secondary schooling in northern Nigeria before entering the University of Ibadan for his BA. He later went to Syracuse University for his MA and PhD, then returned to Nigeria and taught for ten years at the University of Maiduguri. He has been a fellow of the University of Iowa's writing program and also a fellow of the Headlands Center for the Arts in Sausalito, California, as well as a visiting professor of English at Whitman College in Walla Walla, Washington. From 1996 to 1997 he was the NEH professor of humanities at Albright College in Reading, Pennsylvania. He later joined the faculty of the African American and African studies department at the University of North Carolina at Charlotte as a professor. In 2007 he became the Frank Porter Graham Distinguished Professor at the University.

Widely acknowledged as one of the most talented of African poets in the generation following that of Wole Soyinka and Christopher Okigbo, the prolific Ojaide has published several volumes of poetry, an autobiography—*Great Boys: An African Childhood* (1998), a study of traditional performances—*Poetry, Art, and Performance: Udje Dance Songs of the Urhobo People* (2003), and some critical essays, including *The Poetry of Wole Soyinka* (1994) and *Poetic Imagination in Black Africa: Essays on African Poetry* (1996). While his range is broad and his subjects eclectic, he is primarily a poet-activist against the ills that bedevil his country and the larger human community. In titles such as *The Eagle's Vision* (1987), *The Fate of Vultures and Other Poems* (1990), and *Daydream of Ants and Other Poems* (1997), he spells out his perception of his society (and the human community at large) and the role of the poet in it.

Ojaide sees in his country a state of affairs in which the strong victimize the weak, in which self-serving politicians enrich themselves at the nation's expense and military impostors tyrannize the defenseless public. Moreover, in addition to spectacles of humans treating one another with inhumanity, he also records and decries their abuse and pollution of the environment as they exploit its resources and in the process impoverish the people who have to live in it. He also bemoans the estrangement of the present generation from traditional values in a land "where everybody is a king."

Labyrinths of the Delta (1986), whose title recalls Christopher Okigbo's *Labyrinths*, and *Delta Blues and Home Songs* (1998) also testify to a shared attachment between the two poets—to the indigenous culture (in this case Urhobo) and its mythology. Similar to Okigbo's invocation of Idoto, for instance, Ojaide appeals to Aridon, the God of Memory, for the retrieval of stolen wealth from the "rogue-vaults" to which corrupt officials have secreted it. Although he pays homage to Okigbo, though, and despite some similarity in their themes and referents, his poetry is not nearly as self-consciously opaque as Okigbo's. Rather, it is "strong, supple, various, colorful, moving, invariably interesting" (according to a Hayden Carruth blurb), as well as unpretentious and "prosaic" in its accessibility. The 1998 collection of a large number of his poems, *Invoking the Warrior Spirit,* is a sort of retrospective of his oeuvre from his student days up to that point, and a good record of the poet's preoccupations as well as of his development, from his apprentice days to his maturity. In *I Want to Dance and Other Poems* (2003), which is presented as a song cycle, the poet journeys through time and space, absorbing myriads of experiences between setting forth and returning home. Another volume of poetry, *In the House of Words*, followed in 2005.

Ojaide has been honored with many awards: the Commonwealth Poetry Prize in 1987, the All-Africa Okigbo Prize for Poetry awarded by the Association of Nigerian Authors (ANA) in 1988, and the BBC Arts and Africa Poetry Award for same year.

FURTHER READING

Ogede, Ode S. "Tanure Ojaide. *Poetic Imagination in Black Africa: Essays on African Poetry*." *Research in African Literatures* 29, no. 2 (1998): 230–31.

Olafioye, Tayo. *The Poetry of Tanure Ojaide*. Oxford: African Books Collective, 1999.

Sallah, Tijan M. "The Eagle's Vision: The Poetry of Tanure Ojaide." *Research in African Literatures* 26, no. 1 (Spring 1995): 20–29.

Okai, Atukwei (1941–) Atukwei Okai was born in 1941 in Accra, Ghana, and grew up in the northern part of the country. After receiving his early education in Ghana, he went to the Gorky Literary Institute in Moscow, where he received his MA in literature in 1967. On returning to Ghana, he received a University of Ghana scholarship to study for a MPh degree at London University, and in 1968 he became a Fellow of the Royal Society of Arts (UK). Since 1971, when he joined the Institute of African Studies at the University of Ghana, Legon, he has taught at that university, and has held such positions as senior research fellow in African literature and head of the language, literature, and drama unit.

Okai's widely anthologized poetry, which has appeared in numerous international journals such as *The New African Okyeame*, *The New American Review*, *The Atlantic Monthly*, *Black World*, and *Literary Cavalcade*, is noted for its musicality. Fellow Ghanaian poet Kofi Anyidoho describes him as "a poet-cantor with a priest-like function," one whose perception of the reality around him "fills his soul with inner tensions" because of what he perceives as a lack of community and communion among people, and a distancing of people from God. His performances of his poetry are always histrionic and electrifying, accompanied with drumming, dancing, and chanting. His bold experimentation and his efforts to fit African material into the English language in such poems as "Tinkongkong! Ayawaso," in his collected poems *Longorligi Logarithms and Other Poems* (1974), have won him enthusiastic praise from some critics and impatient dismissal from others. While the Nigerian dramatist Femi Osofisan praised him for his percussiveness and deliberate violation of English syntax and lexicon, for example, his fellow Ghanaian K. K. Dei-Annang dismissed him as having been led by hubris "from writing poems *in* Africa into the fatal wish to write '*African*' poetry." Few, though, would question his significance as a poet. His other poetry collections are *Flowerfall* (1969), *The Oath of the Fontomfrom and Other Poems* (1971), and *The Anthill in the Sea: Verses and Chants for Children* (1988).

Okai was actively involved in the formation of the Ghana Association of Writers and was its long-term president (from 1971 to 1991). In 1989 he became the secretary general of the Pan-African Writers' Association (PAWA), effectively the director of the association's affairs, and he has retained the position ever since. PAWA has its headquarters, PAWA House, in Accra, Ghana. Among the honors that he has won are the Iqbal Centenary Commemorative Gold Medal awarded by the government of Pakistan in 1979, and the 1980 International Lotus Prize and Gold Medal of Italy's National Council for Research.

FURTHER READING

Anyidoho, Kofi. "Atukwei Okai and His Poetic Territory." In *Ghanaian Literatures*, ed. Richard K. Priebe, 135–50. New York: Greenwood Press, 1988.

Fraser, Robert, *West African Poetry: A Critical History*. Cambridge: Cambridge University Press, 1986.

Okara, Gabriel (1921–) Gabriel Imomotimi Gbaingbain Okara was born in Bomadi in the Ijo area of Nigeria on April 21, 1921. He attended Government College, Umuahia, and studied journalism at Northwestern University from 1956 to 1959. On his return to Nigeria he took a job as principal information officer in the Eastern Nigeria Ministry of Information. When the Nigerian civil war broke out he joined forces with the Biafrans and worked for the secessionist republic as an information officer. In that capacity he accompanied Chinua Achebe to the United States in 1969 to solicit funds to aid the Biafrans. After the war, he headed the Rivers State Broadcasting Corporation and served as editor of the newspaper, *Nigerian Tide*. He retired in 1975 and became the writer-in-residence for the Rivers State Council for Arts and Culture.

Okara had won the poetry prize in the Nigerian Festival of the Arts in 1953, and he had his debut in print in 1957 in the pages of *Black Orpheus*. He has subsequently been anthologized in a number of books and magazines in Africa and elsewhere. His poems reflect on the impact that the meeting of East and West has had on Africans, much of it detrimental, as he shows in such poems as "Once Upon a Time." He also attempts to forge a synthesis of the two cultural elements, African and Western, as in his poetic account of an African dreaming of Africa while watching snowflakes fall gently down in London, and the poetic blending of piano and drums in harmonious music. *The Fisherman's Invocation*, which was published by Heinemann in 1978 and offers readers a collection of his early poetry, was the joint winner of the Commonwealth Poetry Prize for that year.

Okara believes that an African writer, regardless of what language he or she writes in, must give priority to African thought, philosophy, folklore, and imagery to the full-est possible extent, and that only by literal translation of African expressions into whatever foreign language the African writer is using can he or she effectively communicate them to the reader. His own method of accomplishing that end has been to train himself to stop thinking in English in the first instance, but think instead in his native Ijo. The result is most vividly evident in Okara's one novel, *The Voice* (1964), the story of the rebel Okolo, who takes it upon himself to question the wayward habits of his community. Okara narrates, in English forced into Ijo syntax, Okolo's principled and ultimately fatal search for the mysterious "it." Coming as early as it did in the development of modern Anglophone African writing, many critics believed that it would lead to further bold experimentation in finding viable African alternatives to unalloyed Europhonism, but the trail he blazed has proved a dead end.

Okara's output since the end of the war is slim; unfortunately, he did not pursue the experimentation he began in *The Voice*, but he did produce works for children, like *Little Snake and the Frog* and *An Adventure to Juju Island*, both published 1981.

FURTHER READING

Lindfors, Bernth. "Interview with Gabriel Okara." *Dem-Say: Interviews with Eight Nigerian Writers*, 41–47. Austin: African and Afro-American Studies and Research Center, University of Texas, 1974.
Scott, Patrick. "Gabriel Okara's *The Voice*: The Non-Ijo Reader and the Pragmatics of Translingualism." *Research in African Literatures* 21, no. 3 (Fall 1990): 75–88.
Taiwo, Oladele. *Culture and the Nigerian Novel*. New York: St. Martin's Press, 1976.

Okigbo, Christopher (1932–67) Christopher Ifeanyichukwu Okigbo, a member of the first generation of famous Nigerian writers that includes Chinua Achebe, Wole Soyinka, and Flora Nwapa, was born on August

16, 1932, in Ojoto, in the Onitsha province of the former Eastern Nigeria. His father, Chief James Okoye Okigbo, and his mother, Anna Onugwalobi Okigbo, were both Catholic (his father being a teacher in the Catholic school system), while his grandfather was a priest of the river goddess Idoto. He had his primary education at the Umulobia Catholic School, and in 1945 he was admitted to Government College, Umuahia, for his secondary education. He later gained admission to the University College, Ibadan (now University of Ibadan), to study medicine, but on enrolling he switched to the classics. He received his BA in 1956 and thereupon embarked on sampling a series of occupations, apparently in an effort to determine his true calling. He taught at a grammar school at Fiditi in Western Nigeria and later was an assistant librarian at the new University of Nigeria, Nsukka. He left the position to work at the Nigerian Tobacco Company, thence to the United Africa Company, from where he moved to the federal civil service in Lagos as private secretary to the federal minister of information, and then in 1962 he became the West Africa manager for Cambridge University Press. He also served for a while as editor for the Mbari Press in Ibadan.

While a student at Ibadan, Okigbo showed an interest in translating Greek and Latin poetry, some of which he published along with his own poems in the *Horn*, a student magazine then edited by John Pepper Clark (Bekereremo). It was in 1958, though, that he decided that his chief calling in life was to write poems, and he responded by placing his poems in journals such as *Transition* and *Black Orpheus*, among others. In 1962 he published a pamphlet of poems entitled *Heavensgate*, the first entry of which began with a returning prodigal's invocation of "mother Idoto" (a village stream that in the poem stood for nature and indigenous cultures). The work bears testimony

to his classical education and Catholic background, and it also shows some influence of Igbo mythology.

Heavensgate is mainly about the poet's religious experiences and betrays little preoccupation with political or social problems; *Limits* (1964) also deals with religion, but with art and culture as well. In *Silences* (1965) Okigbo turns his attention to politics, expressing his misgivings and anxiety about events in the country and internationally. These themes continue to preoccupy the poet in *Path of Thunder: Poems Prophesying War* (1967), which contains attacks on colonialists' as well as corrupt politicians' exploitation and foresees the debacle that in fact occurred soon after its publication. By the time of its appearance the war over Biafra's attempt to secede had broken out, and Okigbo enlisted on the Biafran side, where he was given the rank of major. Refusing an administrative job, he opted for combat, and a mere month after his enlistment he was killed near Nsukka in one of the first skirmishes of the war. He received the Biafran National Order of Merit posthumously.

Before he died, Okigbo made a selection of the poems he wished to be remembered by; they were published by Heinemann in 1971 as *Labyrinths*, with the inclusion of *Path of Thunder*. Heinemann also published a volume of his poems as *Collected Poems* in 1986. The poetry typically showcases the influences of his Catholic religion, his classical education, and his familial closeness to traditional deities. That combination makes his poetry as a whole taxing to most readers, especially because it also includes allusions to the poet's private experiences that no reader can decipher without some help from the poet himself. In spite of its difficulty, it is delightful and appealing because of a musicality that recalls traditional singing and suggests that the poet intended his verses to be sung.

Okigbo's output was small because he died so early; but on the strength of what he wrote, much of which was of course published posthumously, he enjoys a reputation as one of the best poets the continent has produced. Already in his lifetime, he had won the Langston Hughes Award, the first prize for poetry, at the 1966 Dakar Festival of African Arts, which he rejected because it was designated for the best *African* poet, while he preferred not to be so pigeonholed.

FURTHER READING

Achebe, Chinua, and Dubem Okafor, eds. *Don't Let Him Die.* Enugu: Fourth Dimension, 1978.

Anozie, Sunday O. *Christopher Okigbo: Creative Rhetoric.* New York: Africana, 1972.

Fido, Elaine Savory. "Okigbo's *Labyrinths* and the Context of Igbo Attitudes to the Female Principle." In *Ngambika: Studies of Women in African Literature,* ed. Carole Boyce Davies and Anne Adams Graves, 223–39. Trenton, NJ: Africa World, 1986.

Okoye, Ifeoma (1937?–) Born in Anambra State in eastern Nigeria, Ifeoma Okoye attended St. Monica's College, Ogbunike, from which she earned a teaching certificate in 1959. She taught at the school from 1960 to 1961, and from 1963 to 1967 at All Saints International School, Enugu. From 1971 to 1974 she ran her own nursery school in Enugu, and in 1974 she enrolled at the University of Nigeria, Nsukka, graduating in 1977 with a BA honors degree in English. She was a postgraduate student in English at Aston University in England from 1986 to 1987, and after completing her course there she took a teaching job at the Institute of Management and Technology, Enugu. In October 1992 she transferred to Nnamdi Azikiwe University at Awka, and remained with that institution until August 2000. She subsequently moved to Enugu.

Okoye began her career writing for children about children, because she was dismayed at the paucity of works that both addressed their experiences and were produced for them. Among her early works in that genre are *The Adventures of Tulu the Little Monkey, Eme Goes to School,* and *Only Bread for Eze* (all 1980) and *The Village Boy* (1981). In 1982 she published her first work for adults, *Behind the Clouds,* a vehement denunciation of the tendency to blame a couple's failure to have children on the woman even when the failure might be on the man's part. The Nigerian National Council for Arts and Culture honored her in 1983 with prizes for both *The Village Boy* and *Behind the Clouds.* In 1985, *Only Bread for Eze* also received an award at the Ife International Book Fair. A later novel, *Men Without Ears* (1984), about the greed that pervaded the country in the oil-boom years, earned her the Association of Nigerian Authors prize for the best fiction of the year, and in 1999 she was joint winner (with South Africa's Esther Zondo and Peggy Verbaan) of the 1999 Commonwealth Short Story Competition for the Africa Region for her short story "Waiting for a Son." Her *Chimere* (1992) is a detective novel in which a young student who does not know who her father is reacts to her colleagues' mockery by embarking on a search for him against the wishes of her mother. With it Okoye combats the opprobrium that society directs at "illegitimate" children.

Okoye has been described by admiring fans as the most important female novelist from Nigeria after Flora Nwapa and Buchi Emecheta, and as a consummate stylist whose language is characterized by delicacy, vigor, and confidence and whose plots are convincingly developed and resolved. Less admiring critics have, however, faulted her for heavy-handed feminist haranguing (as in *Behind the Clouds*), which some characterize as "adolescent" principally because of its blatant didacticism and lack of subtlety.

A work she announced about the difficulties widows face in Nigeria is yet to appear.

Okpewho, Isidore (Oghenerhuele) (1941–)
Born in Abraka in southern Nigeria, Isidore Okpewho was educated at St Patrick's College, Asaba, before he entered the University College, Ibadan, from which he received a BA Honors (First Class) in classics in 1964. He went on to the University of Denver to study comparative literature and earned his PhD in 1976. The University of London awarded him a doctor of letters in humanities in 2000.

Between 1974 and 1976, Okpewho was an assistant professor of English at State University of New York, Buffalo. From there he joined the faculty of the English department at the University of Ibadan as a lecturer. Having achieved the rank of full professor and served as chair of his department from 1987 to 1990, he left the university to spend a year as a visiting professor of English and American literature and language at Harvard University. From there he went to join the faculty of SUNY at Binghamton as professor of Africana studies, English, and comparative literature. He was chair of Africana studies from 1991 to 1997.

Okpewho is best known as the author of highly acclaimed scholarly works on the epic, oral literature, and modern literature in Africa, areas in which his impressive erudition in the classics and close familiarity with modern literary movements stand him in good stead. In his works on the epic and African oral literature he has insisted on correcting the tendency among non-African scholars to deny the existence of the epic in Africa, and to ignore the aesthetic dimensions of African oral narratives and poetry. His fictional works, for their part, have followed an evolutionary pattern that begins with the exploration of individual and domestic tragedies localized in an African village to the examination of large historical events encompassing the transatlantic slave trade and affecting families in both Africa and the United States. Thus *The Victims* (1970) dwells on the devastating consequences of superstition and distrust in a polygamous household, in which Nwabunor attributes her difficulty in having children to the diabolical machinations of Ogugua, her co-wife to Obanua. Her attempt to poison her co-wife's children backfires and destroys the family. *The Last Duty* (1976) is set in the context of the Biafran War, the bloody conflict serving as a backdrop against which Okpewho tells the story of interethnic intrigue and betrayal among a few men and a woman. While still at the manuscript state the novel was awarded the UCLA African Arts Prize in 1972; it has also been translated into French, Russian, Ukrainian, and Lithuanian.

Ethnic conflict also plays a prominent role in *Tides* (1993), a work that dramatizes the struggle of the people of the petroleum-producing Delta area of Nigeria to arrest the pollution and destruction of their streams and farms and secure some commensurate benefits from the exploration of their oil wealth. The experiences of the two journalists, whose correspondence between 1976 and 1978 constitutes the novel, recall the events that engulfed Ken Saro-Wiwa and cost him his life. The work won the 1993 Commonwealth Writers Prize for Africa.

Okpewho's most recent novel, *Call Me By My Rightful Name* (2004), is the story of Otis Hampton, a university student and outstanding basketball athlete in Boston, who suddenly at age twenty-one begins to suffer violent spasms at the sound of African drumming, and to declaim what seems to be poetry in a tongue nobody recognizes. Linguistic and psychiatric consultations result in a journey to a village in Western Nigeria where his true identity is disclosed: he is the reincarnation of a local hero betrayed by rivals and sold into slavery a long while back. Otis's declamations are garbled repetitions of the ritual poetry his ancestor was reciting when he was captured and enslaved. Otis, taking the new name Akimbowale, is instrumental in healing the schism in the community and restoring the rightful lineage to power. After two years in his adopted home he returns to the United States to resume normal life, but as a changed and more purposeful person. In this work Okpewho combines his expertise in folklore with his skills as a novelist to provide readers with a lesson in the functions of oral texts, for example as a source of information about undocumented past events, as well as their affective qualities.

Okpewho has received several honors, including fellowships from the Woodrow Wilson International Center for Scholars (1982), the Alexander von Humboldt Foundation (1982), the Center for Advanced Study in the Behavioral Sciences at Stanford (1988), the W. E. B. Du Bois Institute at Harvard (1990), the National Humanities Center in North Carolina (1997), and the Simon Guggenheim Memorial Foundation (2003). In 1993 the Finnish Academy of Science and Letters named him a full member of the Folklore Fellows International; in the same year he received a Guggenheim Fellowship and was awarded a distinguished professorship by the trustees of SUNY Binghamton. He was also the president of the International Society for Oral Literature in Africa (ISOLA) from 2004 to 2006, and he serves on the Research Advisory Council for Harvard's Center for the Study of World Religions and on the editorial boards of *Oral Tradition* and *Research in African Literatures*.

Okpewho is the editor of *The Heritage of African Poetry: An Anthology of Oral and Written Poetry* (1985); he has also published four scholarly works: *The Epic in Africa* (1979), *Myth in Africa* (1983), and *African Oral Literature* (1992), and *Once Upon a Kingdom: Myth, Hegemony, and*

Identity (1997). He also coedited the volume *The African Diaspora: African Origins and New World Identities* (1999), with Carole Boyce Davies and Ali A. Mazrui, and edited *Chinua Achebe's Things Fall Apart: A Casebook* (2003).

Okpi, Kalu (1947–) Kalu Okpi grew up in southern Nigeria and Cameroon, where he also received his early education. He joined the Biafran army on the outbreak of the civil war and served as an officer. After the conflict he attended New York University, receiving a BA in fine arts in 1974. He returned to Nigeria and took a job as a producer at the Eastern Nigeria Television Service. In 1977 he moved to the Nigeria Television Service, Enugu, as principal producer, and in 1981 he went to London for in-service training at the Television Training Institute and earned a diploma in television drama. In 1987 he moved to Lagos as chief writer for the Nigerian Television Service.

Okpi was one of the original authors for the Macmillan Pacesetter series of popular fiction, which was designed to appeal to affluent young readers. The imprint was a perfect match for him, since he considers writing as primarily a means of entertainment and has little interest in using it as a vehicle for changing people or society. Accordingly, he has refused to join the Association of Nigerian Authors because he considers it too highbrow and does not share its notions about the utilitarian functions of literature.

His first novel, *The Smugglers* (1977), a thriller about an undercover police operation to capture smugglers, is exemplary of his fiction. Among his many other works is the romance *Love* (1991), about the star-crossed lovers Nkem and Love, who were brought together at birth, separated by circumstances despite their love for each other, and reunited in death on the verge of finally finding the happiness that had eluded them in life. He is also the author of *Love Changes Everything* (1994), a novel for young adults.

In 1985 Okpi was the recipient of the African Literature Prize awarded by Deutsche Welle Radio for his story "The Champion Wrestler."

Okri, Ben (1959–) Ben Okri was born in 1959 in Minna, Northern Nigeria, where his father worked as a civil servant. When Okri was eighteen months old he was taken to London, where his father was studying law on a scholarship. In London Okri attended John Donne Primary School, Peckham, an almost exclusively white school where he experienced racism for the first time. But he also developed an avid interest in English classical literature. He returned to Nigeria after five years (1966), and continued his education at the Children Home School, Ibadan, and later at the Mayflower Grammar School, Ikenne. Okri also attended Urhobo College, Warri, where he completed his secondary education in 1972.

Okri then moved to Lagos, where his father had set up his law practice, and studied by correspondence for a diploma in journalism. He also wrote for newspapers, attributing his gravitation to journalism to the anger he felt at the corruption of the politicians in Nigeria at the time. He had begun writing poetry when he was still very young, and had apparently also considered the graphic arts, but by the time he was fourteen, he told an interviewer, he had discovered that his talent was more oriented toward writing than graphics.

In his youth Okri often went to court with his father, who was determined that his son would inherit his law practice, and often sat through his father's interviews with clients in his chambers located in one of the poorer areas of the city. Okri thus became

familiar with different sorts of people in different kinds of circumstances, gaining thus a valuable asset for his later writing.

When he came to consider a university education, Okri thought he might study science, but he could not gain admission to any of the country's universities. He did win a government scholarship to study at the University of Essex, but it was later cancelled. He went to England nonetheless at the age of eighteen to live with an uncle in South London. By then he had completed the manuscript for *Flowers and Shadows*, which was later published in 1980. When his uncle's house was demolished he experienced homelessness and near-starvation, surviving on the charity of friends and by sleeping in railway stations.

Okri completed his studies at Essex University, taking a degree in comparative literature. For a while thereafter he worked as a broadcaster for the BBC and as poetry editor for *West Africa*, but his excessively high standards and consequently high rate of rejecting submissions left him with too few poems to publish, and the paucity caused him his job. He credits several factors for influencing his writing, among them the loneliness of studying at Warri, four hundred miles from his home in Lagos; the experience of the civil war; and the difficult years in England, which brought him nostalgia and fond recollections of the stories that are a prominent feature of African upbringing. All of these are reflected in his works, both in the early realistic novels and in the later works that have earned him a reputation as a leading magical realist among African writers.

Okri's early works of fiction, *Flowers and Shadows* and *The Landscapes Within* (1981), deal realistically with urban problems in modern Nigeria, in the first through the frustrations of the teacher Jeffia Okwe, and in the second through those of the idealistic painter Omovo. His transition from realism to magic realism resulted from a deliberate apprenticeship that he forced himself to undergo at a time when he believed that he had strayed too far into modernism, and realized that his ambition was better than his craft. He stopped writing full-length novels and honed his craft by writing short stories, which were published in *Incidents at the Shrine* (1986) and *Stars of the New Curfew* (1989). The stories collected in the two volumes are bold in their experimentation, and are typically African in their way of perceiving reality, especially in recognizing the continuity of the worlds of the living and the dead, of spirits and humans, and the seen and the unseen. His masterpiece after the apprenticeship, *The Famished Road* (1991), chronicles the experiences of Omovo, an *abiku*, one of those spirit-children believed to maintain contact with their playmates in the spirit world, and who cause their parents great grief by suddenly departing the world of humans to rejoin their spirit playmates. *Songs of Enchantment* (1993) continues in the same vein, although not as successfully as its predecessor.

Okri has earned enthusiastic accolades for his writing, as well as wide recognition and prestigious prizes. He has been both a fellow in creative arts and a visiting writer-in-residence at Trinity College, Cambridge University, and he has won, among several prizes, the 1987 Commonwealth Writer's Prize for Africa, the *Paris Review* Aga Khan Prize for fiction, and the prestigious Booker Prize in 1991 for *The Famished Road*.

FURTHER READING

McCabe, Douglas. "'Higher Realities': New Age Spirituality in Ben Okri's *The Famished Road*." *Research in African Literatures* 36, no. 4 (Winter 2005): 1–21.
Moh, Felicia Oka. *Ben Okri: An Introduction to His Early Fiction*. Enugu, Nigeria: Fourth Dimension Publishers, 2000.
Quayson, Ato. *Strategic Transformations in Nigerian Writing: Orality & History in the Work of Rev. Samuel Johnson, Amos Tutuola, Wole Soyinka & Ben Okri*. Oxford: Oxford University Press, 1997.
Ryan, Alan. "Talking with Ben Okri." *Newsday*, July 19, 1992.
Smith, Andrew. "Ben Okri and the Freedom Whose Walls Are Closing In." *Race & Class* 47, no. 11 (2005): 1–13.

Olafioye, Tayo Pete (1948–) Tayo Olafioye was born in Igbotako in the Yoruba area of Nigeria. He received his high school education at Christ's School, Ado-Ekiti, after which he did an Honors English course at the University of Lagos, earning his BA in 1968. He studied for an MA in English at the University of San Diego, graduating in 1971, later for a PhD in education at the University of Denver, which he received in 1974. He has taught at the University of Ilorin in Nigeria, San Diego State University, California State University, San Marcos, and National University and Southwestern College, San Diego.

Olafioye, a poet, novelist, and critic, is a prolific writer who has published at least nine volumes of poetry and three works of fiction—*The Saga of Sego* (1985), *Bush Girl Comes to Town* (1988), and *Grandma's Sun: Childhood Memoir* (2000)—as well as critical works and a collection of essays. Olafioye's works, most especially his poetry in such collections as *A Carnival of Looters* (2000) and *The Parliament of Idiots* (2002), responds with power and intensity to the disastrous turn of events in his country since independence, the squandering of the hopes and expectations people, Nigerians and non-Nigerians alike, had for the "Giant of Africa" now reduced to a dwarf by rapacious and murderous rulers. In addition to his preoccupation with the sociopolitical problems of his country he also deals with the plight of individuals struggling with private, personal choices, as in his novel *Bush Girl Comes to Town* (1988), a tale of African youths misplaced and misguided in California. Olafioye also communicates with his readers on his own personal experiences, as in *The Parliament of Idiots*, in which he mourns "the death of my two mothers: my biological mother Elizabeth Kehinde, and my natal mother, Nigeria." He lets his readers even more intimately into his experiences in *A Stroke of Hope* (2000), talking them through his harrowing struggle with prostate cancer, his fears and hopes—hopes of survival, but also, failing that, "hope to listen / To the sounds of paradise / If I make it there." Among his several other works are the poetry collections are *Ubangiji: The Conscience of Eternity* (2000); *Town Crier: Selected Poems* (2004); and *Tomorrow Left Us Yesterday* (2004).

Olafioye's critical works include *Critic as Terrorist* (1989) and *Tanure Ojaide: Critical Appraisal* (2000).

Omotoso, Kole (1943–) Bankole Ajibabi Omotoso was born on April 21, 1943, at Akure in the present-day Ondo State of western Nigeria. He attended King's College, Lagos for his secondary education, and the University of Ibadan for his undergraduate education, receiving his BA in French and Arabic in 1968. He later went to the University of Edinburgh to do graduate studies in Arabic literature, and received for his PhD in 1972. He taught Arabic and Islamic studies at the University of Ibadan from 1972 to 1976, and went on to head the department of dramatic arts and to direct the University Theatre at the University of Ife, Ile-Ife (now Obafemi Awolowo University), from 1976 to 1988. He was a visiting professor of English studies at the University of Stirling in Scotland from 1989 to 1990, and a visiting professor of English at the National University of Lesotho in 1990. The following year he worked at the Tawala Theatre in London, then moved to South Africa. He was an English professor at the University of the Western Cape from 1991 to 2000, and is currently a professor of drama at the University of Stellenbosch in Matieland.

Omotoso edited the students' literary magazine while he was a student at King's College, and was a contributor to the literary journal *Horizon* at the University of Ibadan. He was also for a while during the 1970s the literary editor for the Lagos-based news magazine *Afriscope*. He has published several novels and plays, as well as scholarly essays. His novels include *The Edifice* (1971), a tale about an interracial marriage between a Nigerian man and a white woman in England, and its unhappy ending back in Nigeria when the man presumably reverts to type; *The Combat* (1972), an allegory based on the civil war, in which two sides engage in combat for a prize that in the end eludes both; and *Fela's Choice* (1974), a detective novel. A later novel, *Just Before Dawn* (1988), is an epic fictionalization of Nigeria's history, especially during the 1970s and 1980s, but also including the colonial-era inauguration of the forces that would shape that history. *Memories of Our Recent Boom* (1990) is an autobiographical novel.

Omotoso also wrote the plays *The Curse* (1976) and *Shadows in the Horizon* (1977), both of which address the corruption and military dictatorships that have become endemic as a result of the oil boom in Nigeria, and short stories, some of which are collected in *Miracles and Other Stories* (1973). He is also the author of the critical study *Achebe or Soyinka: A Re-interpretation and a Study in Contrasts* (1995).

During his stint at the University of Ife he established himself as one of the socially conscious intellectuals who had a significant impact on the literary discourse in the country in the 1970s and 1980s.

FURTHER READING

Lindfors, Bernth. "Kole Omotoso Interviewed." *Dem-Say: Interviews with Eight Nigerian Writers*. Austin: African and Afro-American Studies and Research Center, University of Texas, 1974.

Msiska, Mpalive Hangson. "Cultural Dislocation and Gender Ideology in Kole Omotoso's *The Edifice*." *The Journal of Commonwealth Literature* 25, no. 1 (1990): 98–108.

Onitsha Market Literature Onitsha market literature is a literary and commercial phenomenon that originated at about the end of the Second World War and flourished until the mid-1970s. It was founded on the production of chapbooks on matters of interest to a new class of urban semiliterate readers, but by the time of its demise it could claim even sophisticated professionals with a high level of literacy among its producers and consumers. Indeed, the author commonly acknowledged as its pioneers, Cyprian Ekwensi, also straddles the divide between popular and highbrow literatures; while his pioneering work *When Love Whispers* (1947) clearly belongs in the popular genre, his most popular work, *Jagua Nana*, is undoubtedly in the literary mainstream, although it manifests a persistence of characteristics reminiscent of the popular genre.

The origin of the phenomenon has been attributed to the character of the town Onitsha at the time and the makeup of its residents. A bustling commercial center with what was regarded as the largest market in West Africa, it was home to a vigorously enterprising population of traders and artisans, many of them illiterate, and many with varying degrees of literacy. It was also a center of primary and secondary educational institutions whose products were employed in various capacities—as shop clerks, trade apprentices, trainee teachers, correspondents for local newspapers, and so forth. The pioneering writers for the popular market emerged from this group, and the group also provided the primary consumers.

Another factor that contributed to the birth of the literature was the return of demobilized soldiers who had fought in India and the Far East during the Second World War. They brought home with them wartime pulp literature that whetted the appetite of those who saw and read them. At about the same time the colonial government's sale of its old printing presses gave entrepreneurs the means to make reading materials available to the public cheaply and in large quantities, a boon to the city dwellers who had developed a taste for literary entertainment in a town that had no public library.

The year 1947 is generally recognized as ushering in the birth of the genre with the publication of Cyprian Ekwensi's novelette *When Love Whispers* and the collection of short stories *Ikolo the Wrestler and Other Igbo Tales*. The first Onitsha chapbooks were quite short, mostly with fewer than twenty pages, and they were hawked along the streets, at market stalls, bookstores, motor parks, and elsewhere. They dealt with a variety of subjects, ranging from love stories, crime stories, instructions on how to write love letters and win lovers, or on how to achieve success. So popular were they that people went to evening literacy schools simply to acquire the ability to read them, and illiterates purchased them and then paid professional "letter writers" to read them.

The literature was at its most popular between the years 1958 and 1962, years that straddled Nigeria's attainment of independence in 1960, when titles published averaged about fifty annually. It is perhaps not irrelevant that the phenomenon originated among the Igbo, one of whose members, Chinua Achebe, gave Anglophone Nigerian literature its greatest impetus with the publication of *Things Fall Apart* (1958). From Onitsha the market literature's influence spread to other Igbo towns like Aba, Enugu, Owerri, to towns in other, non-Igbo parts of Nigeria and Cameroon, and even farther to Accra and other Anglophone West African towns.

Developments in the country after independence inevitably affected the fortunes of Onitsha market literature. Shortly after emerging from colonialism Nigeria embarked on a course of history that would quickly dissipate the optimism and enthusiasm with which its citizens embraced freedom. Six years later the Biafran War broke out, a war that pitted the Igbo against the rest of the country, and that was fought largely on Igbo soil with devastating effects on the Igbo people. The war ended in January 1970, but one of the casualties was the bustling metropolitan and commercial center of Onitsha. And even though by the time the civil war broke out the Onitsha literature had ceased to be a local phenomenon, it is fair to say that it fared even worse than the city of its birth, for while Onitsha has made a significant comeback, the literature associated with it has not. One might also speculate that the increasing number of more sophisticated writers and publishing outlets, some Nigerian-owned and some foreign-owned, was responsible for pushing the market literature off the shelves. Whatever the case, the once-thriving popular tradition was virtually dead by the middle of the 1970s.

FURTHER READING

Lindfors, Bernth, ed. *Critical Perspectives on Nigerian Literatures.* Washington, DC: Three Continents Press, 1976.

Obiechina, Emmanuel N. *Onitsha Market Literature.* New York: Africana, 1972.

Onwueme, Osonye Tess (1955–) Tess Onwueme, as she is popularly known, is widely recognized as the most important, and certainly the best-known African female playwright. She was born in Ogwashi-Uku in the Delta State of Nigeria on September 8, 1955. She earned her BA in education at the University of Ife (now Obafemi Awolowo University) in 1979, her MA in literature from the same university in 1982, and her PhD from the University of Benin (Nigeria) in 1987. She had a number of teaching appointments in Nigeria between 1980 and 1989. She was an assistant lecturer in English at the University of Ife from 1980 to 1982, and an assistant professor of English at the Federal University of Technology at Owerri, Imo State, from 1982 to 1985 before moving to the Imo State University, Okigwe, in 1986 as an associate professor. From 1988 to 1989 she headed the performing arts unit of the university. She left in 1999 when she was appointed a distinguished writer and associate professor of Africana studies at Wayne State University in Detroit, Michigan. In 1990 she left Wayne State to take an associate professorship of English and multicultural literacy at Montclair State University in New Jersey. In 1992 she transferred to Vassar College as an associate professor of English and Africana studies, and in 1994 she was named distinguished professor of cultural diversity and professor of English at the University of Wisconsin, Eau Claire. While still in Nigeria Onwueme served as the vice president of the Association of Nigerian Authors (ANA) from 1987 to 1988, and its acting president from 1988 to 1989.

As a playwright Onwueme has focused her attention on social and political issues, using the stage as a forum to satirize political errancy, decry environmental mismanagement, champion the cause of women, and advance the ideal of Nigerian unity. Four of her plays have won the Drama Prize of the ANA: *The Desert Encroaches* (1985), *Tell It to Women* (1997), *Shakara: Dance-Hall Queen* (2000), and *Then She Said It* (2002). In addition she won the Distinguished Authors'

Prize at the Ife International Book Fair in 1988, and at Wayne State she was honored with the Martin Luther King, Jr., Cesar Chavez, Rosa Parks Distinguished Writer's Award for 1989–1990.

Then She Said It grew out of a project entitled "Who Can Silence the Drum? Delta Women Speak," which Onwueme carried out with the aid of a Ford Foundation grant. In the play, major Nigerian rivers (Oshun, Obida, Koko, Niger, and Benue) are personalized as formidable women characters in the state of Hungaria, leading the cry for emancipation and environmental recuperation from the blight caused by multinational exploitation. In like manner, *What Mama Said* (2003), which is set in the imaginary state of Sufferland, depicts abused and exploited people confronting both their corrupt government and multinational oil exploration companies to seek redress and self-determination. *The Reign of Wazobia* (1993), for its part, employs the powerful heroine Wazobia to promote a pan-Nigeria vision, "Wazobia" being a conflation of the words for "Come" in the country's three major languages, Yoruba, Hausa, and Igbo.

In her other plays, as in her scholarly essays, Onwueme seeks to enlighten her audience and readers about African cultures and the impact of the slave trade on Africa and the African diaspora, and to promote the interests of African women. She typically enriches her plays with traditional resources like proverbs and folk stories, and enlivens their performances with music and dance. In *Why the Elephant Has No Butt* (2000), she moves from drama to fiction. In this novel, which is based on an Igbo folktale, Mother Turkey explains Elephant's plight, using the familiar structure of weak and vulnerable Tortoise getting the better of big and powerful Elephant as a vehicle for giving voice and agency to downtrodden people in their struggle against their powerful exploiters.

FURTHER READING

Amuta, Chidi. "The Nigerian Woman as Dramatist: The Instance of Tess Onwueme." In *Nigerian Female Writers: A Critical Perspective*, ed. Henrietta C. Otokunefor and Obiageli C. Nwodo, 53–59. Lagos: Malthouse, 1989.

Ebeogu, Afam. "Feminism and the Mediation of the Mythic in Three Plays by Tess A. Onwueme." *Literary Griot* 3, no. 1 (1991): 97–111.

Uko, Iniobong. *Gender and Identity in the Works of Osonye Tess Onwueme*. Trenton, NJ: Africa World Press, 2004.

Osofisan, Femi (1946–) Babafemi Adeyemi Osofisan was born on June 15, 1946, in Erunwon, Ogun State, western Nigeria, his father dying only three months after his birth. He received his secondary education at Government College, Ibadan, and in 1966 he was admitted to the University of Ibadan to study French. He received a BA (Honors) in the subject in 1969. He embarked on his graduate studies the following year, and during the same year he had his play, *A Restless Run of Locusts*, produced. He earned his PhD in 1974.

In his professional life Osofisan has worked as an editor and translator for the Ford Foundation, as assistant lecturer in the Modern Languages Department of the University of Ibadan, as professor of drama at both the University of Benin and the University of Ibadan, and as a visiting artist and professor in several universities in Europe and the United States. He has also had an illustrious career as a playwright, actor, and director. In 1971 he was a member of the cast for the premiere production of Wole Soyinka's *Madmen and Specialists* at the Arts Theatre of the University of Ibadan, and in 1977 he assisted Dapo Adelugba in directing Wale Ogunyemi's *Langbodo* as Nigeria's drama entry at the Second World Black Festival of Arts and Culture (FESTAC '77) in Lagos. In

1979 he founded his own theater company, the semiprofessional Kakaun Sela Kompany, at Ibadan.

A prolific writer who has written close to forty plays and published about twenty-five, in addition to fiction, poetry and critical essays, Osofisan has been widely recognized and rewarded for his artistry; in 1983 he won the first Association of Nigerian Authors (ANA) Prize for Literature with *Morountodun and Other Plays*, and the same association's Poetry Prize in 1987 with the collection, *Minted Coins*, which he published under the pseudonym Okinba Launko. In 1993 he added the ANA's Drama Prize to his trophies, and in the same year he founded the literary journal, *Opon Ifa Review*. He served as president of ANA for 1988, and in 1991 he became the vice president of the Pan-African Writers' Association (PAWA) and was named grand patron of the Ghana Association of Writers (GAW).

Osofisan's difficult early years inculcated in him a deep empathy with the less fortunate members of society, and as an admirer of Bertolt Brecht he believes in using the stage for social instruction, with resort to all available traditional resources, including song and dance. He takes his subjects from several sources, including current events, history, and mythology. *Once Upon Four Robbers* (1980) was inspired by the public execution of armed robbers in Lagos in the years following the civil war. The play argues that the crime wave sweeping the country was a result of the social inequities rife in the country. *Morountodun* (1982) is a rewriting of a famous Yoruba myth, but reworked to promote the interest of workers. Among his numerous other works are *The Chattering and the Song* (1977), which he dedicated to Soyinka and Christopher Okigbo. In spite of the dedication, he is critical of both for what he considers their elitism and escapism, revising Soyinka's view of the human

condition (which the latter elaborated in the play *The Strong Breed*) in his own play, *No More the Wasted Breed* (1982). He accorded a similar attention to another older Nigerian dramatist, John Pepper Clark-Bekederemo, correcting Bekederemo's worldview as propounded in *The Raft* in his own *Another Raft* (1988).

Apart from *Morountodun and Other Plays*, other collections of Osofisan's plays are *Birthdays Are Not For Dying and Other Plays* (1990) and *The Oriki of a Grasshopper and Other Plays* (1995). They testify to the playwright's command of humor and other rhetorical devices, but they achieve their greatest impact in performance, especially under Osofisan's own direction when his sense of theater manifests itself.

FURTHER READING

Dunton, Chris. *Make Man Talk True: Nigerian Drama in English Since 1970*. London: Hans Zell, 1992.

Onwueme, Tess Akaeke. "Osofisan's New Hero: Women as Agents of Social Reconstruction." *Sage* 5, no. 1 (1988): 25–28.

Richards, Sandra L. *Ancient Songs Set Ablaze: The Theater of Femi Osofisan*. Washington, DC: Howard University Press, 1996.

Osundare, Niyi (1947–) Niyi Osundare is considered among the most accomplished of contemporary African poets, and along with the likes of Tanure Ojaide and Odia Ofeimun is included among the Nigerian poets of the "alternative tradition" of committed social criticism.

Osundare was born on March 12, 1947, in Ikere, in the Ondo State of western Nigeria. His father practiced traditional medicine, and by observing him at work, Osundare became familiar with the incantations that would later enrich his writing and performances. He attended Amoye Grammar School in Ikere for his secondary education, and later the University of Ibadan, from which he received his honors English degree in 1972. He earned an MA from Leeds University in 1974 and his PhD from York University in Toronto in 1979. Having taught at the University of Ibadan and as a visiting professor at the University of Wisconsin at Madison, he is currently a professor of literature at the University of New Orleans. Flooded out of New Orleans by Hurricane Katrina in 2005, Osundare took up a visiting professorship and residency at the Franklin Pierce College in Manchester, New Hampshire.

Osundare started out as a playwright, but after writing some plays he discovered that his true métier was poetry, specifically a "poetry of performance" that incorporates drama. In keeping with his attraction to drama, rather than reading his poems he *performs* them, a practice that for him better accords with the Yoruba tradition, and he also often accompanies his performances with different kinds of drums, each with a specific symbolic message. Moreover, so important is the performance aspect for him that when he publishes his poems he sometimes includes musical directions.

Osundare is always mindful of community—community of singers, hearers and composers—when he writes, because of his belief that the audience is the most important part of any artistic performance. He also believes that poetry should be accessible, and not a conundrum; in this view he aligns himself with the *bolekaja* critics who dismiss the "Hopkins' disease" of poets such as Clark-Bekederemo, Okigbo, and Soyinka, while nonetheless holding those poets in high esteem. In addition to its accessibility, his poetry is also relevant, reflecting the experiences of the turbulent years of Nigerian politics, especially the 1980s and 1990s, the murderous tyranny of dictators such as Sani Abacha, and the privations the regime imposed on the people. In such a climate, according to him, a poet had no choice but

to be political. His political activism, not surprisingly, earned him the dangerous and unwelcome attention of the security forces, who enlisted some of his students at Ibadan to spy on him. He was able, though, to stump them with his cryptic words.

Osundare has been the recipient of many honors. His collection *The Eye of the Earth* (1986) earned him both the poetry prize of the Association of Nigerian Authors and the Commonwealth Prize for Poetry (1986), and *Waiting Laughters* (1990) won the prestigious Noma Award, making Osundare the first Anglophone poet to win that prize. Among his other honors was an honorary doctorate from the University of Toulouse, which he received in 1999.

Some of his other publications are *Songs of the Marketplace* (1983), *Songs of the Season* (1990), *Midlife* (1993), *Pages from the Book of the Sun: New and Selected Poems* (2002), and *The Word Is an Egg* (2005). He is also the author of the critical volume *Thread in the Loom: Essays on African Literature and Culture* (2002).

FURTHER READING

Mowah, Frank Uche. "Seeking a Way Across the Wilderness: Niyi Osundare's *Songs of the Marketplace*." *Journal of African Studies* 15 (1988): 76–79.

Na'Allah, Abdul-Rasheed, ed. *Emerging Perspectives on Niyi Osundare, the People's Poet.* Trenton, NJ: Africa World Press, 2003.

Nwachukwu-Agbada, J. O. J. "Post-war Nigeria and the Poetry of Anger." *Wasafiri* 12 (1990): 3–6.

Our Sister Killjoy, or Reflections from a Black-Eyed Squint (1977) Ama Ata Aidoo copyrighted *Our Sister Killjoy, or Reflections from a Black-Eyed Squint* in 1966, but it was not published until 1977. It tells the story of Sissie's travel to Europe, first to Germany on scholarship and then to England on her way home. Divided into four parts, "Into a Bad

Dream," "The Plums," "From Our Sister Kill-joy," and "A Love Letter," it serves as a vehicle for Aidoo to examine a wide range of issues and voice her disapproval of actions and attitudes, both of Africans and of Europeans, both past and present. These include the European slave trade, whose reminders still litter the West African coastline in the shape of castles, and neocolonialism, to which African "pseudo-intellectuals" such as Sammy consent with their mimicry of Western ways and values and their acceptance of Western culture as superior to African ones. She had met Sammy, a young man she concluded had been brainwashed and taken in by Western claims of superiority to the rest of humanity.

Her experiences once she arrives in Germany offer Sissie many more reasons to be uncomfortable, and also critical of Europeans. She finds that they are astonishingly insular and ignorant about other peoples, and that the individualistic pursuit of material well-being has rendered human contact inconsequential. Moreover, both in her German acquaintance Marija and at the castle where she goes for a youth camp she is reminded of European violence and tradition of injustice. Marija's husband and son are both named Adolf, a name Sissie connects with Germany's Nazi past, a past that made her refuse Marija's invitation to visit Munich. The castle, for its part, reminds her that such structures were erected with the slave labor that the nobles extorted from the serfs.

In England en route to Ghana, Sissie is involved in arguments with Africans living there on a number of issues, principally the duty that the educated African owes to his or her people. Her interlocutors are professionals, many medical doctors, who would rather remain in England after completing their training instead of returning home to help their societies. She returns to the subject in the "love letter" she writes to her boyfriend (with whom she has broken up because he has decided to remain in England), in which she discusses an eminent African surgeon who would not return home because he would not have access to the cutting-edge equipment available to him in Europe. A discussion of Dr. Christiaan Barnard's successful transfer of an African's heart into a white man in South Africa enables Sissie (and Aidoo) to use the operation to symbolize Europe's harvesting of Africa's human resources for the benefit of Europe.

Aidoo's novel ranges over several other issues, including the use of European languages by African writers, the imposition of European names and prejudices on young Africans in Christian schools, the abuse of women in medieval Europe, and the planting of an automatic revulsion to lesbianism in the minds of African women. Stylistically, the work is highly innovative, combining verse and prose, and featuring other devices that jolt the reader out of any complacency, such as the use of capitals for whole sentences and the dedication of an entire page to a single word.

FURTHER READING

Chetin, Sara. "Reading from a Distance: Ama Ata Aidoo's *Our Sister Killjoy*." In *Black Women's Writing*, ed. Gina Wisker, 146–59. New York: St. Martin's, 1993.

Nwankwo, Chimalum. "The Feminist Impulse and Social Realism in Ama Ata Aidoo's *No Sweetness Here* and *Our Sister Killjoy*." In *Ngambika: Studies of Women in African Literature*, ed. Carole Boyce Davies and Anne Adams Graves, 151–59. Trenton, NJ: Africa World Press, 1986.

Owusu, Kofi. "Canons Under Siege: Blackness, Femaleness, and Ama Ata Aidoo's *Our Sister Killjoy*." *Callaloo* 13, no. 2 (1990): 341–63.

Owusu, Martin Okyere (1943–) Born in Agona Kwaman in colonial Gold Coast, Martin Owusu went to Mfantsipim School, Cape Coast, for his secondary education, and the Presbyterian Teacher Training College,

Akropong-Akuapem, to train as a teacher. Having been influenced by the dramatist Joe de Graft, under whom he had studied in his secondary-school days, he proceeded to the School for Music and Drama at Legon after qualifying as a teacher, and there earned a diploma in theater studies. He later studied drama at Bristol University, receiving a master's degree in literature in 1973, and also at Brandeis University, where he took his PhD in 1979, with a focus on Western influences on African theater. He returned to Ghana to teach drama and theater, and he is currently the director of the School of Performing Arts at the University of Ghana.

Owusu is one of the most prominent dramatists in his native Ghana where he has published several plays, some of which, in the tradition of his older compatriot Efua Sutherland, are derived from folktales. His reputation however rests more on his achievements as an actor, a director, and an academic, than as a writer. Examples of his writings are the short plays collected in *Adventures of Sasa and Esi* (1968) and *The Story Ananse Told* (1970). In the same folk vein is *The Sudden Return and Other Plays* (1973), which includes his much-admired historical play *The Mightier Sword*, about the Asante-Denkyira war. Owusu has also tried his hands at adaptations, for example rewriting W. E. B. Yeats's "The Pot of Broth" as *The Pot of Okro Soup*.

His major scholarly publication, *Drama of the Gods: A Study of Seven African Plays* (1983), is based on his PhD dissertation.

Oyeyemi, Helen (1984–) Helen Oyeyemi was born in Nigeria in 1984. Her family moved to London when she was four, and there her father studied social sciences at Middlesex University. Helen herself studied social and political sciences at Corpus Christi College, Cambridge, graduating in 2006. She is the author of the critically acclaimed first effort, *The Icarus Girl* (2005), which she wrote at eighteen while she was supposed to be studying for her A-level examinations.

Oyeyemi grew up in Lewisham in a strictly religious home in which belief in superstitions, especially her mother's, had a serious impact on her upbringing. For example, in her household you could not write a person's name in red, otherwise the person would die, and you could not whistle in the house lest you summon spirits; breaches of these cautions invited commensurate repercussions from her mother. Her childhood difficulties were compounded by her experiences in school: her schoolmates considered her a weird social misfit and picked on her, and she often spent her lunch hours crying. These problems she coped with by inventing a playmate she named Chimmy, who helped keep her naughtiness in check until she had him run over and killed when she was eight. When she succumbed to depression her parents were not in a position to help her, because such problems are a rare experience for Nigerians to cope with. When at fifteen she attempted suicide, a psychiatrist suggested a trip to Nigeria as a possible therapeutic, and it both proved beneficial for her mental health and gave her the ideas for her highly successful novel.

The Icarus Girl is about the troubled young life of eight-year-old Jessamy, who lives with her English father and Nigerian mother in suburban Kent. Because she is unable to cope socially and psychologically, her mother takes her to Nigeria as a possible therapy, and there she makes the acquaintance of the imaginary Titiola (Tilly Tilly), who will thereafter play a major role in her life both in Nigeria and back in Britain. The novel, Oyeyemi has admitted, is more about her than she initially thought. Like the precocious Jessamy in the novel, she is herself unusually bright and well read for her age. It was in fact reading that proved most therapeutic for her while she was home recovering from the overdose she took in her suicide attempt. It was a much easier option than trying to relate with people (because she has difficulty verbalizing her thoughts) as well as being a means to fill the hours she had to herself at home, since her parents would not let her and her two siblings play in the nearby playgrounds. And although already a successful writer, Oyeyemi considers herself more a reader than a writer.

Although a reporter wrote that Oyeyemi completed the novel in a sudden burst of creativity in seven weeks, she says it actually took her seven months. In an explanation that is reminiscent of the main reason Chinua Achebe has given for beginning to write novels about Igbo people, Oyeyemi recalls that while growing up in Lewisham she never saw her likeness in the books she read; they were all about white people, and they eventually got her thinking she was white. Then she discovered Simi Bedford's *Yoruba Girl Dancing* and realized that a Yoruba girl living in England could have an interesting life.

Oyeyemi has also published two plays, *Juniper's Whitening* and *Victimese* (2005), and a second novel, *The Opposite House* (2007), which is about Cuban mythology. She was nominated for the 2006 British Book Awards Decibel Writer of the Year Award, and *The Icarus Girl* was nominated for the 2006 Commonwealth Writer's Prize and featured on the BBC *Page Turner* program.

P

Palm-Wine Drinkard and His Dead Palm-Wine Tapster in the Dead's Town, The (1952) Amos Tutuola's earliest work, *The Palm-Wine Drinkard and His Dead Palm-Wine Tapster in the Dead's Town*, was also his most popular and most successful. It had the advantage of novelty, which his later works lacked. It is indeed fair to say that Tutuola devoted the rest of his career to attempts to live up to the expectations *Drinkard* had created in his admirers, a feat that he was never to accomplish.

The story is about the quest of a young "palm-wine drinkard" to find his dead palm-wine tapster and persuade him to return from "the Dead's Town" and continue his tapping service, because no other tapster can match his skills. In the quest the drinkard must necessarily journey to the land of the dead in order to press his suit with his tapster, and, as one would expect, the journey is fraught with danger and full of excitement. The plot is indeed a compilation of episodes in which the drinkard, accompanied by the wife he gained en route, encounters and overcomes a variety of life-threatening dangers. Fortunately for him, he had had the presence of mind on leaving home to take with him all his native juju and his father's as well.

Tutuola took many of his episodes either directly from Yoruba folktales or based them on materials from such tales. For example, at the beginning of his adventures the drinkard discovered the direction to Death's house by adopting a tried and true folkloric strategy: he lay at a fork in the road, pretending to be asleep, with his head and his legs each pointing in one direction, and a wayfarer who came upon him casually remarked that the sleeper's head was pointed in the direction of Death's house. The adventure that resulted in his acquiring a wife also came from a folktale about a beautiful young woman who spurned all offers of marriage only to throw herself at a handsome stranger, in the end discovering that he was nothing but a skull who had borrowed all other parts of his body. Other materials came from the writings of D.O. Fagunwa, who had written and published several Yoruba-language adventures that were highly popular in the 1950s.

The language of the novel is spectacularly substandard, not because (as some early critics thought) Tutuola was experimenting, but because he had very limited formal education and his command of English was little better than rudimentary. Describing the "complete gentleman" (the skull) who won the young woman's heart, Tutuola tells his readers, "if I were a lady, no doubt, I would follow him to where-ever he would go, and still as I was a man I would jealous him more than that." The famous poet Dylan Thomas described the style as "young English," and its appeal was such that, according to Harold Collins, Tutuola admirers adopted "Tutuolese" to amuse themselves.

Tutuola also adopted certain Yoruba usages in his work that persuaded non-African readers of the depth of his creativity. These included the animation of inanimate objects (Drum beating itself, Song singing, Dance dancing, and Laugh laughing), and the materialization of abstract concepts, such as fear, which could consequently be vacated and lent out. The central concept of the book itself—the notion that there is no existential barrier between the lands of the living and the dead—is of course a Yoruba (and African) concept that has now entered into the realm of common knowledge for European readers of African fiction, such that the fictional works of the Ghanaian Kojo Laing (*Search Sweet Country*), the Sierra Leonean Syl Cheney-Coker (*The Last Harmattan of Alusine Dunbar*), and the Nigerian Ben Okri (*The Famished Road*) do not seem as strange or bewildering as they might otherwise have been. *The Palm-Wine Drinkard* at least prepared the way for them.

FURTHER READING

Collins, Harold R. *Amos Tutuola*. New York: Twayne, 1969.

Lindfors, Bernth. *Critical Perspectives on Amos Tutuola*. Washington, DC: Three Continents Press, 1975.

Owomoyela, Oyekan. *Amos Tutuola Revisited*. New York: Twayne, 1999.

Peters, Lenrie (1932–) Lenrie (Leopold Wilfred) Peters was born in Bathurst, Gambia, in 1932, and had his early education there and in Sierra Leone before going to Cambridge University to study natural science, and later to University College Hospital in London to study medicine. After receiving his medical degree in 1959, he underwent specialist training in surgery at Guildford, finishing in 1967. He embarked on his writing career while in Cambridge, writing some poetry and starting on the novel *The Second Round*, which was published in 1965. After his move to London he began to broadcast on the BBC's Africa and World services. He returned to The Gambia in 1972 to practice medicine.

Far from being hostile to what colonialism has done to his country and its cultures, Peters finds the latter stultifying, and is nostalgic about his experience in England, although he continues to embrace his Africanness. His writing is quite innocent of traditional influences, a fact that earned him the reputation of cosmopolitanism, and his poetry that of intellectualism. His poetry collection *Satellites* (1967) deals with a variety of human and personal experiences, while *Katchikali* (1971), whose title refers to a famous Gambian shrine, encompasses Gambian realities and themes. The title poem celebrates the shrine but also laments the destruction of its grove by "those who ignore [its] mysteries." His one novel, *The Second Round*, is largely autobiographical. It is the story of Dr. Kawa, who after his medical studies in England returns to Sierra Leone but has difficulties fitting back into an African lifestyle or adjusting to its expectations.

He eventually escapes from Freetown to set up a practice in the interior of the country.

Peters, whom the younger Gambian writer Tijan Sallah describes as "that paterfamilias of a national Gambian literature in English," is acclaimed the father of Gambian literature, not only because of his pioneering writing but also because of his encouragement and nurturing of younger writers.

FURTHER READING

Sallah, Tijan M. "The Dreams of Katchikali: The Challenge of a Gambian National Literature." www.Gambia.com.

Publishing Until the 1960s, the book trade in Anglophone West Africa was confined to the marketing of books for educational purposes, that is, either for use in the schools or by individuals undergoing a variety of correspondence courses. These were books published by such houses as Evans, Heinemann, Longman, Macmillan, Nelson, and Oxford University Press, and, needless to say, they were by English authors. The publication of African creative writing was a late development, although on rare occasions British publishers had issued African creative writing, such as Joseph Casely-Hayford's *Ethiopia Unbound*, which was published in 1911 by C. M. Phillips of London, R. E. Obeng's *Eighteenpence*, published in Ilfracombe, Devon, in 1943 by Stockwell, and Cyprian Ekwensi's *People of the City*, which Andrew Dakers of London published in 1954. In 1952 Faber and Faber published Amos Tutuola's *The Palm-Wine Drinkard and His Dead Palm-Wine Tapster in the Dead's Town*, but it was the entry of Heinemann in the 1960s into the business of publishing creative works by African authors for sale primarily in Africa that proved the greatest incentive for African literature. Its African Writers Series, launched in 1962 with Cyprian Ekwensi's *Burning Grass*, a new edition of Chinua Achebe's *Things Fall Apart*,

his *No Longer at Ease*, and Kenneth Kaunda's *Zambia Shall Be Free*, soon became the arbiter of African literary standards, being the most prestigious imprint in fiction, poetry, and drama at the time.

More recently other foreign publishers have entered into the African market, for example Allison and Busby, Hutchinson, and Andre Deutsch, all of London, and such North American houses as E. P. Dutton, Random House, and George Braziller. In order to facilitate their operations, some publishers set up African subsidiaries and even imprints targeting particular audiences, such as the Pacesetter imprint that Macmillan set up in 1977 to attract young readers who were looking for racy entertainment and were indifferent to high literary quality. The move was one way of getting around a problem that began to plague most African countries, certainly as early as the 1970s: economic depression and foreign-exchange problems, which made the importation of books difficult and expensive. By the 1980s a "book famine" had gripped most of the continent, leaving even university libraries incapable of building or maintaining their holdings and scholars unable to publish their research or gain access to scholarly works. Indigenous publishers have attempted to take up the slack, but with only mixed success.

The pioneers of indigenous literary publishing in Anglophone West Africa (if we discount newspapers that as early as the late nineteenth century sometimes published short stories and poems) were the entrepreneurs of the popular chapbook industry, notably the Onitsha market literature. Cyprian Ekwensi's *When Love Whispers*, though published in Yaba in 1947 by Chuks, belongs in this genre. Whereas in Nigeria the Nigerian Printing and Publishing Service in Lagos had published Timothy Mofolorunso Aluko's *One Man One Wife* in 1959, the first serious private publisher in Anglophone West Africa was Mbari Publications, which was established in 1961 by the Mbari Artists' and Writers' Club. By 1965 it had published as many as thirty works from the pens of writers from across Africa, but by 1975 it had folded, leaving the field to the aforementioned major metropolitan publishers.

Indigenous publishing received a boost in Nigeria during the oil-boom years when numerous imprints emerged, but they typically thrived for only a short while before being forced to shut down; they, too, could not weather the problems that confronted the foreign-based houses—the inadequate market for literary works as opposed to educational books (due to the scarcity of surplus money and lack of leisure time to devote to reading for pleasure), and the logistical difficulties of stocking and marketing books. Local publications also suffered in comparison to foreign ones because of their usually inferior quality (in terms of production and proofing), and relations between publishers and authors were not always the best because publishers often neglected to pay royalties to their authors.

Nonetheless a number of publishers have survived and even flourished, some of them established by creative writers, for example Ken Saro-Wiwa's Saros International (Port Harcourt) and Flora Nwapa's Tana Press (Enugu), in Nigeria, and Afram Publications (Accra) in Ghana, which was incorporated in 1973 through the efforts of Efua Sutherland and others. Other flourishing publishers include, in Nigeria, Fourth Dimension Publishing Company (Enugu), Malthouse Press (Lagos), Spectrum Books (Ibadan), and in Ghana, Sub-Saharan Publishers, and Woeli Publishing Services, all in Accra.

One major boost for African publishing houses was the founding of the African Books Collective in 1989 by a group of seventeen African publishers. Registered in the United Kingdom and based at Oxford, its purpose is to promote the marketing of the publishers' books in Europe, North America, and other parts of the Commonwealth, a goal that it has spectacularly achieved. In January 2003 Michigan State University Press became the sole distributor of the collective's books in North America. Another incentive for publishing in Africa, and a boon to African publishers, was the institution in 1979 of the Noma Award for Publishing in Africa by the Japanese publisher Shoichi Noma. It has served as a counterweight to the numerous foreign awards that attract African authors to publishers in Europe and North America.

FURTHER READING

Neame, Laura. "Saro Wiwa the Publisher." In *Ken Saro Wiwa: Writer and Activist*, ed. Craig McLuckie and Aubrey McPhail, 153–75. Boulder, CO: Lynne Rienner, 2000.
Zell, Hans M. "Publishing in Africa: The Crisis and the Challenge." In *A History of Twentieth-Century African Literatures*, ed. Oyekan Owomoyela, 369–87. Lincoln: University of Nebraska Press, 1993.

Rotimi, Ola (1938–2000) Olawale Gladstone Emmanuel Rotimi was born on April 13, 1938, in Sapele, in what used to be Western Nigeria. His father was an Egba Yoruba and a trade unionist, while his mother was Ijo. Rotimi grew up, therefore, speaking Yoruba and Ijo as well as Igbo, and became quite conversant with the different cultures.

From 1945 to 1949 Rotimi underwent primary education at St Cyprian's School in Port Harcourt and continued at St Jude's School Lagos from 1951 to 1952, after which he went to the Methodist Boys' High School in Lagos for his secondary education. In 1959 he embarked on his undergraduate studies at Boston University, earning his BA in 1963. From there he went to Yale University to study drama, receiving his MA in 1966. On his return to Nigeria he joined the University of Ife (now Obafemi Awolowo University) as a research fellow. He founded the Ori Olokun Theater, and became the head of the department of dramatic arts in 1975, serving in that capacity until 1977, when he moved to the University of Port Harcourt. In 1991 he returned to Obafemi Awolowo University, and founded the African Cradle Theatre (ACT).

In 1963, while he was still a student in the United States, Boston University's Drama School produced his play *To Stir the God of Iron.* Set in a Nigerian village in wartime, the play set the pattern he would maintain in his career as a playwright and director, namely, the use of traditional settings, cultural resources, and themes. *Our Husband Has Gone Mad Again* was also an early play of his that saw performance by the Yale Drama School in 1966. It was later published in 1974. The play is about the domestic turmoil that results from a military officer's decision to become involved in politics.

In *The Gods Are Not to Blame,* which had its premiere in 1968 during the Ife Festival of the Arts at the Ori Olokun Cultural Center (a part of the University's Institute of African Studies), Rotimi adapted the Oedipus myth into a Yoruba setting that gave him opportunities to feature such things as traditional divination and military regalia. It won the first prize at the festival and was later published in 1971. His most famous play, *Kurunmi,* a dramatization of the life and fortunes of a famous Yoruba general that also makes full use of Yoruba cultural materials, was published in the same year, but had earlier been performed with another of his plays, *The Prodigal,* at the Ife Festival of the Arts in 1969. *Ovonramwen Nogbaisi,* a play about the sacking of Benin by British troops

in 1895, premiered at the fourth Ife Festival in 1971 and was published the same year. His other plays include *Holding Talks* (1979), *If: A Tragedy of the Ruled* (1983), and *Hopes of the Living Dead* (1988).

Rotimi was undoubtedly one of the most successful Nigerian dramatists, and his plays were popular both on stage and as set texts in Nigerian schools. His frequent attention to traditional celebrities and their problems earned him the criticism of some progressive scholars who would rather he paid more attention to the plight of the common people. Perhaps as a response to such criticisms, he concentrated in *If* on the economic and political exploitation of the working class, and in *Hopes of the Living Dead* he dealt with the efforts of a marginalized group (in this case lepers) to stop official actions that would have worsened their condition.

Rotimi died in 2000.

FURTHER READING

Banham, Martin. "Ola Rotimi: Humanity as My Tribesmen." *Modern Drama* 33, no. 1 (March 1990): 67–81.

Johnson, Alex C. "Ola Rotimi: How Significant?" *African Literature Today* 12 (1982): 137–53.

S

Sallah, Tijan (1958–) Born in Serrekunda, Gambia, in 1958, Tijan Sallah received his early education in both secular and religious (Quranic as well as Christian) schools. Later, at Saint Augustine's High School, he became interested in both Francophone and Anglophone Africans' writing about Africa, and he also began writing poetry, his first poem being "The African Redeemer," a memorial to Kwame Nkrumah, the first president of Ghana. Sallah left his country for the United

States and attended Rabun Gap Nacoochee High School in Georgia, where he edited the student paper, *The Silent Runner*. From there he went to Berea College, where he studied economics and business while continuing to pursue his writing interests. From Berea he went on to Virginia Polytechnic Institute, and there, still pursuing his literary inclinations, he inaugurated the student publication *Kaleidoscope*, serving as its editor. After receiving his MA and PhD, Sallah took a few teaching jobs before joining the World Bank. He has continued to work at the World Bank as a senior economist.

Sallah has published at least six books of poetry that speak eloquently of his Gambian and African attachments, and in which he sometimes ventures into metaphysical and mystical explorations. His poetry bears witness to a deep commitment to the welfare and well-being of Africans struggling with the prolonged aftermath of colonization—the dislocations whose seeds were sown during colonialism and the homegrown ills for which the flawed character and questionable performance on the part of independent Africans are responsible. He is equally concerned, though, with the imbalances in the relationship between the industrialized West and the rest of the world, which the former exploits, misunderstands, and denigrates. Whatever his subject, the poetry has an easy grace; it is sonorous and lucid, and free of the self-consciousness that sometimes interposes itself between some poets and their audiences.

The aforementioned quality and characteristics are evident from his first volume of poems, *When Africa Was a Young Woman* (1980). The title poem, which represents Africa as a voluptuous woman who refused all suitors but was raped by foreigners, owes a great deal to the negritude poets. Having thus violated her, the poet says, Africa's abusers left her a wrinkled hag and her children

speaking in foreign tongues. Sallah poetically advocates the abandonment of imported vices and a return to roots, and he gives the lie to those who slander Africa as the land of Tarzans instead of the land of gold and ivory that she is. In this and later volumes—*Before the New Earth* (1988), *Koraland* (1989), and *Dreams of Dusty Roads* (1993)—Sallah laments white minority rule in South Africa and Zimbabwe (before the fall of apartheid in the former and its imitation in the latter), ridicules the piglike occupants of statehouses who are good only for gorging themselves and being duped by foreigners, enjoins African youths to respect their elders, and decries social inequity, injustice, violence, and the scourge of both poverty and beggary in African cities. His attentiveness to matters concerning women's welfare finds expression in such poems as "Cry Not," which consoles women who have lost their men to wanderlust, and whose title reminds one of Bob Marley's "No Woman, No Cry."

Sallah's short story "Weaverdom," a biting satire on colonialism and its co-opted Africans, is anthologized in *Contemporary African Short Stories* (1992), edited by Chinua Achebe and C. L. Innes. He has also edited a volume of poetry, *New Poets of West Africa* (1995), and a monograph on the life and works of the slave/poet Phillis Wheatley.

FURTHER READING

Gurren, Samuel Baity. "Exile and Return: The Poetry and Fiction of Tijan Sallah." *Wasafiri* 15 (Spring 1992): 9–14.

Jagne, Siga Fatima. "Tijan Sallah (1958–)." In *Postcolonial African Writers*, ed. Pushpa Naidu Parekh and Siga Fatima Jagne, 408–12. Westport, CT: Greenwood Press, 1998.

Saro-Wiwa, Ken (1941–95) Ken Saro-Wiwa was a prolific writer of plays, novels, and short stories (with twenty-three books to his name) and was greatly admired by television viewers, principally because of the immensely popular fifty-episode series *Basi and Company* that ran on Nigerian television from 1985 to 1990.

He was born Kenule Benson Tsaro-Wiwa on October 10, 1941, at Bori in the Ogoni area of the Nigerian delta region. His father, Chief J. B. Wiwa, was a forest ranger and a businessman, while his mother Widu was a trader and farmer. After receiving his early education at the Native Authority School in Bori, Saro-Wiwa gained admission to Government College, Umuahia, in 1954, finishing there in 1961. He then entered the University of Ibadan to study English. At the university he served as editor of the student magazine *The Horizon*, in which he published some of his earliest works such as "High Life," later included in O. R. Dathorne and Willfried Feuser's *Africa in Prose* (1969). He was also president of the student dramatic society as well as a performing member of the university's traveling theater. After graduating from Ibadan in 1965 he took a teaching job at Stella Maris College, Port Harcourt, and later at Government College, Umuahia. He was working as a graduate assistant at the University of Ibadan in 1966 when the political crisis in the country erupted. He joined the general exodus of easterners back to the Eastern Region and took up another assistantship at the University of Nsukka, but when Colonel Odumegwu Ojukwu declared the secessionist republic of Biafra and the civil war broke out, he escaped to the Ogoni area because of his allegiance to the federal side.

In 1967 he moved to Lagos and became active in groups working toward the creation of a Rivers State. His involvement in the Interior Advisory Council and the Rivers State Study Group led to his appointment as administrator of Bonny, in the Delta area, a post he assumed early the following year after its liberation. From serving at that post he went on to become a member of the Ex-

ecutive Council for Rivers State as a commissioner, holding first the portfolio of works, land, and transportation, and later that of education. He remained in government service until 1973 when he was relieved of his duties; he was to serve once more in another administration, that of the military dictator Babangida, who in September 1987 named him executive director of the Directorate for Mass Mobilization for Self-Reliance, Social Justice and Economic Recovery.

During his service in the Rivers State government, Saro-Wiwa cultivated the contacts that would later prove helpful to his business ventures, and he also continued to pursue his literary interests. For example, he entered the BBC Africa Service competition in October 1971 and was a joint winner of the fourth prize. His prizewinning play, *Transistor Radio*, was broadcast on the BBC Theatre Series in 1972. He wrote commentaries for the national newspaper *Punch*, and in 1973 Longman (Nigeria), published two of his books, *Tambari* and *Tambari in Dukana*. Longman's editors were not particularly enthusiastic about the next manuscript he delivered to them, however. Their foot-dragging on the project prompted him to start his own publishing venture as part of Saros International Limited, which he had earlier established as a transportation and grocery concern. It issued *Sozaboy* (Soldierboy) in 1985. The highly entertaining story in "rotten English," about naive Mene and his harrowing experiences during the Nigerian civil war, has proved immensely successful; it won honorable mention by the Noma Award selection committee in 1987.

In 1985, Saro-Wiwa began writing and producing the television series *Basi and Company*. Begun in response to a friend's challenge, the series became a huge success and ran from October 1985 to October 1990. It also generated the book *Basi and Company: A Modern African Folktale* (1987), a collection of fourteen episodes from the series. In a preface, the author notes that the episodes and the series itself are modern versions of the traditional folktale featuring Kuru the Tortoise (a trickster), Basi being the human incarnation of the trickster. Two other books based on the series followed: *Basi and Company: Four Television Plays* (1988) and *Four Farcical Plays* (1989). In all of these Saro-Wiwa employs his sharp wit to lampoon social and political deviancy. In *Adaku and Other Stories* (1989), he turns with both understanding and humor to the difficulties that women face in the society, and his twenty-poem collection *Songs in a Time of War* (1985) is based on his experiences during the civil war. His collection of short stories, *A Forest of Flowers* (1986), was short-listed for the Commonwealth Writers Prize. It was largely because of his reputation as a writer that he was invited to the United States in 1990 in the visiting-fellow program of the United States Information Agency.

Saro-Wiwa was an artist of considerable versatility, with an especially keen ear for humor and satire. The popularity of the *Basi* television series testifies to his ability to read his people's anxieties and aspirations and to speak to them. He was also an effective stylist, whether in formal or "rotten" (pidgin) English. The critic Craig McLuckie has commented that the satire is so precise and telling because the author knew the events and characters he portrayed intimately, since he was himself implicated in the sort of schemes they pursued. Unfortunately, his involvement in civil activism at a dangerous time eventually cost him his life. Almost as a rehearsal for his eventual execution the Sani Abacha dictatorship arrested him and held him in detention for a month and a day from June to July 1993 for his activities on behalf of the Movement for the Survival of Ogoni People (MOSOP), which he had helped organize in 1991. He was arrested again in May

1994 on a trumped-up charge of murder, and despite loud international outcry, he was hanged with eight other Ogoni activists on November 10, 1995. A biographer, Femi Ojo-Ade, cites his fate as an example of what happens when "potentially progressive elements within the African intelligentsia" permit themselves to be lured into the embrace of military dictators, obviously a reference to Saro-Wiwa's stint as an administrator during the civil war and director during the Babangida dictatorship. The same critic also offers the opinion, which few will feel inclined to challenge, that talented though Saro-Wiwa was as a writer, he would have been far less prolific as a published author had he not owned his own publication company.

FURTHER READING

McLuckie, Craig W., and Aubrey McPhail, eds. *Ken Saro-Wiwa: Writer and Political Activist*. Boulder, CO: Lynne Rienner, 2000.

Nnolim, Charles E. *Critical Essays on Ken Saro-Wiwa's Sozaboy: A Novel in Rotten English*. Toronto: Saros International, 1992.

Ojo-Ade, Femi. *Ken Saro-Wiwa: A Bio-Critical Study*. Lagos: Africana Legacy Press, 1999.

Okome, Onookome, ed. *Before I Am Hanged: Ken Saro-Wiwa, Literature, Politics, and Dissent*. Trenton, NJ: Africa World Press, 2000.

***Search Sweet Country* (1986)** *Search Sweet Country*, a novel by B. Kojo Laing, is the first evidence of a new style in African creative writing that, originating in the 1980s, presents readers with the depiction of a universe at variance with that of ordinary experience, a universe, that is, in which there is no clear demarcation between the real and the imaginary, the human and the spiritual, the mundane and the ethereal. In its converging world, witches fly around, people disappear at will, and long-dead ancestors mingle with the living in the marketplace. It is set in Accra in the 1970s during the corrupt administration of Colonel

Kutu Acheampong. The country was then in the throes of food scarcity, and the Colonel had launched his Operation Feed Yourself, which was supposed to alleviate the shortage of food. The plot centers on the importation of agricultural horses, which the officials claim would make agriculture more efficient and productive. When the horses arrive, though, they somehow get loose and stampede through the airport, shocking spectators and officials alike. It became obvious that the animals were racehorses, not agricultural horses, and a campaign was set in motion by which the officials sought to cover up the whole fraudulent business.

The drama, involves such characters as Dr. Boadi, a corrupt intellectual co-opted by the government, Professor Sackey, another intellectual but an honest one, and Boadi's adversary, Kofi Loww, Professor Sackey's ally, and Okay Pol, the airport administrator who is caught up in the intrigue, as well as the mysterious 1/2-Allotey, a farmer and a medicine man. The story is as a vehicle by which Laing mounts a critique of the culture of corruption in the country, and of the ineffectuality and lack of direction of the Ghanaian intellectual elite.

The intellectuals' problem, as enunciated by Professor Sackey, is principally a failure of perception, the failure to see the necessary complementarity of phenomena and to make the connections that will transform seemingly random and disparate elements into meaningful wholes. They habitually separate the world into opposing categories, like the contemporary and the traditional, the indigenous and the foreign, the Western and the Africans, and opportunistically skip from one category to the other instead of forging usable syntheses of them. Their inability in this regard breeds moral inertia or deficiency, Laing suggests.

Laing presumably focuses on the intellectuals as much as he does because he was working in the administration of the University of Ghana and living on campus when he wrote the novel. His critique, of course, extends to public-service functionaries, who apart from their responsibility for the policies that resulted in the food shortage inculpate themselves even more by using an ostensibly ameliorative project to defraud the country and people. In the bargain, they show their contempt to their people by expecting them to believe whatever the government wishes them to despite of the evidence of their own senses.

Laing borrows words liberally from a variety of African languages and pidgin English, and he experiments by blurring the distinction between poetry and prose. This experimentation, no doubt, is in quest of an answer to the puzzle of writing African literature in a non-African language, one that the Nigerian Gabriel Okara had also attempted to solve by similar experimentation in *The Voice* (1964). In addition to the foregoing, his idiosyncratic English usage—his penchant for neologisms, unconventional syntax, obscure and tortuous imagery, and the like—makes his writing quite taxing for the average reader.

Laing's conflation of worlds aligns his vision with what is characteristic of traditional African narrative art. Readers already familiar with Tutuola's works would be prepared for the sort of universe Laing created in *Search Sweet Country*, and even for such a name as 1/2-Allotey; Tutuola, after all, had already familiarized us with a half-bodied baby (in *The Palm-Wine Drinkard*), and Wole Soyinka later with a Half-Child (in *A Dance of the Forests*).

FURTHER READING

Wright, Derek. "Imagined and Other Worlds: Magic History in Kojo Laing's *Search Sweet Country* and Ben Okri's *The Famished Road.*" *New Directions in African Fiction*, 140–61. New York: Twayne, 1997.

***Second-Class Citizen* (1974)** In her second
autobiographical novel, *Second Class Citizen*, Buchi Emecheta recounts the story of
strong-willed Adah Ofili, later Adah Obi, a
woman determined to succeed (according
to her definition of success) no matter what
obstacles might lie in her path. Her conception of what constitutes success develops
early, when she is eight or thereabouts, and
practically all the residents of Lagos who hail
from her hometown of Ibuza put on quite a
to-do to welcome Mr. Nweze back from the
United Kingdom, where he has studied law.
From that time London beckons to her, and
she knows that to get there she has to be educated. But although her father would have
opted to educate her along with her brother
Boy, her mother does not believe in educating girls. Not surprisingly, therefore, when
her father dies and she goes with her mother
to live with her late father's brother (who inherits her mother according to custom), she
becomes virtually a servant, and her father's
savings are assigned to Boy's education. Her
schooling is not terminated immediately
only because her people calculate that she
will fetch a more substantial "dowry" later
on if she has some education. Undaunted,
Adah enrolls herself in a primary school in
spite of her mother, and later, urged on by
her Presence (an inner goad), she steals the
money to sit the entrance examination to a
high school. Fortunately for her, she is bright
enough to win a scholarship that frees her
from parental support. She eventually completes her high-school education and immediately marries Francis, a young man doing independent study in accountancy. Her
well-paying job at the American Consulate
enables her to send Francis to England to
pursue his studies, and herself to follow him
a short while later.

The better part of the novel is about
Adah's difficult life in London, made even
more difficult than what awaits most Africans in that city and in England as a whole
because Francis turns out to be the worst
kind of husband imaginable. Not only does
he prove a failure as a student, but he is also
a philanderer, a deadbeat, and an incorrigible wife abuser. Adah has to earn the money
to support the family (they have four children in rapid succession), and to endure the
beatings he deals out to her whenever she
says or does anything to displease him, yet
all the while she continues her self-improvement through education.

Eventually she can take no more of
Francis's abuse, and she leaves him. The last
straw is his destroying her first full-length
fiction manuscript, which she has given
him to read. She has sought escape from her
hard life by reading novels, works by such
Igbo writers as Flora Nwapa and Chinua
Achebe, and the African American James
Baldwin. Reading them has prompted her to
write about her own experiences, which she
does in a manuscript she entitled *The Bride
Price*. "I felt so fulfilled when I finished it,"
she says, "just as if I had just made another
baby." When Francis burns the manuscript,
therefore, she feels as though he has killed
her baby. She takes her children and walks
out on him. Francis's later actions justify
her decision: he disowns both her and the
children in court, after he has burned her
passport, their marriage license, and the
children's birth certificates.

The novel bears all the hallmarks of the
project Emecheta has devoted her career to
pursuing—the exposure of the seemingly
pathological misogyny of Igbo men in particular, but African men in general. She asserts at the beginning that Adah's birth date
was uncertain because her parents had not
bothered to record it; girl children were
worthless, she says, and their births not
worth recording—that despite the information that her father practically worshiped her
because he believed her to be the reincarna-

tion of his mother. A little later Emecheta writes that "among the Ibos [Igbo] in particular, a girl was little more than a piece of property." She also attributes the abuse Adah suffers at Francis's hands to changes that had taken place in the lives of Igbo men. In the past the men had other diversions; they had their "tribal dances" to occupy them, and moreover their wives knew that they were "bought, paid for and must remain like that, silent obedient slaves." The men no longer had such diversions, the logic goes, and took up beating their wives instead, and the wives themselves had ceased to regard themselves as bought and paid-for slaves.

Much as Emecheta tries to demonize Francis, though, she does, in spite of herself, offer some details that redeem him somewhat. Despite Emecheta's portrayal of Francis as a man who subjects Adah to closely paced pregnancies, either as a means of keeping her incapacitated or because of his insatiable sexual appetite, she also writes that the day after she arrived in England Francis had taken her to see a female gynecologist because he did not want her getting pregnant, and she had been set up with all sorts of gadgets to help her avoid having babies. She also writes of Adah's frequent use of sex to get him to see things her way. And as for the claim that Francis forced babies on Adah, she apparently derived a sense of fulfillment herself from "making" babies, and described the completion of her first novel as giving her the same sort of fulfillment she derived from "making" a baby. With regard to his burning her book, his explanation was that his family would be outraged if they found out that his wife had written the sort of book Adah had written. We may decry his action, but there is a point to his argument: he burned the manuscript because it had portrayed his family in an unacceptably scandalous light.

Finally, given the actions she permitted herself to take to get her way—stealing the

money to pay for the high-school entrance examination, marrying Francis because she needed a place to study, forging Francis's signature to obtain birth-control pills, and so forth—one suspects that Emecheta herself considers Adah to be not quite the innocent victim she might at first glance appear to be.

Sofola, Zulu (1938–95) Born on June 22, 1938, in Issele-Uku in the present-day Edo State of Nigeria, Nwazuluoha Okwumabua later shortened her first name to Zulu. After finishing her secondary education in Nigeria she went first to the Southern Baptist Seminary in Nashville, Tennessee, and later to Virginia Union University, where she obtained her BA in 1960. In 1965 she earned her MA in drama at the Catholic University of America in Washington, D.C. On her return to Ibadan she took a job at the University of Ibadan from 1968 to 1970, while also working toward her PhD from the same university, which she completed in 1977. Sofola joined the faculty of the University of Ilorin, and from 1989 she served as the head of the department of performing arts. She was on a visit to the United States when she died in 1995.

Sofola, who said that she took up writing plays as a means of providing answers to the questions put to her about her country and culture when she was a student in the United States, wrote, published, and directed several topical plays that both portrayed her understanding of reality in Africa, ancient and modern, and criticized what she saw amiss in contemporary Nigeria. These include *Wedlock of the Gods* (1973), *King Emene* (1975), *Old Wines Are Tasty* (1981), and *Song of a Maiden* (1986). In her works she focused attention on the place of women in traditional African cultures, and on that issue she differed substantially from many female Anglophone African writers, especially those such as Buchi Emecheta who represent women as the benighted victims of the men in their lives. Sofola maintained that traditional African cultures held women in high esteem and had a prominent place for them in society's affairs, but that they lost that place as a result of the distortions the colonizers enabled and abetted when they controlled the affairs of the continent.

FURTHER READING

Dunton, Chris. "Zulu Sofola." *Make Man Talk True: Nigerian Drama in English Since 1970,* 32–46. London: Hans Zell, 1992.
Ezenwa-Ohaeto. "Interview with Zulu Sofola." *Sage* 5 (Summer 1988): 66–67.
Fido, Elaine Savory. "A Question of Realities: Zulu Sofola's *The Sweet Trap.*" *ARIEL: A Review of International English Literature* 18, no. 4 (1987): 53–66.

Soyinka, Wole (1934–) In 1986, Wole Soyinka became the first African writer to win the Nobel Prize in Literature. The award acknowledged his unassailable position as the most important writer the continent had produced as of that date, and no realistic challenge to that status has since arisen. Certainly no other African writer is (or has been) more studied, written about, and interviewed than he, and no other writer approaches anything like his range or his mastery of the diverse literary genres on which he has brought his talent to bear. An authority on his work and career, Biodun Jeyifo, describes him as "one of the most influential of writers of Africa and the developing world," and further states that practically every one of his works is a remarkable achievement.

Born on July 13, 1934, in Abeokuta to S. A. Soyinka, a Christian mission-school headmaster, and his wife Eniola, Akinwande Oluwole grew up in a privileged home within the sequestered compound of the mission at Aké. He received his high school education at Government College, Ibadan, and

went on to University College, Ibadan (now the University of Ibadan), in 1952. There he studied Greek, English, and history until 1954, when he left for Leeds University for an honors course in English. At Leeds he was a member of the theater group, and after graduating in 1957 he worked as a play reader for the Royal Court Theatre in London, where he had opportunities to produce his own plays.

During his student days at Leeds and later during his stint with the Royal Court Theatre, Soyinka made a close study of classical Greek, Japanese Noh, and Irish drama and was exposed to the works of such contemporary "angry" playwrights as John Osborne and Harold Pinter. It was during this period that he wrote his first play, *The Swamp Dwellers,* a tragedy about the destruction of a family by a combination of natural disasters and human duplicity; it had its premiere in 1959. In the same year the play was also performed at the Arts Theatre of the University College, Ibadan, along with another play by him, *The Lion and the Jewel,* a comedy in which a lecherous traditional chief seduces a vain, streetwise, but naive young woman. Together they had the distinction of being the first works by an African playwright ever performed on that stage.

The preparations for Nigeria's independence were underway when Soyinka returned to the country in 1960. With a grant from the Rockefeller Foundation to do research into traditional rituals, he joined the English department at his alma mater in Ibadan as a research fellow, and also founded a theatrical company, the 1960 Masks. Its first feature production was *A Dance of the Forests,* which had been commissioned for the country's independence festivities in October 1960 but was later considered inappropriate for the occasion. Soyinka, however, arranged its premiere performance to coincide with the independence celebrations, and to the consternation of the planners of the festivities, the play, with its denunciation of the African heritage as one riddled with murderous corruption and its promise of little hope that the future would be any better, injected an unwelcome note of discordance into the prevailing euphoric mood. "Unborn generations," one of the characters declares, "will be cannibals.... Unborn generations will, as we have done, eat up one another."

Soyinka proved himself equally comfortable writing dark and serious plays and turning out light comedies and satires. His *Collected Plays 1* (1973) includes the already mentioned dark plays *A Dance of the Forests* and *The Swamp Dwellers*, as well as *The Strong Breed* (in which "the strong breed" acts as a sacrificial carrier for the evil in the offing for a community), *The Road* (an exploration in the liminal space between living and dying, and of the meaning of those phenomena), and the adaptation *The Bacchae of Euripides*; the second volume, *Collected Plays 2* (1974), combines the comedies *The Lion and the Jewel*, the Jero plays—*The Trials of Brother Jero* and *Jero's Metamorphosis* (both of which dramatize the antics of a wily Lagos beachfront prophet)—the political satire *Kongi's Harvest*, the first of the plays in which he will anatomize Africa's crop of diabolical dictators, and *Madmen and Specialists*, a scathing indictment of the authorities responsible for the state of anomie that flowered in the country and was highlighted by the bloody war of Biafran secession. In this last play he echoes his prediction (in *A Dance of the Forests*) of ever recurring cannibalism with the promise, "*Bi o ti wa / Ni yio se wa*" ("As Was the Beginning, As Is, Now, As Ever Shall Be, World Without").

The Interpreters, a novel about the ineffectuality of the new elite, appeared in 1965 and added to the general impression that Soyinka did not intend his writing for readers without an uncommon command of English. The aforementioned *Kongi's Harvest*, about the demented and megalomaniacal dictator Kongi, was far more successful, although a film version under the direction of Ossie Davies (with Soyinka in the title role) proved an embarrassing disaster. That same year, Soyinka was arrested and charged with taking over a radio station during the political upheavals in the Western Region of Nigeria, but he was soon discharged and acquitted. He was arrested again in 1967, this time for allegedly aiding the rebel Biafrans after the country had become embroiled in its civil war. He served three years in detention, although no charges were ever filed against him, and the experience formed the basis for several later works, including *Madmen and Specialists* (1970), the volume of poetry *A Shuttle in the Crypt* (1971), the memoir *The Man Died: Prison Notes of Wole Soyinka* (1972), and the novel *Season of Anomy* (1973).

After his release from prison in October 1969 Soyinka assumed the position of chair of the department of theater arts at the University of Ibadan, but he soon abandoned the post to go into voluntary exile in Europe. During his exile he served as editor for the cultural journal *Transition*, and when he returned to Nigeria in 1975, he took a job as a professor of English at the University of Ife, where in 1978 he founded the Unife Guerilla Theatre. Its métier was street theater, and it served as a vehicle for the playwright's attacks on corruption and misgovernment.

Soyinka's unrelenting and outspoken criticism got him into trouble again in the mid-1990s with General Sani Abacha, the Nigerian military dictator at the time, who issued an order for his arrest. Soyinka was able to skip the country, and he further infuriated Abacha with the essay *The Open Sore of a Continent: A Personal Narrative of the Nigerian Crisis* (1996) and the play *The Beatification of Area Boy* (1996), an enactment of Abacha's bloody slum-clearance operation in Lagos. He added to his anti-Abacha repertoire the play *King Baabu* (2002), also a satire on the dictator's ignominious rule. Patterned after Alfred Jarry's *Ubu Roi*, the hero—the grotesquely inhuman General Basha Bash of Guatu—seizes power in a coup and gives himself the title King Baabu. Soyinka lampoons like Baabu (the name means something like "None" or "Nothing" in Hausa) and the other characters (like General Uzi and Potipoo), whose speech patterns show their intelligence to have stagnated at a childish level.

Soyinka's first poetry collection, *Idanre and Other Poems*, came out in 1967, the title poem being a celebration of Ogun, the Yoruba god with whom he is powerfully fascinated, and who also features in the title of his third collection, *Ogun Abibiman* (1976). Ogun's fascination for him stems from what he regards as the god's combination of creative and destructive powers, a quality that in Soyinka's opinion makes him the patron god of artists. Soyinka's interest in and use of mythology, especially Yoruba mythology, somewhat balances the profound influence of Western writers and thinkers on him and in his work. Among the western influences are Bertolt Brecht, Euripides, William Faulkner, John Gay, James Joyce, and J.M. Synge. His versatility and eclectic sensibility are, to say the least, profoundly impressive, but they have not earned him universal praise. To some critics they are evidence of ambivalence, even escapism, that militates against commitment. Moreover, his tendency to flaunt his virtuoso command of the English language and his flair in forcing it into unfamiliar shapes make interpreting him a challenge, and have prompted some critics (Chinweizu and company) to label his uneasy style as an affectation and a proof of an affliction they have labeled "Hopkins' disease." The tendency to obscurantism,

critics have charged, militates against the playwright's social-ameliorative purposes, Jeyifo, for example, commenting that many of his works "seem to embody attitudes to language, style, communication, and artistic vision which are calculated to alienate or perplex readers and audiences, thereby often subverting … Soyinka's progressive, revolutionary intentions." In his own defense, Soyinka acknowledges the difficulty of his style, which he says is inadvertent: "I have to concede … I tend toward what's called the elliptical style of writing. That's not deliberate, it's just a quirk about which I can't do much. But I deny absolutely any attempt to mystify or create obscurities."

Soyinka has written three autobiographical works: *Aké: The Years of Childhood* (1982), an account of his first eleven years growing up at Aké in Abeokuta; *Ìbàdàn: The Penkelemes Years: A Memoir, 1946–1965* (1994), which covers the period of political activity leading up to Nigeria's independence and thereafter the inauguration of what Soyinka would later describe as a season of anomy; and *You Must Set Forth at Dawn* (2006), as much a celebration of his friendship with the late Femi Johnson as a testimony to Soyinka's extremely eventful life spanning the 1960s to the early years of the new century, including his capture of the Nobel Prize in Literature in 1986. In addition he also wrote *Ìsarà: A Voyage Around Essay* (1989), a tribute to his father, Essay (for S.A.), as he was called, and his ability to affect his present and future even without the benefit of a foreign education. Soyinka has also written important critical studies, among them *Myth, Literature, and the African World* (1976), *The Critic and Society* (1980), and "The Autistic Hunt; Or, How to Marxmise Mediocrity" (1988), an in-kind rejoinder to attacks on him by leftist critics such as Chinweizu and Geoffrey Hunt.

Soyinka's literary practice has been closely wedded to his social activism, as his perennial involvement in real-life political controversies attests. The importance he attaches to political involvement is evident in his dedication of the volume of poetry, *Mandela's Earth* (1988), to the anti-apartheid activist and statesman to whom he also dedicated his 1986 Nobel Award speech, "This Past Must Address Its Present." His political and social consciousness in combination with a flair for the dramatic surfaced early—in his days as one of the pioneering students of the University College, Ibadan. There in 1952, in association with six fellow students, he founded the National Association of Sea Dogs, also known as the Pyrates Confraternity. The students' aim was to rid the campus, and the nation, of what they saw as the blight of tribalism, which was gaining ground in campus as well as national politics. The Pyrates' adoption of pirate regalia and the skull-and-bones insignia, as well as the exclusiveness of the confraternity, made it in time the most attractive association in the university. As he reveals in *You Must Set Forth at Dawn*, the organization is still very much alive, and its members are to be found in influential positions in various spheres of the country's life, positions that they use to foment necessary political action at moments of national crisis.

Soyinka's political awareness in later life has tended, though, to be or seem to be limited to the anomie of the African present and its African authors, with first causes appearing to weight little with him. His criticism of African leaders has accordingly been sharp and unrelenting while he has at the same time demonstrated a studied lacuna for the assault on the African space by European colonizers. Rather than take the colonial rapaciousness to task he has instead been more interested in castigating Africans for their postcolonial missteps and chiding them for continuing to dwell on the evils of colonialism instead of looking to their own contribution to their present malaise. Even the

admiring Jeyifo finds this aspect of Soyinka's output "remarkable," commenting that "unlike what we encounter in the works of fellow African writers like Achebe, Ousmane Sembene, Ngugi wa Thiong'o, Ama Ata Aidoo, and the late Mariama Bâ, the metanarratives that legitimated the struggles of these social movements [anticolonial revolutions, the struggles of working people and the poor for better conditions, the fight for gender equity, and the general striving for agency] appear in Soyinka's works mostly as fragments, and nearly always in ironic deformations."

To Soyinka's credit, however, in addition to lambasting erring politicians and lampooning the foibles of both lowly and highly placed Nigerians (and Africans), he has also been involved in practical projects of social amelioration, prominent among them being his organizing and directing the Road Safety Corps in the early 1980s, as a means of instilling discipline into Nigerian drivers and thus reducing the carnage for which Nigerian roads are world-famous. Of course, that activity during a military regime has laid him open to the charge of collaborating (in whatever guise) with dictators, but he has rationalized the Road Safety Corps as an outgrowth of his dismay at seeing so many of his students (at Ife) lose their lives on the famished roads leading to and from the city.

Since fleeing Nigeria under threat from Sani Abacha, Soyinka has effectively made his home in the United States, where he has been a visiting professor at Emory and other universities. In 2004 he delivered the BBC Radio 4 Reith Lectures, which he gave the title *Climate of Fear*. It addresses the paranoia that has gripped the West, especially the United States after the Al Qaeda attack on the country in September 2001. In the lectures he takes issue with President George Bush's contention that the attack was an unprecedented phenomenon that changed the world. Such a view, in Soyinka's opinion, evinced ignorance of the experiences of societies outside the United States (and Europe), and the mistaken assumption that the United States of America is coextensive with the world.

FOR FURTHER READING

Agetua, John. *When the Man Died: Views, Reviews, and Interview on Wole Soyinka's Controversial Book.* Benin, Nigeria: Agetua, 1975.

Gibbs, James. *Wole Soyinka.* Basingstoke: Macmillan Education, 1986.

Gibbs, James, Ketu H. Katrak, and Henry Louis Gates Jr. *Wole Soyinka: A Bibliography of Primary and Secondary Sources.* Westport, CT: Greenwood Press, 1986.

Jeyifo, Biodun, ed. *Perspectives on Wole Soyinka: Freedom and Complexity.* Jackson: University Press of Mississippi, 2001.

——. *Conversations with Wole Soyinka.* Jackson: University Press of Mississippi, 2001.

——. *Wole Soyinka: Politics, Poetics and Postcolonialism.* Cambridge: Cambridge University Press, 2003.

Jones, Eldred D. *The Writing of Wole Soyinka.* London: Heinemann, 1983.

Katrak, Ketu. *Wole Soyinka and Modern Tragedy: A Study of Dramatic Theory and Practice.* New York: Greenwood Press, 1986.

Maduakor, Obi. *Wole Soyinka: An Introduction to His Writing.* New York: Garland, 1986.

Olayebi, Bankole, ed. *WS: A Life in Full.* Ibadan: Bookcraft, 2004.

Page, Malcolm. *Wole Soyinka: Bibliography, Biography, Playography.* London: TQ Publications, 1979.

Wright, Derek. *Wole Soyinka Revisited.* New York: Twayne, 1993.

Sozaboy: A Novel in Rotten English (1985)

Sozaboy: A Novel in Rotten English, Ken Saro-Wiwa's most impressive work, is a powerful indictment of war, its senselessness and indiscriminate destructiveness, and of its deceitfully attractive glamour for the naive. The hero is the young apprentice driver Mene, whose home is the village of Dukana. He is nicknamed Sozaboy (Soldier Boy) because of his resolve to become a soldier. Persuaded of the glorious adventurousness of war by the accounts of a veteran of the Second World War, he is further enticed into the soldier's life when a war breaks out, because he wants to impress his new girlfriend, Agnes, with the irresistible J. J. C. (voluptuous breasts), and nothing impresses women like a soldier's uniform. He duly joins the army, having paid for the privilege, leaving behind his newly married wife and a mother who reluctantly acquiesces to his desire because Agnes supports it also.

Sozaboy's war experiences include, apart from drills and long-delayed deployment, being taken prisoner and pressed into duty as a driver for the enemy side, a switch that causes him no discomfort, one side being just as good (or bad) as the other. He eventually deserts because he wants to find his family, and in the process sees the extreme devastation and privation that the war has caused in the villages and the countryside. He also sees other signs of human depravity—people in positions of trust profiteering from the war at the expense of those entrusted to their care. When they find that he has discovered their perfidy they betray him as a deserter, and he barely escapes being shot only because the executioner runs out of ammunition. In the end, finally back home in Dukana, Sozaboy discovers that his mother and wife have been killed in an enemy raid. What more, the people of Dukana are convinced that he has long died, and that what they are seeing is a ghost that must be killed to ward off whatever evil its appearance might portend. He again escapes with his life, vowing that henceforth, "if anybody say anything about war or even fight, I will just run and run and run and run and run. Believe me yours sincerely."

Saro-Wiwa relied on his firsthand knowledge of the civil war (although nowhere is that war specifically mentioned) to craft a story that is compelling in its depiction of the inanity and insanity of war. This particular war has no well-defined casus belli, sides, or goals, Sozaboy's reasons for enlisting apparently being typical for most soldiers. As the rumors of war gather at the beginning of the narration Mene visits his favorite palm-wine bar, the African Upwine Bar in Diobu. It is there that he meets Agnes as well as a man he later recognizes as Manmuswak (the name means "Man must eat") who enunciates the common soldier's attitude: if he is told to fight, he fights; if he is told to stop fighting, he stops. Incidentally, when the two meet later during the fighting, Manmuswak is on the other side, and it is he who later attempts to execute Mene.

What endears *Sozaboy* to readers, though, is its "rotten English," which some critics see as an instance of linguistic resistance to corrupt and murderous authority. Saro-Wiwa describes it as "disordered and disorderly. Born of a mediocre education and severely limited opportunities." The language, he adds, "has the advantage of having no rules and no syntax. It thrives on lawlessness, and is part of the dislocated and discordant society in which Sozaboy must live, move and have not his being." It is a deliberate and artistic creative achievement unlike the naive and inadvertent linguistic errors of his older compatriot Amos Tutuola.

As a story of the exploitation and victimization of the young and naive, *Sozaboy* has been variously compared to Voltaire's *Candide*, Jaroslav Hasek's *The Good Soldier Schweik*, and Joyce Cary's *Mister Johnson*.

Stillborn, The (1984) *The Stillborn* is the story of Li (short for Libira, meaning needle), and secondarily of her sister Awa and friend Faku. A young, needle-thin girl, Li returns, full of dreams, to her village after graduating from a boarding school. She wants to escape from her home, which is dominated by un-

loving parents, and experience the freedom of the city. Along comes the dashing Habu Adams, who has his own dreams of becoming a doctor in the city. Two years of illicit abandon later the two are married, and Habu moves to the city by himself. He does not become a doctor, however, but a salesman, and he does not seem overly anxious to have Li around. When Li does join him in the city after four years of separation she finds that he is not the man of her dreams; he is more interested in his drunken city trysts than in her, although in one night of drunken lovemaking he does impregnate her.

Li returns to the village to find that her friend Faku's marriage to Garba, another city man, is no more fulfilling than hers. Although she is Garba's second wife, who would normally be presumed to have more claim to his attention than the first (senior) wife, Faku has not in fact been able to supplant the other woman in their husband's mind or bed. After six years of marriage she has had only one child, conceived in the days of their courtship, a testimony to the distant intimacy that has had no reprise. Li finds, too, that her sister Awa's marriage to the Headmaster Dan Fiama is also a fiasco. The discoveries galvanize her, and she resolves to pursue her dreams without relying on a husband.

Li completes her teacher-training course while living apart from Habu, spurning his pleas for reconciliation as well as other men's suits. Her success is confirmed when after her grandfather dies her sister refers to her as "the man of the house." Alkali, however, has no intention of proving the legendary feminist dictum that a woman without a man is like a fish without a bicycle, but rather to make a heartwarming statement of the possibility, perhaps even the necessity, of rapprochement between man and woman. When Habu is injured in an accident and loses both the use of his limbs and the will to live, Li opts to return to him, to be his crutch and share his crutches with him, so that together they can learn to walk again.

Sutherland, Efua (1924–96) Born Efua Theodora Morgue on June 27, 1924, in Cape Coast, colonial Gold Coast, Sutherland was educated at St. Monica's Training College before going on to Homerton College, a teacher-training institution in Cambridge. She also studied at the School of African and Oriental Studies, University of London, graduating with a BA in education. She returned home in 1951 and embarked on a career as a teacher at St. Monica's Training College and later at other schools, and she joined in the founding of the literary magazine *Okyeame*.

In 1958 she founded the Experimental Theatre Players, housed where the National Theatre now stands in Accra. In 1960, with funding from the Rockefeller Foundation and the Ghanaian government, the troupe became the Ghana Drama Studio, and in 1963 it became affiliated with the University of Ghana, by which time Sutherland had joined the faculty of the School of Music and Drama. Although her Drama Studio started as a workshop for children, it became the grooming ground for adult playwrights and dramatists. When its downtown theater was demolished in 1990 to make room for the National Theatre, an exact replica was erected near the Institute of African Studies at the University in Legon.

In 1968 Sutherland founded the Kusum Agoromba traveling theater at the School of Drama and the Ghana Society of Writers (later Writers' Workshop) in the Institute of African Studies at the university. Outside the university, she established the community theater Kodzidan (story house) in Ekumfi-Atwia. Her use of Ghanaian languages in these ventures enabled her to reach and involve a wide and varied audience around the country, who would have been excluded by English-language performances or performances confined exclusively to the city.

An accomplished playwright, poet, fiction writer, and biographer, Sutherland was adept at combining European and African elements in her writings, especially materials from Akpan folktales, *anansesem*. Typical is the play *The Marriage of Anansewa* (1975), about Ananse the trickster's scheme to marry his daughter Anansewa to the highest bidder, without the suitors' knowing they are in a bidding war. The plot serves as a vehicle for subtle criticism of the exploitation of women in patriarchal societies. Best known among her other works are *Foriwa* (1962), which expressed the ideals of national unity and progress by uniting a woman from the south with a man who had come there from the north to work for development, and *Edufa* (1967), a story of venality in which Edufa sacrifices his loving wife Ampoma to prolong his own life.

Sutherland wrote for children in both English and Akan, because she was insistent that Ghanaian children grow up bilingual. Representative of her works for children are *The Roadmakers* (1961), *Playtime in Africa* (1962), *Vulture! Vulture!* and *Tahinta* (both 1968), and *The Voice in the Forest* (1983).

Honored in her lifetime with a doctorate from the University of Ghana and appointment as an adviser to President Jerry Rawlings, Sutherland died on January 2, 1996.

FURTHER READING

Ankumah, Adaku T. "Efua Theodora Sutherland (1924–1996)." In *Postcolonial African Writers*, ed. Pushpa Naidu Parekh and Siga Fatima Jagne, 455–59. Westport, CT: Greenwood Press, 1998.

Pearce, Adetokunbo. "The Didactic Essence of Efua Sutherland's Plays." *African Literature Today* 15 (1987): 71–81.

Wilentz, Gay. "Writing for the Children: Orature, Tradition and Community in Efua Sutherland's *Foriwa*." *Research in African Literatures* 19, no. 2 (1988): 182–96.

T

Things Fall Apart (1958) The educational-books division of Heinemann published Chinua Achebe's pioneering work as the first title in its African Writers Series, which played a major role in the development of Anglophone African literature. Achebe has explained that his motivation for writing the novel was his dissatisfaction with the portrayal of Africa and Africans in such colonial novels as Joyce Cary's *Mister Johnson* and Joseph Conrad's *Heart of Darkness*, among others. He had read these works as a student of English at the university, and he was determined to counter their erroneous and demeaning portrayal of the people and world he knew by providing readers with more authentic and authoritative images. In addition, he resolved to challenge the colonizers' claims that their intervention in African life was for altruistic purposes, and that as a result of their presence and activities on the continent the people had experienced an amelioration of their circumstances. He would show that instead of a boon to Africans, European colonization had been, on balance, a disaster.

Achebe's approach to his corrective effort is to depict the everyday life of a traditional African community, the village of Umuofia, before it came into contact with European influences, and later to show the effects of the Europeans' arrival on the community. He therefore tells the story in two parts, the first being an exposé of the working of the traditional society, the second a depiction of the community under the stress of coping with an intrusive and overbearing European presence. The strategy enables the author to demonstrate, in the first part, the highly developed institutions that Umuofia had in place to deal with any eventuality it could imagine, from the familial to the communal, and from the routine to the extraordinary. The reader is able to observe relationships among members of a polygamous household—among the wives and with the husband as well as between parents and children—and among friends; to witness communal cooperation in such matters as preparing for a wedding and celebrating funerals; to watch its justice system as it deals with domestic abuse and inadvertent homicide; and to see how it negotiates conflicts with its neighbors. He is thus able to place the disruption of traditional life occasioned by European activities in a context that casts grave doubts on the presumed incoherence of traditional life and the beneficence of European colonization.

Religion plays an important role in the story, a vindication of the truism that religion pervades all aspects of traditional African life. The vanguard of the European advance is constituted by the European Christian missionaries and their African helpers, the elaboration of the superiority of European ways to African ones is in religious terms, and the decisive, final confrontation between the two forces is over religious matters—the unmasking of a traditional spirit by a Christian convert and its consequences. In these events Achebe's champion of tradition is the imposing Okonkwo, a man driven as much by the need to achieve success, gargantuan enough to erase the memories of his feckless father, as by his fanatical devotion to his traditional gods. The defection of his firstborn son Nwoye to the Christian ranks is thus a fitting symbol for the falling apart of the traditional community. Furthermore, Okonkwo's suicide and the minimization of his demise by the gloating District Commissioner also demonstrate the colonizer's lack of regard for matters that are of consequence to Africans. Confronted by an agitated Umuofian who rails at him for having driven one of the greatest men of Umuofia to suicide and consequently to a dog's burial, the District Commissioner sees only a trivial event that might merit "perhaps not a whole chapter but a reasonable paragraph" in his projected book, *The Pacification of the Primitive Tribes of the Lower Niger.*

The author's intent of providing his readers with authentic images of traditional life as a vindication of their coherence and as a rebuttal to colonialist claims of disorder inevitably gives a significant anthropological dimension to the story. Along with the painstaking depiction of traditional ceremonies and the protocols of everyday transactions, it attempts to capture the manner and cadence of traditional (in this case Igbo) verbal exchanges, including the copious use of proverbs. The text is also sprinkled with Igbo words and expressions, each of which is accompanied with its English gloss. These features are consistent with Achebe's goal of educating a world ignorant of African realities, although these features would also seem to call into question another of his professed desires: to convince his own people that they had a culture they could be proud of even before the arrival of the Europeans.

A measure of the significance of *Things Fall Apart* in the development of modern Anglophone African literature is its service as a model for later writers, especially with regard to the recuperation of traditional cultures. The authors who have emulated it include, apart from such Igbo writers as Flora Nwapa and Onuora Nzekwu, the Kenyan James Ngugi (Ngugi wa Thiong'o), especially in such early works as *Weep Not Child* (1964) and *A Grain of Wheat* (1967).

FURTHER READING

Jeyifo, Biodun. "Okonkwo and His Mother: *Things Fall Apart* and Issues of Gender in the Constitution of African Post-Colonial Discourse." *Callaloo* 16, no. 4 (1993): 847–58.

Lindfors, Bernth, ed. *Approaches to Teaching Things Fall Apart.* New York: Modern Language Association of America, 1991.

Quayson, Ato. "Realism, Criticism, and the Disguises of Both: A Reading of Chinua Achebe's *Things Fall Apart* with an Evaluation of the Criticism Relating to It." *Research in African Literatures* 25, no. 4 (1994): 117–36.

This Earth, My Brother… **(1971)** Kofi Awoonor's *This Earth, My Brother …* bears the subtitle *An Allegorical Tale of Africa*, and the dust jacket describes it as "an allegory of the African predicament … a fictional evocation of the quintessence of life in Africa … the spectre of people, existing, suffering, and dying." It narrates the experiences of Amamu, a young lawyer in Accra, who, overwhelmed by the decay and corruption he sees in his society, loses his mind and dies.

Set mostly in Accra where Amamu works, the work also features some details of his youthful days in his hometown of Theme. It is unconventional in some important regards: for most of its length it alternates prose and verse, the prose segments dealing with plot development and the verse passages constituting evocative commentary. Awoonor has said, however, that he intended the prose passages to be of secondary importance to the verse ones. The plot itself dispenses with chronological development and jumps back and forth in time.

The narrative line is quite slight, comprising Amamu's encounter with assorted manifestations of the dysfunction of his country's institutions (such as the police system), the corruption and irresponsibility of the elite and professional classes (such as his fellow patrons of the National Club), and the ubiquitous and growing filth that threatens in time to overwhelm the city and country, beginning with Nima, the city within the city of Accra. It includes a record of his unsatisfactory marriage and the more fulfilling affair with the prostitute Adisa. It also features glimpses of such wasted lives as Abotsi's: he had fought for the empire against the Japanese in Burma, and he had returned eccentric, salvaging dead goats and chickens from the dunghills that abound in the city. When his stomach was killing him the hospital would not treat him, and when he died the church would not bury him.

In flashbacks we see the already established pattern of abuse and degeneration during the colonial period, a state of affairs that implicates colonizer and colonized alike: in his Catholic primary school, Deme Primary School, Mr. Agbodzan and the staff teach Christian faith and values through the catechism, but the example Mr. Smith, the inspector of schools, sets is decidedly un-Christian as he is voluble with public insult directed at Agbodzan; Geoffrey Allen, the district engineer, is "degenerate and stupid," and "sleeps with native girls," and so does Mr. Henry Douglas, the district commissioner. He neglects his wife Mary to take up with an African concubine upcountry, leaving Mary to seek consolation in the bed of Gary Arnold of the police force, until Arnold returns from leave with a wife.

The most significant detail from the past, though, is the death of Dede, Amamu's cousin who died at age twelve; she had also succumbed to an ailment that consumed her stomach. Although dead, she had remained with Amamu all his life, and in fact symbolized the redemption he was straining toward throughout what the author represents as Amamu's pilgrimage through life. At the end, after he has wandered distracted through the night and arrived at the beach near Denu, Dede is the woman of the sea who rises out of the waters to enfold him in her embrace and symbolically grant him rest and solace.

The African world Awoonor portrays in his novel recalls that of Armah's *The Beautyful Ones Are Not Yet Born*, with which it also shares scatological language—it is one of filth and decay, death, and corruption, with the exception that Awoonor's ending at least offers the hero a peaceful cloture.

Transition In 1961, Rajat Neogy, a Ugandan of Indian descent, inaugurated the literary magazine *Transition* in Kampala. He modeled it after *Black Orpheus* (published in Ibadan, Nigeria) and intended to make it a forum to explore intellectual and other preoccupations that would be open to thoughtful and creative contributions in diverse disciplines. It quickly distinguished itself in terms of the contributors it attracted, a lineup that included African heads of state such as President Julius Nyerere of Tanzania, and famous writers from Africa and elsewhere such as Chinua Achebe, James Baldwin, and Langston Hughes. It also cultivated a reputation for being fearless and controversial, both in the subject matters of the articles it published, including such things as race, sex, and politics, and in its daring confrontations with powerful figures. It was such a confrontation with president Milton Obote over his political decisions that got Neogy in trouble in 1968. He wound up in jail, and his magazine went into abeyance.

After his release from prison, Neogy resuscitated *Transition* in Ghana in 1971, and when Wole Soyinka became the editor in 1973, rechristening it *Ch'indaba*, it became even more vocal and frontal in its attacks on political figures and institutions, but by 1976 it had spent its force and it ceased publication. It was revived in 1991 thanks to the efforts of Henry Louis Gates of Harvard University, who had studied under Soyinka at Cambridge University and had contributed to the magazine while Soyinka was the editor. With Soyinka as the chairman of the editorial board and Gates teaming up as co-editor with his Harvard colleague, the Ghanaian scholar Kwame Anthony Appiah, the new *Transition*, published by Duke University Press, is intended to serve as "an international review of politics, culture, and ethnicity from Beijing to Bujumbura." Its relocation from the African continent to the United States signaled much more than a geographical relocation, though, because it also represented a decided de-emphasis on the old *Transition*'s focus on Africa. The shift is deliberate and in keeping with the substitution of diaspora for continent, and also the growing attraction of internationality, hybridity, and the other concepts consonant with postcoloniality.

FURTHER READING

Benson, Peter. *Black Orpheus, Transition, and Modern Cultural Awakening in Africa.* Berkeley: University of California Press, 1986.

Echeruo, Michael J.C. "From *Transition* to *Transition.*" *Research in African Literatures* 22, no. 4 (Winter 1991): 135–45.

Tutuola, Amos (1920–97) Faber and Faber published Amos Tutuola's *The Palm-Wine Drinkard* in 1952, six years before the publication of Chinua Achebe's first novel, *Things Fall Apart*. Although he was thus among the first generation of modern Nigerian writers, unlike the others he was not a product of Nigeria's elite educational system. In fact his education was quite minimal, a total of six years, and it did not include a high-school education. His uncertain command of his chosen medium of English, despite persistent efforts at improvement, attests to that lack. He nonetheless achieved immense popularity worldwide as a literary genius, especially in the early part of his career, and his accomplishments continue to spark contentious debate on their implications for the nature of creativity and the legitimate criteria for determining literary excellence.

Tutuola was born in 1920 in Abeokuta, in what is now the Ogun State of western Nigeria. His primary education was at the Salva-tion Army School, where he enrolled at the relatively advanced age of twelve, and for a brief period when he was a houseboy in Lagos in a school in that city, and finally back at his old school in Abeokuta. The death of his father when he was nineteen put an end to his formal schooling and he moved to Lagos in 1940 to live with a brother. Two years later he found employment with the British Royal Air Force in Lagos as a blacksmith. He stayed at the job for the duration of the Second World War, after which he was demobilized. In 1946 he took another job in the civil service as a messenger in the federal labor department.

Tutuola's new job often left him sitting idle for hours at his desk outside the office of the officer to whom he was assigned, and he relieved the boredom by jotting down remembered folktales on ledger sheets. These he submitted in response to an advertisement of religious literature, which he mistook for an invitation for manuscripts. A series of unlikely accidents ensued that led to the publication of *The Palm-Wine Drinkard and His Dead Palm-Wine Tapster in the Dead's Town* (1952). It tells of the adventures of a palm-wine addict who goes to the land of the dead in an attempt to bring his dead tapster back to life. Dylan Thomas's enthusiastic review of the "brief, thronged, grisly and bewitching story, or series of stories … in Young English" was the first of many such in Europe and the United States that made the book a sensational success. In Nigeria, however, critics, especially Yoruba ones, dismissed Tutuola as a poor raconteur of Yorba tales, and an equally bad reproducer in English of the earlier Yoruba masterpieces of D. O. Fagunwa.

Undeterred by such criticisms, Tutuola went on to publish eight other "novels" (which some critics prefer to characterize as "romances") and two collections of short stories. The other works are variations on the formula so successful in *Drinkard*: a hero's and/or heroine's quest that entails horrific encounters with frightful creatures but ends with some sort of boon. After his second book, *My Life in the Bush of Ghosts* (1954), the international adulation accorded him waned somewhat, but he retained a corps of devoted admirers, among them Nigerians converted from their earlier skepticism. An adaptation of *Drinkard* for the stage by the Yoruba opera artiste Kola Ogunmola enjoyed tremendous success in 1962; that production, for whose success some critics mistakenly credit Tutuola, also marked the high point of his career. Tutuola's other works, which return to the fantasy world that had served him well in earlier works (as the titles attest), include *Simbi and the Satyr of the Dark Jungle* (1955); *The Brave African Huntress* (1958); *Feather Woman of the Jungle* (1962); *Ajaiyi and His Inherited Poverty* (1967); *The Witch Herbalist of the Remote Town* (1981); and *Pauper, Brawler, and Slanderer* (1987). His collection of folktales, *Yoruba Folktales*, was published in 1986.

Tutuola was named a writer-in-residence at the University of Ife (now Obafemi Awolowo University) in 1979, and in 1983 he participated in the USIA International Visitor Program, and was a Fellow of the Iowa Writing Workshop. While in the United States he visited New Orleans, and the city made him an honorary citizen. In 1989, the Modern Language Association named him an honorary fellow, and in 1992 the Pan-African Writers Association awarded him its Diploma of Native Patrons.

Inasmuch as Tutuola, because of the paucity of education, never mastered English thoroughly enough to use it as well as one would normally expect of a fiction writer, the significance of his acclaim in spite of that limitation continues to be the subject of debate, especially regarding the criteria by which to assess literary excellence, the role of non-African readers and critics in determining African literary standards and achievements, and the claims of English as a legitimate medium for African writing.

Tutuola spent his waning years in neglect and died in poverty on June 7, 1997. The Association of Nigerian Authors (ANA) did not think him worthy of an award in his lifetime, but many of its luminaries decried the failure of his country to recognize and honor him adequately while he lived. He did however have some influence on younger writers, which is evident in Ben Okri's short story "What the Tapster Saw" and in Ken Saro-Wiwa's use of "rotten English" in *Sozaboy* (1985).

FURTHER READING

Collins, Harold R. *Amos Tutuola.* New York: Twayne, 1969.

Lindfors, Bernth, ed. *Critical Perspectives on Amos Tutuola.* Washington, DC: Three Continents Press, 1975.

Owomoyela, Oyekan. *Amos Tutuola Revisited.* New York: Twayne, 1999.

Two Thousand Seasons (1973) Ayi Kwei Armah's *Two Thousand Seasons* is an allegory of the abuse the African continent has endured at the hands of foreign adventurers, first "predators" (Arabs) from the desert and later "destroyers" (Europeans) from the sea. It is also a tale of Africans' eager collaboration with the invaders—either as *askaris* (hired bodyguards and mercenaries only too eager to turn their weapons against their own people and to imagine the most gruesome methods of dealing death) or as kings whose depravity and greed induce them to welcome the invaders in the first place in return for paltry payments, and even to collude with the foreigners in the killing and enslavement of their own people. Most of all, though, the work is a ringing declaration of the essential virtue and purity of women in contrast to the essential evil and corruption of men. For example, the story claims that in the beginning men ruled, but their rule was ruined by paralyzing jealousy and the slaughter of the innocent in unending struggles for power; it took the intervention of the women who displaced the men to restore tranquility and usher in a period of peace, equity, and reciprocity.

The prophets and visionaries also come from among the women, like the young clairvoyant Anoa, who even in the peaceful time saw the impending visitation by white invaders. The book's title refers to her prediction that the people of "the way" were doomed to two thousand seasons of suffering: a thousand seasons of slavery and another thousand of climbing back from enslavement. The plot is the enactment of the prophecy.

The visitation by predators and destroyers is a punishment for the people's abandonment of "the way" (which is variously defined as reciprocity, connectedness, and creation), and indulging in "the generosity of fools" towards foreigners. But part of the abandonment of "the way" is also the pursuit of selfish interests, especially on the part of the men in positions of power, and yet another the abuse of women by the patriarchs, who left all productive work to the women while they sat around getting drunk, and also contrived to turn the women into housekeeping baby makers. Indeed, with the notable exception of the righteous and ascetic counselor Isanusi, all the grown men are depraved, the worst lot being the kings, whose interest in kingship in the first place is an emblem of spiritual deformity. For example, King Koranche of Anoa, far from opposing the white destroyers from the sea, about whose fiery destruction of Enchi and its recalcitrant people he and his subjects had heard, actually yearned for their arrival and colluded with them once they arrived in the bloody suppression of the people's resistance, and the plot to sell them

into slavery. Before him there was King Jonto, who had erected a special enclosure to confine virgins and young boys for his perverse sexual pleasure.

In addition to castigating selfishness and extolling communalism Armah lashes out against the pursuit of foreign habits, manners, and practices. He pours ridicule and contempt on Islam, a slave religion in his view, and Christianity, whose claims he dismisses as childish and laughable. He is also disgusted by the growing attractiveness of foreign names, and the ominous advent of the time when people will forget African names, "when you will call your brother not Olu but John, not Kofi but Paul; and our sisters will no longer be Ama, Naita, Idawa and Ningome but creatures called Cecilia, Esther, Mary, Elizabeth and Christina." No hybridity or internationality for Armah.

In keeping with his conviction that the African writer has inherited the mantle of the biblical prophet, Armah uses language that evokes the denunciatory manner in which biblical prophets tended to confront and harangue erring Israelite kings and their people. The sustained poetic cadence is intended to add weight and authority to the work's vision and message, but its artifice does call attention to itself and sometimes proves bothersome. Also, the work's effectiveness as a call to virtue and regeneration is severely undercut by the author's penchant for name-calling and his weakness for inventing and detailing gruesome methods of inflicting violence and death.

The novel does hold out some hope in the youth, both male and female, to whom he gives names such as Abena, Dedan, Efua, Irele, Kimathi, Mofolo, Okai, Soyinka (names that pay homage to famous writers and, along with Isanusi, span the entire continent), who rebel against kingly corruption during their initiation and lead the journey back to "the way."

FURTHER READING

Abety, Peter. "Women Activists in Ayi Kwei Armah's *Two Thousand Seasons* and Ousmane Sembene's *God's Bits of Wood*: A Study of the Role of Women in the Liberation Struggle." *Bridges: An African Journal of English Studies* 4 (1992): 19–33.

Evans, Jenny. "Women of 'The Way': *Two Thousand Seasons*, Female Images and Black Identity." *ACLALS Bulletin* 6, no. 1 (1982): 17–26.

FURTHER READING

Ogunyemi, Chikwenye Okonjo. *Africa Wo/Man Palava: The Nigerian Novel by Women.* Chicago: University of Chicago Press, 1996.

Taiwo, Oladele. *Culture and the Nigerian Novel.* New York: St. Martin's Press, 1976.

———. "Adaora Ulasi." *Female Novelists of Modern Nigeria.* London: Macmillan, 1984.

Ulasi, Adaora Lily (1932–) Adaora Ulasi was born in 1932 in Aba, in eastern Nigeria. She received her early education in Nigeria before moving to Los Angeles, where she attended Pepperdine University and the University of Southern California. She received her BA in journalism at the latter in 1954. After returning to Nigeria she worked for a time as the editor of the women's page for *Daily Times* and *Sunday Times*. In 1967 she left Nigeria to live in the United Kingdom, and has lived there since. In 1972 she became the editor of the magazine *Woman's World.*

Ulasi is the acknowledged pioneer of the detective fiction genre among Nigerian writers. Her first two works bear titles in Pidgin English: *Many Thing You No Understand* (1970) and *Many Thing Begin for Change* (1971). They are both set in the Igbo area of Nigeria in 1935, and apart from pursuing the solution of crimes they also attempt to show the people's lifestyle. The author gives the impression, though, that she is either unfamiliar with the area or is not interested in accuracy. The same carelessness is evident in *The Man from Sagamu* (1978), which is set in the Yoruba-speaking area of western Nigeria.

Ulasi's other works include *The Night Harry Died* (1974) and *Who Is Jonah?* (1978), both published in Nigeria.

***Violence* (1979)** Festus Iyayi's first published novel is a commentary on political, social, and economic life in Nigeria during the oil-boom years, especially the mid-1970s to the early 1980s. It focuses on the impossible struggles of a destitute young couple, Idemudia and his wife Adisa. Idemudia grew up in an abusive home where his father grossly mistreated his mother. Unable to continue living under his father's roof, he drops out of secondary school and moves to the city. There his inability to provide adequately for his wife in the midst of affluence and conspicuous consumption earns him her constant taunts.

Iyayi represents Idemudia's difficulties as resulting from class exploitation, the exploiting class being represented by Obofun, a corrupt and rich businessman, and his wife Queen, an equally corrupt cement contractor. She employs Idemudia and his friends to help her offload cement but is reluctant to pay them, accusing them instead of stealing her cement. She also offers herself to Idemudia as a means of gaining control over him, while her husband takes advantage of Adisa's desperation to gain her sexual favors. The plot's main argument is couched in the form of a play within the novel. The scene is the hospital, to which Idemudia has gone after falling ill while working for Queen. Poor hospital patients have to sleep on the floor of the crowded wards or share beds (and inevitably their diseases) while the VIPs' opulent ward remains empty. The play, appropriately titled *Violence* and written by a former hospital patient, is the accusatory entertainment the poor patients mount to mark the occasion of a commissioner's official visit to the hospital. It dramatizes the trial of poor people accused of assorted crimes against society. In his defense of the accused the defense lawyer indicts society itself for inflicting violence on the lowly in the form of poverty and social oppression, and argues that when desperate people are driven to antisocial acts they are merely answering the violence society has visited upon them with another form of violence.

An adaptation of *Violence* for video, financed and produced by Clement T. Ofuani, was presented for public showing in 2006 in Nigeria and South Africa.

Voice, The (1964) *The Voice* advances the interesting proposition that modern-day elders have departed from the path of rectitude that their predecessors hewed to and bequeathed to them, and that moreover it is the modern-day youth who must remind them of the old ways and urge their return to it. The hero is Okolo, who on finishing school and returning to his town of Amatu ruins the people's festivities in anticipation of "the coming thing" when he questions all and sundry if they have got "it." Some people attribute his disruptive behavior to "too much book," suggesting that education has robbed him of his senses. Chief Izongo and Elders will have none of his inconvenient probing, and the "think-nothing people," happiest when nobody calls their attention to what might be amiss around them, want nothing of his pessimism either. His only ally is another outcast in the community, the witch Tuere. Izongo and the Elders have him arrested, telling him he will be untied only if he gives up his questioning and joins them. He decides instead

to leave the town and go to the city, Sologa, where, he says, "my inside tells me, I will find persons whose insides are like mine."

What he does find, though, is that things are not much different in Sologa. Even before he arrives there, he gets into trouble trying to be a Good Samaritan. His acquired notoriety makes him *non grata* in Sologa, and his return to Amatu leads to his execution along with Tuere, who instructs her helper, Ukule the cripple, to "stay in the town and in the days to come, tell our story and tend our spoken words." The two go to their deaths with Ukule's words ringing in their ears: "Your spoken words will not die."

Since Okolo's mission is the restoration of a state of virtue that he asserts the ancestors maintained but the current elders have lost, and since the people of Amatu attribute his troublesome quest to his Western education (up to secondary school level), the suggestion is that the same Western education that is usually equated with alienation and loss of mooring is precisely what qualifies him (and by extension the educated youth) for the corrective and restorative task. But Okara does not seem to subscribe to the equation of education with moral vision, for when Abadi, Izongo's chief supporter, boasts that he has been to England, America, and Germany and that he has his MA and PhD, Okolo responds, "You have your M.A., Ph.D., hut you have not got *it*." Having "*it*" thus has nothing to do with formal education.

The Voice occupies a special place in Anglophone West African fiction more for its experimentation with language than for its thesis or worldview; that the political leadership was corrupt and the general public sheepishly complacent at the time of independence was a fairly common perception among Anglophone writers. Moreover, Okara wrote his novel at a time when a spirited debate was underway about the propriety of writing African literature in non-African languages. One of the recommendations advanced to surmount the problem posed by the absence of any African language spoken (or read) by enough people to make writing in it feasible was that writers use Africanized versions of English. While some writers experimented with pidgin, Okara chose to marry English vocabulary and the syntax of his native Ijo, and also to transliterate Ijo expressions into English.

FURTHER READING

Anozie, Sunday O. "The Theme of Alienation and Commitment in Okara's *The Voice*." *Bulletin of the Association for African Literature in English* 3 (1965): 54–67.

Ashaolu, Albert Olu. "A Voice in the Wilderness: The Predicament of the Social Reformer in Okara's *The Voice*." *International Fiction Review* 6 (1979): 111–17.

Farid, Maher S. "Gabriel Okara, *The Voice*." *Lotus: Afro-Asian Writing* 13 (1972): 180–83.

Iyasere, Solomon. "Narrative Techniques in Okara's *The Voice*." *African Literature Today* 12 (1982): 5–21.

Webb, Hugh. "Allegory: Okara's *The Voice*." *English in Africa* 5, no. 2 (1978): 66–73.

Yoruba Girl Dancing **(1991)** Simi Bedford's *Yoruba Girl Dancing*, like Soyinka's *Ake*, offers readers a glimpse of the sort of mandarin upbringing that a few privileged Africans enjoyed during the height of the colonial period. The story, which starts out in Lagos, begins during the Second World War (there is reference to her Uncle George who was off flying planes in the war) when the heroine Remi Foster is six. Soon thereafter the scene shifts to England, where she experiences her late childhood and grows through adolescence to adulthood, becoming an Englishwoman in the process. The brief glimpse the reader gets of her life in Lagos is of life in the household of one the richest men in the city, her grandfather, a merchant who even during colonialism employed white men in his businesses. A descendant of one of the slaves who had fought on the British side against the Americans and as a reward had been freed and sent to Sierra Leone, the grandfather, Elias Foster, had moved from there to Lagos to become a successful trader in palm oil. The four-story family mansion is located on upscale Broad Street, from which the family goes to church at the Lagos Cathedral in a procession of four cars or takes daily constitutionals along the Marina, returning home to enjoy such delicacies as homemade ginger beer and chin-chin pastries.

The scene shifts to England because Remi's father Simon, a High Court judge, wants his daughter to enjoy the sort of education that will equip her to play a leadership role in her soon-to-be-independent country. Her experiences in a variety of English schools and communities are a revealing catalogue of what Africans were exposed to in England during the period. These include the assertion that the black of the skin runs, personal affronts such as strangers getting a feel of their hair without leave, and assumptions that all Africans naturally sing well. A side trip to Germany serves to show that the English are not unique, and also that Germans see the black woman as a sex object.

Although the heroine celebrates her Yoruba heritage, interestingly expressed in the form of exquisite dancing ("Is there anything more beautiful … than a Yoruba girl dancing?"), the story does not return to Nigeria but ends at the residence of the Western High Commissioner in London, where Remi's childhood friends from Lagos—with such hybrid names as Akin Williams, Olu Thompson, Wole Grant, Ayo Smith, Dele Hopkins, and Alaba Jones—are assembled for year-end festivities and dancing.

PART THREE

Writers and Selected Works

Abani, Chris

NOVELLAS

Becoming Abigail (2006)
Song for Night (2007)

NOVELS

Masters of the Board (1985)
GraceLand (2005)
The Virgin of Flames (2007)

POETRY

Kalakuta Republic (2001)
Daphne's Lot (2003)
Dog Woman (2004)
Hands Washing Water (2006)

Abdallah, Mohammed Ben

DRAMA

The Slaves (1972)
The Trial of Mallam Ilya (1987)
The Verdict of the Cobra (1987)
The Fall of the Kumbi (1989)
Land of a Million Magicians (1993)

Abruquah, Joseph Wilfred

NOVELS

The Catechist (1965)
The Torrent (1968)

Achebe, Chinua

AUTOBIOGRAPHY

Home and Exile (2000)

CHILDREN'S STORIES

How the Leopard Got His Claws,
    with John Iroaganachi (1972)
The Drum (1977)
The Flute (1977)

ESSAYS

Morning Yet on Creation Day (1975)
The Trouble with Nigeria (1983)
Hopes and Impediments (1988)

NOVELS

Things Fall Apart (1958)
No Longer at Ease (1960)
Arrow of God (1964)
A Man of the People (1966)
Anthills of the Savannah (1987)

POETRY

Beware Soul Brother and Other Poems (1971)
Christmas in Biafra and Other Poems (1973)

SHORT STORIES

Girls at War and Other Stories (1972)

Acholonu, Catherine

DRAMA

Into the Heart of Biafra (1985)
The Deal and Who Is the Head of State (1986)

LITERARY CRITICISM

Motherism: The Afrocentric Alternative to Feminism (1995)

POETRY

Nigeria in the Year 1999 (1985)
The Spring's Last Drop (1985)

Acquah, Kobena Eyi

POETRY

The Man Who Died: Poems 1974–1979 (1984)
Music for a Dream Dance (1989)
No Time for a Masterpiece: Poems (1995)
Rivers Must Flow (1995)

Adichie, Chimamanda Ngozi

NOVELS

Purple Hibiscus (2003)
Half of a Yellow Sun (2006)

Aidoo, Ama Ata

CHILDREN'S STORIES

The Eagle and the Chicken (1986)

DRAMA

The Dilemma of a Ghost (1965)
Anowa (1970)

NOVELS

Changes: A Love Story (1991)
Our Sister Killjoy; Or, Reflections From a Black-Eyed Squint (1977)

POETRY

Someone Talking to Sometime (1985)
Birds and Other Poems (1987)
An Angry Letter in January (1991)

SHORT STORIES

No Sweetness Here (1970)
The Girl Who Can and Other Stories (1999)

Aig-Imoukhuede, Frank

POETRY

Pidgin Stew and Sufferhead (1982)

Aiyejina, Funso

POETRY

A Letter to Lynda and Other Poems (1989)
The Legend of the Rockhills and Other Stories (1999)
I, The Supreme and Other Poems (2004)

Alkali, Zeynab

NOVELS

The Stillborn (1984)
The Virtuous Woman (1987)

SHORT STORIES

The Cobwebs and Other Stories (1997)

Aluko, T. M.

AUTOBIOGRAPHY

My Years of Service (1994)

NOVELS

One Man, One Wife (1959)
One Man, One Matchet (1964)
Kinsman and Foreman (1966)
Chief the Honorable Minister (1970)
His Worshipful Majesty (1973)
Wrong Ones in the Dock (1982)
A State of Our Own (1986)
Conduct Unbecoming (1993)

Amadi, Elechi

DRAMA

Dancer of Johannesburg (1979)

NOVELS

The Concubine (1966)
The Great Ponds (1969)
Sunset in Biafra (1973)
The Slave (1978)
Estrangement (1986)

Aniebo, I. N. C.

NOVELS

The Anonymity of Sacrifice (1974)
The Journey Within (1978)

SHORT STORIES

Of Wives, Talismans and the Dead (1983)
Man of the Market (1994)
Rearguard Action (1998)

Anyidoho, Kofi

ESSAYS

*The Word Behind Bars and the Paradox of
  Exile* (1997)
*Beyond Survival: African Literature & the
  Search for New Life* (1998), with Abena
  Busia and Anne Adams

POETRY

Elegy for the Revolution (1978)
A Harvest of Our Dreams and *Earth Child*
  (1985)
The Fate of Vultures (1989)
Ancestral Logic and Caribbean Blues
  (1993)
*Praise Song for the Land: Poems of Hope and
  Love and Care* (2002)

Armah, Ayi Kwei

NOVELS

The Beautyful Ones Are Not Yet Born (1969)
Fragments (1970)
Why Are We So Blest? (1972)
Two Thousand Seasons (1973)
The Healers (1979)
Osiris Rising (1995)
KMT: In the House of Life (2002)

Attah, Sefi

NOVEL

Everything Good Will Come (2005)

Awoonor, Kofi

LITERARY CRITICISM

*The Breath of the Earth: A Critical Survey of
  Africa's Literature, Culture and History*
  (1976)

NOVELS

*This Earth My Brother … An Allegorical Tale
  of Africa* (1971)
*Comes the Voyager at Last: A Tale of Return to
  Africa* (1992)

POETRY

Rediscovery and Other Poems (1964)
Night of My Blood (1971)
Messages: Poems from Ghana (1971; editor,
  with A. Adali-Mortti)
Ride Me, Memory (1973)
Guardians of the Sacred Word (1974)
The House by the Sea (1978)

Until the Morning After: Collected Poems
  (1987)

Bandele-Thomas, Biyi

DRAMA

Marching for Fausa (1993)
Two Horsemen (1994)
Death Catches the Hunter / Me and the Boys
  (1995)

NOVELS

*The Man Who Came in from the Back of
  Beyond* (1991)
*The Sympathetic Undertaker and Other
  Dreams* (1991)
The Street (2000)
Burma Boy (2007)

Besong, Bate

DRAMA

The Most Cruel Death of the Talkative Zombie
  (1987)
Change Waka & His Man SawaBoy (2003)
Three Plays (The Achwiimgbe Trilogy) (2003)

POETRY

Polyphemus Detainee & Other Skulls (1980)
*Obasinjom Warrior with Poems After
  Detention* (1991)
*Just Above Cameroon (Selected Poems 1980–
  1994)* (1998)

Blay, J. Benibengor

NOVELS

Emilia's Promise and Fulfilment (1944)
After the Wedding (1967)
Dr. Bengia Wants a Wife (1967)
Coconut Boy (1970)
The Story of Tata (1976)

POETRY

Immortal Deeds (1940)
Memoirs of the War (1946)
Ghana Sings (1965)

SHORT STORIES

Be Content with Your Lot (1947)
Operation Witchcraft (1956)
Love in a Clinic (1957)
Tales for Boys and Girls (or *Folk Tales*)
  (1966)

Cheney-Coker, Syl

NOVEL

The Last Harmattan of Alusine Dunbar
  (1990)

POETRY

Concerto for an Exile (1973)
The Graveyard Also Has Teeth with *Concerto
  for an Exile* (1980)
The Blood in the Desert's Eyes (1990)

Chinweizu

LITERARY CRITICISM

*Toward the Decolonization of African Litera-
  ture* (1980), with Onwuchekwa Jemie and
  Ihechukwu Madubuike
*Voices from Twentieth Century Africa: Griots
  and Towncriers* (1988)

POETRY

Energy Crisis (1978)
Invocations and Admonitions (1986)

SHORT FICTION

The Footnote (1981)

Clark-Bekederemo, J. P.

AUTOBIOGRAPHY

America, Their America (1964)

DRAMA

Song of a Goat (1961)
The Raft (1964)
Ozidi (1966)
The Boat (1981)
*The Bikoroa Plays: The Boat, The Return
  Home,* and *Full Circle* (1985)
All for Oil (2000)

POETRY

Poems (1961)
A Reed in the Tide (1965)
Casualties: Poems 1966–68 (1970)
A Decade of Tongues (1981)
State of the Union (1985)
Mandela and Other Poems (1988)
Once Again a Child (2004)

Conteh, J. Sorie

NOVEL

The Diamonds (2001)

Conton, William (Farquhar)

NOVELS

The African (1960)
The Flights (1987)

Darko, Amma

NOVELS

Beyond the Horizon (1995)
The Housemaid (1998)
Faceless (2003)

De Graft, Joe (Joseph Coleman)

DRAMA

Sons and Daughters (1963)
Through a Film Darkly (1970)

POETRY

Beneath the Jazz and Brass (1975)

Dei-Anang, Michael Francis

DRAMA

Okomfo Anokye's Golden Stool (1960)
*Cocoa Comes to Mampong: Brief Dramatic
  Sketches Based on the Story of Cocoa in the
  Gold Coast* (1971)

POETRY

Wayward Lines from Africa (1946)
Africa Speaks (1962)
Ghana Semi-Tones (1962)
*Ghana Glory: Poems on Ghana and Ghanaian
  Life* (1965), with Yaw Warren

Dipoko, Mbella Sonne

NOVELS

A Few Nights and Days (1966)
Because of Women (1969)

POETRY

Black and White in Love (1972)

Djoleto, Amu

CHILDREN'S BOOKS

Kofi Loses His Way (1996)
Akos and the Fire Ghost (1998)
The Frightened Thief (1992)
The Girl Who Knows About Cars (1996)
Twins in Trouble (1991)

NOVELS

The Strange Man (1967)
Money Galore (1975)
Hurricane of Dust (1987)

POETRY

Amid the Swelling Act Haps (1992)

Easmon, Sarif

DRAMA

Dear Parent and Ogre (1961)
The New Patriots (1966)

NOVEL

The Burnt-Out Marriage (1967)

SHORT STORIES

The Feud and Other Stories (1981)

Echeruo, Michael Joseph Chukwudalu

LITERARY CRITICISM

Chinua Achebe Revisited (1999)

POETRY

Distanced: New Poems (1975)
Mortality and Other Poems (1995)

Echewa, T. Obinkaram

CHILDREN'S BOOKS

*Mbi, Do This; Mbi, Do That: A Folktale from
    Nigeria* (1998)
The Magic Tree: A Folktale from Nigeria (1999)

NOVELS

The Land's Lord (1976)
The Crippled Dancer (1986)
I Saw the Sky Catch Fire (1992)
*How Tables Came to Umu Madu: The
    Fabulous History of an Unknown Continent*
    (1993) with Elanim Ekeh and Efanim Ekeh

Egbuna, Obi

DRAMA

The Ant Hill (1965)

NOVELS

Wind Versus Polygamy (1964)
The Minister's Daughter (1975)
The Madness of Didi (1980)

SHORT STORIES

Daughters of the Sun and Other Stories (1970)
Emperor of the Sea and Other Stories (1974)

Ekwensi, Cyprian

CHILDREN'S BOOKS

The Passport of Mallam Ilia (1960)
An African Night's Entertainment (1962)
Trouble in Form Six (1966)

NOVELS

When Love Whispers (1947)
The Leopard's Claw (1950)
People of the City (1954; rev. 1969)
Jagua Nana (1961)
Burning Grass (1962)
Survive the Peace (1976, 1979)
Divided We Stand (1980)
Jagua Nana's Daughter (1986)
King for Ever (1992)

SHORT STORIES

Ikolo the Wrestler and Other Ibo Tales (1947)
Lokotown and Other Stories (1966)
Restless City and Christmas Gold (1975)

Emecheta, Buchi

AUTOBIOGRAPHY

Head Above Water (1986)

NOVELS

In the Ditch (1972)
The Bride Price (1975)
Second-Class Citizen (1975)
The Slave Girl (1977)
Double Yoke (1982)
The Rape of Shavi (1984)
A Kind of Marriage (1986)
The Family (1989)
The Joys of Motherhood (1994)
Kehinde (1994)
The New Tribe (2000)

Enekwe, Ossie Onuora

NOVEL

Come Thunder (1984)

POETRY

Broken Pots (1977)

SHORT STORIES

The Last Battle and Other Stories (1996)

Fatunde, Tunde

DRAMA

Blood and Sweat (1985)
No Food, No Country (1985)
No More Oil Boom (1985)
Oga Na Tief Man (1986)
Water No Get Enemy (1989)
Shattered Calabash (2002)

Fyle, Clifford Nelson

NOVELS

The Conquest of Freedom (containing *Blood Brothers, These Colonial Hills: The Odyssey of a People,* and *The Alpha*) (1998)

Garuba, Harry Oludare

POETRY

Shadow and Dream and Other Poems (1982)

Habila, Helon

NOVELS

Waiting for an Angel (2003)
Measuring Time (2007)

Henshaw, James Ene Ewa

DRAMA

This Is Our Chance: Three Plays from West Africa (*This Is Our Chance, The Jewel of the Shrine,* and *A Man of Character*) (1956)
Children of the God and Other Plays (*Children of the God, Companion for a Chief,* and *Magic in the Blood*) (1964)
Medicine for Love: A Comedy in Three Acts (1964)
Dinner for Promotion (1967)
Enough Is Enough (1976)
A Song to Mary Charles (1985)

Ike, Chukwuemeka

NOVELS

Toads for Supper (1965)
The Naked Gods (1970)
The Potter's Wheel (1973)
Sunset at Dawn: A Novel About Biafra (1976)
The Chicken Chasers (1980)
Expo '77 (1980)
To My Husband from Iowa (1996)

Iroh, Eddie

CHILDREN'S BOOK

Without a Silver Spoon (1984)

NOVELS

Forty-Eight Guns for the General (1976)
Toads of War (1979)
The Siren in the Night (1982)

Iweala, Uzodinma Chukuka

NOVEL

Beasts of No Nation (2005)

Iyayi, Festus

NOVELS

Violence (1979)
The Contract (1982)
Heroes (1986)

SHORT STORIES

Awaiting Court Martial (1996)

Johnson, Lemuel

POETRY

The Sierra Leone Trilogy: Highlife for Caliban (1973), *Hands on the Navel* (1978), and *Carnival of the Old Coast* (1995)

Konadu, Samuel Asare

NOVELS

Wizard of Asamang (1964)
The Lawyer Who Bungled His Life (1965)
Come Back Dora! (1966)
Shadow of Wealth (1966)
A Woman in Her Prime (1967)
Ordained by the Oracle (1969)

Laing, B. (Bernard Ebenezer) Kojo

NOVELS

Search Sweet Country (1986)
Woman of the Aeroplanes (1988)
Major Gentl and the Achimota Wars (1992)

POETRY

Godhorse (1989)

Maddy, (Pat) Yulisa Amadu

DRAMA

Obasai (with *Alla Gbah*, *Gbana-Bendu*, and
  Yon-Kon) (1971)
Naw We Yone Dehn See (1975)
Take Tem Draw Di Rope (1975)
A Journey Into Christmas (1980)
Big Berrin (1984)
Big Breeze Blow (1984)
Drums, Voices and Worlds (1985)

LITERARY CRITICISM

*African Images in Juvenile Literature: Com-
  mentaries on Neocolonialist Fiction*, with
  Donnarae MacCann (1995)
*Ambivalent Signals in South African Young
  Adult Novels*, with Donnarae MacCann
  (1998)
*Apartheid and Racism in South African
  Children's Literature, 1985–1995*, with Don-
  narae MacCann (2001)

NOVEL

No Past, No Present, No Future (1973)

Mezu, Sebastian Okechukwu

NOVEL

Behind the Rising Sun (1970)

POETRY

The Tropical Dawn (1966)

Moore, Bai T. J.

NOVELS

Murder in the Cassava Patch (1963)
The Money Doubler (1976)

POETRY

Ebony Dust (1962)

Munonye, John

NOVELS

The Only Son (1966)
Obi (1969)
Oil Man of Obange (1971)
A Wreath for the Maidens (1973)
A Dancer of Fortune (1975)
Bridge to a Wedding (1978)

Ndibe, Okey

NOVEL

Arrows of Rain (2000)

Ndu, Pol Nnamuzikam

POETRY

Golgotha (1971)
Songs for Seers (1974)

Nwankwo, Nkem

CHILDREN'S BOOKS

Tales Out of School (1963)
More Tales Out of School (1965)

NOVELS

Danda (1963)
My Mercedes Is Bigger Than Yours (1975)
The Scapegoat (1984)

Nwapa, Flora

CHILDREN'S BOOKS

Mummywater (1979)
Cassava Song and Rice Song (1986)
The Adventures of Deke (1980)

NOVELS

Efuru (1966)
Idu (1969)
Never Again (1975)
One Is Enough (1981)
Women Are Different (1986)

SHORT STORIES

This Is Lagos and Other Stories (1971)
Wives at War and Other Stories (1980)

Obafemi, Olu

DRAMA

The New Dawn (1986)
Nights of a Mystical Beast (1986)
Naira Has No Gender (1993)
Suicide Syndrome (1993)
Dark Times Are Over? A Tropical Drama
  (2005)

LITERARY CRITICISM

Nigerian Writers on the Nigerian Civil War
  (1992)
New Introduction to Literature (1994)
*Contemporary Nigerian Theatre: Cultural
  Heritage and Social Vision* (1996)

Ofeimun, Odia

POETRY

The Poet Lied (1980)
A Handle for the Flutist and Other Poems
　(1986)
Under African Skies (1990)
London Letter and Other Poems (2000)

Oguibe, Olu

LITERARY CRITICISM

The Culture Game (2003)

POETRY

A Song from Exile (1990)
A Gathering Fear (1992)
Songs for Catalina (1994)

Ogundipe, Omolara

POETRY

Sew the Old Days and Other Poems (1985)

Ojaide, Tanure

AUTOBIOGRAPHY

Great Boys: An African Childhood (1998)

LITERARY CRITICISM

*Poetic Imagination in Black Africa: Essays on
　African Poetry* (1996)
The Poetry of Wole Soyinka (1994)
*Poetry, Art, and Performance: Udje Dance
　Songs of the Urhobo People* (2003)

POETRY

Labyrinths of the Delta (1976, 1986)
The Eagle's Vision (1987)
The Endless Song (1989)
The Fate of Vultures (1990)
The Blood of Peace (1991)
Delta Blues and Home Songs (1995)
The Daydream of Ants (1997)
Delta Blues & Home Songs (1998)
Invoking the Warrior Spirit (1998)
In the Kingdom of Songs (2002)
In the House of Words (2006)

Okai, Atukwei

POETRY

Flowerfall (1969)
The Oath of the Fontomfrom and Other Poems
　(1971)
Longorligi Logarithms and Other Poems (1974)
*The Anthill in the Sea: Verses and Chants for
　Children* (1988)

Okara, Gabriel

CHILDREN'S BOOKS

An Adventure to Juju Island (1981)
Little Snake and the Frog (1981)

NOVEL

The Voice (1964)

POETRY

The Fisherman's Invocation (1978)

Okigbo, Christopher

POETRY

Heavensgate (1962)
Limits (1964)
Silences (1965)
Path of Thunder: Poems Prophesying War
　(1967)
Labyrinths / Path of Thunder (1971)
Collected Poems (1986)

Okoye, Ifeoma

CHILDREN'S BOOKS

The Adventures of Tulu the Little Monkey
　(1980)
Eme Goes to School (1980)
Only Bread for Eze (1980)
The Village Boy (1981)
Behind the Clouds (1982)

NOVELS

Men Without Ears (1984)
Chimere (1992)

Okpewho, Isidore (Oghenerhuele)

LITERARY CRITICISM

Chinua Achebe's Things Fall Apart: *A Case-
　book* (2003)

NOVELS

The Victims (1970)
The Last Duty (1976)
Tides (1993)
Call Me By My Rightful Name (2004)

Okpi, Kalu

NOVELS

The Smugglers (1977)
Love (1991)
Changes Everything (1994)

Okri, Ben

NOVELS

Flowers and Shadows (1980)
The Landscapes Within (1981)
The Famished Road (1991)
Songs of Enchantment (1993)

SHORT STORIES

Incidents at the Shrine (1986)
Stars of the New Curfew (1989)

Olafioye, Tayo Pete

LITERARY CRITICISM

Critic as Terrorist (1989)
Tanure Ojaide: Critical Appraisal (2000)

NOVELS

The Saga of Sego (1985)
Bush Girl Comes to Town (1988)
Grandma's Sun: Childhood Memoir (2000)

POETRY

A Carnival of Looters (2000)
A Stroke of Hope (2000)
Ubangiji: The Conscience of Eternity (2000)
The Parliament of Idiots (2002)
Tomorrow Left Us Yesterday (2004)
Town Crier: Selected Poems (2004)

Omotoso, Kole

DRAMA

The Curse (1976)
Shadows in the Horizon (1977)

LITERARY CRITICISM

*Achebe or Soyinka? A Re-interpretation and a
Study in Contrasts* (1995)

NOVELS

The Edifice (1971)
The Combat (1972)
Fela's Choice (1974)
Just Before Dawn (1988)
Memories of Our Recent Boom (1990)

SHORT STORIES

Miracles and Other Stories (1973, 1978)

Onwueme, Osonye Tess

DRAMA

The Desert Encroaches (1985)
The Reign of Wazobia (1993)

Tell It to Women (1997)
Shakara: Dance-Hall Queen (2000)
Then She Said It (2002)
What Mama Said (2003)

NOVEL

Why the Elephant Has No Butt (2000)

Osofisan, Femi

DRAMA

A Restless Run of Locusts (1970)
The Chattering and the Song (1977)
Once Upon Four Robbers (1980)
No More the Wasted Breed (1982)
Morountodun and Other Plays (1983)
Birthdays Are Not for Dying and Other Plays
  (1990)
The Oriki of a Grasshopper and Other Plays
  (1995)

POETRY

Minted Coins (1987)

Osundare, Niyi

LITERARY CRITICISM

*Thread in the Loom: Essays on African Litera-
ture and Culture* (2002)

POETRY

Songs of the Marketplace (1983)
The Eye of the Earth (1986)
Songs of the Season (1990)
Waiting Laughters (1990)
Midlife (1993)
*Pages from the Book of the Sun: New and
Selected Poems* (2002)
The Word Is an Egg (2005)

Owusu, Martin Okyere

DRAMA

Adventures of Sasa and Esi (1968)
The Story Ananse Told (1970)
The Sudden Return and Other Plays (includ-
ing *The Mightier Sword*) (1973)

LITERARY CRITICISM

*Drama of the Gods: A Study of Seven African
Plays* (1983)

Oyeyemi, Helen

NOVEL

The Icarus Girl (2005)

Peters, Lenrie

NOVEL

The Second Round (1965)

POETRY

Satellites (1967)
Katchikali (1971)

Rotimi, Ola

DRAMA

Our Husband Has Gone Mad Again (1966)
The Gods Are Not to Blame (1971)
Kurunmi (1971)
Ovonramwen Nogbaisi (1971)
Holding Talks (1979)
If: A Tragedy of the Ruled (1983)
Hopes of the Living Dead (1988)

Sallah, Tijan

POETRY

When Africa Was a Young Woman (1980)
Before the New Earth (1988)
Koraland (1989)
Dreams of Dusty Roads (1993)

Saro-Wiwa, Ken

DRAMA

*Basi and Company: A Modern African Folk-
tale* (1987)
Basi and Company: Four Television Plays
(1988)
Four Farcical Plays (1989)

NOVELS

Tambari (1973)
Tambari in Dukana (1973)
Sozaboy: A Novel in Rotten English (1985)

POETRY

Songs in a Time of War (1985)

SHORT STORIES

A Forest of Flowers (1986)
Adaku and Other Stories (1989)

Sofola, Zulu

DRAMA

Wedlock of the Gods (1973)
King Emene (1975)
Old Wines are Tasty (1981)

Song of a Maiden (1986)

Soyinka, Wole

AUTOBIOGRAPHY

The Man Died: Prison Notes of Wole Soyinka
(1972)
Aké: The Years of Childhood (1982)
*Ìbàdàn: The Penkelemes Years: A Memoir,
1946–1965* (1994)
You Must Set Forth at Dawn (2006)

BIOGRAPHY

Ìsarà: A Voyage Around Essay (1989)

DRAMA

A Dance of the Forests (1963)
The Lion and the Jewel (1963)
The Strong Breed (1963)
The Swamp Dwellers (1963)
The Trials of Brother Jero (1963)
Kongi's Harvest (1965)
The Road (1965)
Jero's Metamorphosis (1972)
The Bacchae of Euripides (1973)
Madmen and Specialists (1974)
Death and the King's Horseman (1975)
A Play of Giants (1984)
The Beatification of Area Boy (1996)
King Baabu (2002)

LITERARY CRITICISM

Myth, Literature, and the African World (1976)
The Critic and Society (1980)

NOVELS

The Interpreters (1965)
Season of Anomy (1973)

POETRY

Idanre and Other Poems (1967)
A Shuttle in the Crypt (1971)
Ogun Abibiman (1976)
Mandela's Earth (1988)

TRANSLATIONS

Daniel Orowole Fagunwa, *The Forest of a
Thousand Daemons* (1968)

Sutherland, Efua

CHILDREN'S BOOKS

The Roadmakers (1961)
Playtime in African (1962)

Vulture! Vulture! (1968)
Tahinta (1968)
The Voice in the Forest (1983)

DRAMA

Foriwa (1962)
Edufa (1967)
The Marriage of Anansewa (1975)

Tutuola, Amos

NOVELS

The Palm-Wine Drinkard and His Dead Palm-Wine Tapster in the Dead's Town (1952)
My Life in the Bush of Ghosts (1954)
Simbi and the Satyr of the Dark Jungle (1955)
The Brave African Huntress (1958)

Feather Woman of the Jungle (1962)
Ajaiyi and His Inherited Poverty (1967)
The Witch Herbalist of the Remote Town (1981)
Pauper, Brawler, and Slanderer (1987)

SHORT STORIES

Yoruba Folktales (1986)

Ulasi, Adaora Lily

NOVELS

Many Thing You No Understand (1970)
Many Thing Begin for Change (1971)
The Night Harry Died (1974)
The Man from Sagamu (1978)
Who Is Jonah? (1978)

Index